"What an incredibly sobering and detailed examination of denominations and their future role! The authors of this volume challenge us to evaluate the reasons for the ongoing existence of denominations, exploring whether they still serve a purpose. Ultimately, this book is a call to priorities: We must keep our denominations focused on the ministry of rebirth and redemption, not on the business of enforcing rules and rituals. An honest reading will help churches and denominations strive to do more than just survive, but, rather, to play a transformational role in a world that needs Christ."

—Kevin Ezell, President, North American Mission Board
of the Southern Baptist Convention

"There can be little doubt that the two great movements that have shaped American religious life are evangelicalism and denominationalism. And the largest and most influential American denomination is, without a doubt, the Southern Baptist Convention. Understand these two movements, and you understand much of the heart of American religious life. Together they form the Rocky Mountains, so to miss them would be to miss the landscape of our nation. Any exploration of the relationship between these two movements, and particularly one as informed and incisive as what is found in this volume, is worth the time and investment to read. Particularly when the future of both, in light of the ever-changing cultural landscape, is very much in question. Which means the future of American religious life rests significantly in this discussion."

—James Emery White (www.churchandculture.org)
Founding and Senior Pastor, Mecklenburg Community Church
Charlotte, North Carolina

"Every once in a while a book comes along that is a must read. This is one of them. Edited by David Dockery, *Southern Baptists, Evangelicals, and the Future of Denominationalism* helps us to understand better not only the history and present state of the Southern Baptist Convention but the future of denominationalism. It throws helpful light upon the various ways Southern Baptists and 'Evangelicals' have interacted with each other. Its authors possess an unfailing confidence in the power of Christ's gospel, a belief in the truthfulness of Scripture and a conviction that Christ is building His church. This book neither glosses over present problems, nor despairs that these problems are insuperable. It calls upon believers to follow Christ faithfully, to think biblically and to spread the marvelous gospel of Christ.In a word, this is an instructive, encouraging, and inspiring book—one not to miss."

—John Woodbridge, Professor of Church History
and Christian Thought, Trinity Evangelical Divinity School

edited by David S. Dockery

Southern Baptists, Evangelicals,
and the Future of Denominationalism

with Ray Van Neste and Jerry Tidwell

ACADEMIC

NASHVILLE, TENNESSEE

Southern Baptists, Evangelicals,
and the Future of Denominationalism

Copyright © 2011 by David S. Dockery

ISBN: 978-1-4336-7120-3

Published by B&H Publishing Group
Nashville, Tennessee

Dewey Decimal Classification: 280
Subject Heading: SOUTHERN BAPTISTS\PROTESTANT
CHURCHES\ EVANGELICALS

Printed in the United States of America

1 2 3 4 5 6 7 8 • 16 15 14 13 12 11
VP

To the Next Generation
of Southern Baptist and Evangelical Leaders:
May God grant you wisdom and grace
to care for that which
has been entrusted to you (1 Tim 6:20).

Contents

Southern Baptists: Understanding the Past in Order
to Explore the Future

List of Contributors

Daniel L. Akin (PhD, University of Texas System) serves as president of Southeastern Baptist Theological Seminary. A much-sought-after speaker, he is a respected theologian, preacher, and evangelical leader. He is the editor of *A Theology for the Church* (2007) and author of *God on Sex: The Creator's Ideas About Love, Intimacy, and Marriage* (2003), and *1, 2, 3 John* in the New American Commentary.

Mark DeVine (PhD, The Southern Baptist Theological Seminary) is associate professor of divinity at Beeson Divinity School. Dr. DeVine teaches church history and doctrine. He is the author of *Bonhoeffer Speaks Today: Following Jesus at All Costs*, and has written extensively for theological journals and contributed to *The Disciple's Study Bible*. He writes and speaks regularly on the emerging and emergent church movements.

David S. Dockery (PhD, University of Texas system) is president of Union University in Jackson, Tennessee, where he has served since December 1995. Dockery is the author or editor of more than 30 books including *Southern Baptist Consensus and Renewal, Renewing Minds, Biblical Interpretation Then and Now, Interpreting the New Testament, Theologians of the Baptist Tradition, Shaping a Christian Worldview, Holman Bible Handbook, Foundations for Biblical Interpretation, Southern Baptists and American Evangelicals, New*

Dimensions in Evangelical Thought, and *Christian Scripture: An Evangelical Perspective on Inspiration, Authority and Interpretation.* He is a consulting editor for *Christianity Today* and serves on editorial boards for a variety of periodicals and publishing houses. Dockery has served as chair of the board of directors for the Council for Christian Colleges and Universities, as well as the Consortium for Global Education.

Nathan A. Finn (PhD, Southeastern Seminary) serves as assistant professor of church history and Baptist studies at Southeastern Baptist Theological Seminary. Dr. Finn is coeditor of *Domestic Slavery Considered as a Scriptural Institution* (2008) and has contributed to *Calvinism: A Southern Baptist Dialog* (2008) and *Southern Baptist Identity: An Evangelical Denomination Faces the Future* (2009). He also serves as associate editor of *The Journal for Baptist Studies.*

Timothy George (ThD, Harvard University) is founding dean at Beeson Divinity School, Samford University. Dr. George serves as executive editor for *Christianity Today* and on the editorial advisory boards of *The Harvard Theological Review, Christian History,* and *Books & Culture.* He serves as general editor of the *Reformation Commentary on Scripture.* Dr. George has written more than 20 books and regularly contributes to scholarly journals.

D. Michael Lindsay (PhD, Princeton University) is the author of *Faith in the Halls of Power,* which was named one of the best books of 2007 by *Publishers Weekly.* Dr. Lindsay has worked for the Gallup Institute as a researcher, author, public speaker, and consultant. He has cowritten two books with George Gallup. A member of the sociology faculty at Rice University, Dr. Lindsay is the faculty associate of Leadership Rice and assistant director of the Center on Race, Religion, and Urban Life.

Duane Litfin served for seventeen years as president of Wheaton College. He holds an undergraduate degree in biblical studies and a master's degree in theology. His two doctorates are from Purdue University (PhD, Communication) and Oxford University (DPhil, New Testament). Dr. Litfin is the author of several books, most recently *Conceiving the Christian College* (2004), and his writings have appeared in numerous journals and periodicals.

R. Albert Mohler Jr. (PhD, The Southern Baptist Theological Seminary) serves as the ninth president of The Southern Baptist Theological Seminary, the flagship school of the Southern Baptist Convention and one of the largest seminaries in the world. Dr. Mohler has been recognized by such influential publications as *Time* and *Christianity Today* as a leader among American evangelicals. In fact, Time.com called him the "reigning intellectual of the evangelical movement in the U.S." He is the author of eight books and a contributor to several others.

James A. Patterson (PhD, Princeton Theological Seminary) serves as university professor of theology and missions and associate dean of the School of Theology and Missions at Union University. A native of New Jersey, Dr. Patterson previously taught at Toccoa Falls College and Mid-America Baptist Theological Seminary. The author of several articles, chapters in books, and 25-year institutional histories of Mid-America and the Council for Christian Colleges and Universities, he is completing a volume on the patriarch of Landmarkism, J. R. Graves.

Harry L. Poe (PhD, The Southern Baptist Theological Seminary), serves as Charles Colson Professor of Faith and Culture at Union University. Dr. Poe has published over 100 articles and reviews and has written or contributed to over twenty-five books, including *The Inklings of Oxford* (2008), *What God Knows* (2005), *See No Evil: The Existence of Sin in an Age of Relativism* (2004), *Christianity in the Academy: Teaching at the Intersection of Faith and Learning* (2004), *Christian Witness in a Postmodern World* (2001), *The Gospel and Its*

Meaning (1996), *The Fruit of Christ's Presence* (1990), and three books on science and religion with Dr. Jimmy H. Davis: *Chance or Dance* (2008), *Designer Universe* (2002) and *Science and Faith* (2000). He is coeditor with his daughter, Rebecca, of a book of recollections by former students of C. S. Lewis, *C. S. Lewis Remembered* (2006). Dr. Poe serves on several boards, including the Edgar Allan Poe Foundation and Museum of Richmond, Virginia, where he serves as president. He also is president of the Academy for Evangelism in Theological Education and the C. S. Lewis Foundation of Redlands, California, and Oxford, England.

Ed Stetzer (PhD, The Southern Baptist Theological Seminary) is the vice president of Research and Ministry and president of LifeWay Research. Dr. Stetzer has planted churches in New York, Pennsylvania, and Georgia, and has transitioned declining churches in Indiana and Georgia. He has trained pastors and church planters on five continents, and has written dozens of articles and books. Recognized as a leader in church planting and church trends, Dr. Stetzer is the author of *Planting New Churches in a Postmodern Age* (2003), *Perimeters of Light: Biblical Boundaries for the Emerging Church* (with Elmer Towns, 2004), *Strategic Outreach* (with Eric Ramsey, 2005), *Breaking the Missional Code* (with David Putman, 2006), *Planting Missional Churches* (2006), *Comeback Churches* (with Mike Dodson, 2007), and *11 Innovations in the Local Church* (with Elmer Towns and Warren Bird, 2007).

Jerry N. Tidwell (DMin, Southwestern Baptist Theological Seminary) is senior vice president for university relations and assistant professor of pastoral ministry at Union University. Dr. Tidwell is best known across the Southern Baptist Convention as the author of *Outreach Teams that Win: GROW!* which has been used in over 8,000 churches in the United States as well as in foreign countries. Dr. Tidwell served as president of the Tennessee Baptist Convention from 1999–2000, and was chairman of the board of trustees of Union

University from 2001–02. He has served on the executive committee of the Southern Baptist Convention, and serves on the board of the Southern Baptist Foundation.

Ray Van Neste (PhD, University of Aberdeen) serves as associate professor of theology and missions and director of the Ryan Center for Biblical Studies at Union University. His published works include a monograph and various articles on the Pastoral letters, including the study notes on these letters in the ESV Study Bible. He also serves as one of the pastors at a local Southern Baptist congregation and writes a regular blog on pastoral ministry titled, "Oversight of Souls."

Preface

The twenty-first century has ushered in cultural, societal, and structural changes at an exponential rate. We are watching as organizational systems designed for the nineteenth and twentieth centuries are being pushed to their limits. Some are collapsing. New paradigms are being introduced, creating much anxiety about the future. The world is much different than it was 50 years ago. Unfortunately, most denominations reached their peak 50 or so years ago and have been struggling in recent years to envision a new course to chart as we enter the second decade of the twenty-first century.

Change is not new to the church, nor is it new to most fields of study. Thomas Kuhn brought to our attention almost 40 years ago the importance of paradigmatic shifts in science and other areas, which helped us understand how change is perceived and interpreted generation after generation. Peter Toon and Jaroslav Pelikan have provided brilliant analyses of theological development and its impact on the church through the years.[1] Pelikan has reminded us that development includes not only change and diversity, but also continuity. Thus our recognition of change, paradigmatic shifts, and development is not the equivalent of a biological concept of evolution. Our recognition

---

[1] See Thomas Kuhn, *The Structure of Scientific Revolutions* (Chicago: University of Chicago Press, 1970); Jaroslav Pelikan, *Development of Christian Doctrine* (New York: Yale University Press, 1969); and Peter Toon, *The Development of Doctrine in the Church* (Grand Rapids: Eerdmans, 1979).

of change and development includes broader ideas than movement from the simple to the complex, or the basic to the advanced. Nevertheless, change is all about us and it has significant implications for Southern Baptists, for Evangelicals, and for the future of denominationalism in general.

The contributors to this volume are not pessimistic about the future; we are hopeful, largely because of Christ's promise to His church (Matt 16:18). Yet, we recognize that we find ourselves at a propitious moment when important questions about change, continuity, unity, and diversity need to be raised in light of the challenges around us. We not only want to raise the questions but look for answers that are faithful to our confession and our heritage. Many of the chapters take a long look at history in order to shape proposals for the future. Winston Churchill is credited with saying, "The farther back you look, the farther forward you are likely to see." We trust that will be the case for our readers as they work through the chapters that follow.

What is obvious at this time in Southern Baptist life, and in that of many other denominations, is a numerical decline in membership and a seeming disconnect from the denominational traditions for the generation of younger leaders. The disconnect has been created by rapid changes in our culture, which have been understood by a younger generation of leaders who desire greatly to engage these cultural shifts and respond to them in a gospel-focused manner. Times have changed. The contributors to this volume seek to advance the conversation with a recognition of this reality. We want to listen and invite others into the conversation to dream of a preferred future, with God's providential enablement, for Southern Baptists, Evangelicals, and churches around the globe. To the degree that we can embrace change while remaining faithful to Christ and His kingdom (Matt 6:33), we believe we can move forward together in faith and with hope toward the challenges and opportunities that await.

In doing so we acknowledge our limitations in seeing the present challenges clearly, much less their implications for the future. We do, however, recognize that we have been given a sacred trust. We have been "entrusted with God's work" (Titus 1:7 NIV). We have been entrusted with "the faith that was once for all delivered to the saints" (Jude 3 ESV). We have been entrusted with "the glorious gospel of the blessed God" (1 Tim 1:11 HCSB). And we have, therefore, been exhorted to "guard what has been entrusted" to our care (1 Tim 6:20). In many ways, it is this exhortation that serves as the motivation for putting together this volume of essays. We want to encourage the next generation of Baptist and Evangelical leaders toward wise stewardship of that which has been entrusted to them. We pray that God would favor them with great wisdom and abundant grace. We offer this volume in that hope.

I am grateful to all the contributors for their partnership in this work. I am deeply appreciative of the collaborative colleagueship of Jerry Tidwell and Ray Van Neste, who coordinated the conference on the Union campus, from which most of the chapters in this book originated. I am incredibly appreciative of the excellent work provided by Cindy Meredith and Melanie Rickman in the preparation of this book. It has been a delight to work with Brad Waggoner, Jim Baird, and Dean Richardson. For their friendship and invaluable support, I am certainly grateful. For the prayerful and loving encouragement that my wife Lanese has provided throughout this process, I am most thankful. May God's blessings rest on this effort. We pray that this volume will be used for good in the lives of many in the months and years to come.

Soli Deo Gloria
David S. Dockery

Denominationalism:
Historical Trends, Future Challenges

Chapter 1

So Many Denominations: The Rise, Decline, and Future of Denominationalism

DAVID S. DOCKERY, PRESIDENT, UNION UNIVERSITY

In this initial chapter we are going to explore the issues associated with the rise and decline of denominationalism, the shaping of American Evangelicalism, and what these shifts might mean for the future of Southern Baptists and Evangelicals around the world. We are going to begin by providing a sociological and historical overview of the development of denominations before we look ahead to what might be coming down the pike in the twenty-first century. I invite you to join me as we attempt to think together about these important matters. First, however, a hermeneutical caveat: I am both a Baptist Evangelical and an Evangelical Baptist, and I affirm both of these descriptions simultaneously. At times, however, the noun selected seems more important than the adjective. This chapter is shaped by my convictions as a Baptist Evangelical, more so than as an Evangelical Baptist, which would have resulted in a slightly different emphasis to and for this chapter. Yet, in the conclusion, you will see in some of the implications that I can't altogether avoid the "Evangelical Baptist" lens.

Let's begin by looking at Eph 4:1–6 as background for our reflections in this chapter.

> As a prisoner for the Lord, then, I urge you to live a life worthy of the calling you have received. Be completely humble and gentle; be patient, bearing with one another in love. Make every effort to keep the unity of the Spirit through the bond of peace. There is one body and one Spirit—just as you are called to one hope when you were called—one Lord, one faith, one baptism; one God and Father of all, who is over all and through all and in all. (NIV)

Introduction: An In-house Conversation

A Gallup Poll in January of 2010 asked about the importance of religious and denominational identity for Americans. It seems that fewer Americans than ever think that religious or denominational identity is important for them. Denominational identity and religious identity are seemingly on the decline in this country. I'm going to try to paint with a broad brush in this chapter so we will not get bogged down in details, but I want to help us see how we have arrived at this situation and where we might be able to go from here.

On the *Christianity Today* website in the middle of 2009 was a story that claimed that in 1990 there were about 200,000 people in the United States who classified themselves as "nondenominational." By 2009 that number exceeded 8 million.

Most people today think that denominationalism is on the decline. Some things about that decline may be good; other aspects may not be. The question is this: if the denominational structures that have carried Protestant Christianity since the sixteenth century are on the decline, what will carry the Christian faith forward in the twenty-first century? How are we going to respond to the changes all around us? But, before rushing to answer that question, we need to review our denominational history to see where various traditions originated. In doing so, we will try to connect the links of history to see how we arrived at this point.

In the 1987 publication by neurologist Oliver Sacks called *The Man Who Mistook His Wife for a Hat*, Dr. Sacks wrote about patients with a neurological illness characterized by profound amnesia, a syndrome that describes those who do not know what they are doing at any given time; therapists do not know why these patients wander around in a state of profound disorientation. In losing their memories, these people have lost themselves. I fear that American Christianity is on the verge of losing its hope and its identity in a similar kind of disorientation. The problem for many is not so much doubt, but loss of memory. The history of Christianity is best understood as a chain of memory, and we need to reconnect some aspects of that chain.

Going back to the eighteenth century, at the time of the First Great Awakening, there was already a movement toward a non-denominational identity. A forerunner in that century of what is happening in our day was George Whitefield, the great preacher of the First Great Awakening. While preaching in Philadelphia in 1740, Whitefield—who was known for theatrics—called out, "Father Abraham, who have you in heaven? Any Episcopalians?" The answer came back "No." "Any Presbyterians?" "No." "Any Independents?" "Any Baptists?" "Any Methodists?" "No, no, no." "Then who have you in heaven?" The answer came back, "We don't know those names here. All here are Christians." "Then God help us to forget party names and to become Christians in deed and in truth."

Whitefield's message is very similar to the statement of a century ago by one of the key editors of the volumes known as The Fundamentals, R. A. Torrey, who described himself as an "Episcopresbygationalaptist." That description may still typify many. C. S. Lewis, in describing denominational issues, said that our divisions should never be discussed except in the presence of those who have come to believe there is one God, and that Jesus Christ is His only Son.

Therefore, the discussions in this book are best understood as in-house, intramural family conversations.

History of Denominationalism

The idea of a denomination, which comes from the Latin word meaning "to name," is a negative concept for some people. Granted that there is no biblical mandate to establish denominations, they have, however, been important for the history of Christianity as the structures, the organization to carry forward the work of those who come together around shared beliefs and practices. Denominations have historically provided accountability, connection, coherence, structure, and organization to support churches, benevolent work, missions, and educational institutions.

In the history of Christianity there have been three major branches: Roman Catholic, Eastern Orthodox, and Protestant. The contributors to this volume come from the Protestant tradition, which began in 1517 with the posting on the Wittenberg Castle church door of 95 theses penned by Martin Luther.

We all know there are more than three groups within Christianity. There are hundreds, even thousands of denominations. Let's take a quick look at how the various movements developed.

Early Church

The early church was more unified than what we experience today, particularly as it came together following the great councils of the fourth and fifth centuries. There were four major councils from Nicea in AD 325 to Chalcedon in AD 451, and the bishops gave strong leadership and organization to bring about a sense of unity in the church. But, by 1054, there was a break between the East and the West, between Orthodox and Roman Catholic churches, which had been brewing for some time, particularly divisions over the use of icons and the infallibility of popes. Protestantism made a further break from Catholicism in 1517.

The Reformation

We trace the birth of Protestantism to 1517, where we find a monk with a mallet who seemingly had no intention of starting a new denomination; yet, that is exactly what happened when Martin Luther nailed his 95 theses to the Wittenberg Castle church door. From that initiative, denominations began to proliferate. As this movement began in Germany in the early sixteenth century, something similar was taking place across the border in Switzerland. Martin Luther and Ulrich Zwingli came together to see whether they could bring together the two movements often referred to as the German Reformation and the Swiss Reformation. They were able to agree on a number of points such as the Holy Trinity, the person of Jesus Christ, and the nature of salvation. Significant differences were uncovered, however, over their understanding of the Lord's Supper, and the groups went their separate ways. From this fracture came a proliferation of breakaway groups, not only those that followed Luther, Zwingli, and the Swiss Anabaptists, but also groups that followed John Calvin and others. A "third way" group developed in England, known as the Church of England or Anglicans. While there was much general agreement among all these groups, they were not able to agree on key details; new movements were spawned around the key points of their disagreement.

From these movements arose a concern regarding the growing fragmentation of the body of Christ. Philipp Melancthon and Martin Bucer, followers of Luther and Calvin, began to raise questions about this proliferating fragmentation. They issued fresh calls for unity, reminding others of their shared confession around the Nicene Creed: "We believe the church is one, holy, catholic and apostolic." But their calls went largely unheeded.

Seventeenth Century: Expanding Denominational Differences

The seventeenth-century Puritan movement hurried things along rather than slowing them down. If new movements began to take off during the sixteenth century in the Protestant Reformation, they went into an accelerated pace in the seventeenth century as the Puritans sought to purify the churches with a focus on preaching and experiential Christianity, or what they called experimental religion.

From the Puritans or Separatists came other breakaway groups: Baptists, Congregationalists, Presbyterians, and Quakers. By the seventeenth century the church looked something like this: The apostolic church developed from NT times to 1054, with Catholicism going in one direction, Orthodox churches another; Lutheranism and Reformed groups were heading in different directions; with Anglicanism developing as a "third way." The breakaway groups that developed within Anglicanism moved in multiple directions.

Eighteenth Century: Awakenings

The eighteenth century saw the awakenings springing forth in Europe and America. From these movements came the Wesleyans or Methodists; they were influenced by John and Charles Wesley, who preached thousands of sermons and wrote hundreds of hymns, many of which we sing today. John Wesley was an organizational genius, and his emphasis on methods led to use of the term "Methodist."

Nineteenth Century: Revivalism

In the early nineteenth century there were great revivals, including the Cane Ridge Revival in Kentucky led by Barton Stone and Alexander Campbell, who started what is often called the Restoration Movement; we sometimes call the resulting denominations the Churches of Christ and Disciples of Christ. The Holiness Movement was also a breakaway renewal movement, one that made the denominational picture look even more complicated. Each group attempted to purify what had come before, with the Restorationists doing an end run around all the others seeking to return to the ideal of NT times. They all claimed they did not come from Catholics or Lutherans or Anglicans or Reformed in any way, that their roots could be traced to something more pure, to NT times.

Twentieth Century: The Holy Spirit and Sign Gifts

In the twentieth century came yet another movement, the Pentecostals, who trace their origins to Topeka, Kansas (although something similar took place about the same time during the Azusa Street revival in Southern California). This sectarian group was not accepted by any denomination in the early twentieth century, but now they are by most accounts the fastest-growing movement in American Christianity and around the world.

Now at the beginning of the twenty-first century, Pentecostals have evolved from the Holiness Movement, and the emphasis on "distinctives" of each group has led to an unbalanced emphasis on our differences rather than our commonalities.

Denominational Distinctives

Roman Catholics emphasize both sacrament and tradition. The Orthodox highlight liturgy and mystery. Lutherans center on Word and faith. Presbyterians cling to the sovereignty of God. Anglicans focus their forms of worship around the Book of Common Prayer. Baptists place their priorities on Scripture, conversion, and baptism. Quakers appeal to the inner light, while Methodists proclaim a heartfelt religion. Holiness movements stress piety and separatism. Restorationists trace their roots to the NT church, and Pentecostals amplify on the power and manifestation of the Spirit.

So many groups, so many distinctives, so many distinctions. Can we say that these are all true to the words in Ephesians 4 that proclaim

there is one Lord, one faith, one baptism? There are dozens of varieties of each of these major groups, so that today there are thousands
of denominations in this country and around the world. Some have
given up on how to figure out these things, weary with the questions
about history and heritage.

So Many Denominations

The First Great Awakening, however, with George Whitefield's
emphasis, was, as we have noted, a step toward a kind of generic
Evangelicalism that came to prominence in the twentieth century.
The response to an important book in the early twentieth century
by H. Richard Niebuhr confirmed for many the problem of "so many
denominations." It reflects the overriding thinking today that denominationalism as a whole is a failure; some have gone so far as to say
it is sinful, divisive, and harmful. Many acknowledge that fragmentation, especially unnecessary fragmentation, is not good. But we must
recognize that Niebuhr's words that "denominationalism represents
the moral failure of Christianity" represented a focus more on the
sociological differences and ethnic identities within each denomination rather than doctrinal differences.[1]

Theological Differences

Theological differences are often thought to help people understand
and define denominations. But theological issues such as Calvinism and Arminianism are not the only ways to view denominational
developments. Some doctrinal emphases, it is true, are very difficult to
bridge. Perhaps it is better to understand denominational differences
not by asking who's a Calvinist and who's an Arminian, or who's a
Premillennialist and who is not, but rather to discern our differences

---

[1] See H. Richard Niebuhr, *The Social Sources of Denominationalism* (New York:
World, 1929).

from the vantage point of church polity, how churches are organized, how they structure and govern themselves.

Denominational Polity

History reveals that Presbyterians, Anglicans, and Baptists alike have maintained some kind of Calvinist heritage, yet they are quite different in the way they govern the church or churches (and, yes, there are Arminian Baptists and Presbyterians as well). We think of Episcopalians or Anglicans as those who emphasize governance from the top down, a hierarchical structure. Presbyterians have synods and/or general assemblies with external authority, as well as elders who are part of the church and who rule and lead from within. Congregationalists and Baptists, with their emphasis on voluntarism and the priesthood of believers, have developed something more akin to a bottom-up approach to leadership. Polity certainly seems to be a preferred way of understanding how these denominational differences came about.

Liturgical Practices

Another way, however, is to understand the development of denominations through the window of liturgy and worship. Roman Catholics understood the Lord's Supper in one way with their approach of transubstantiation, while Lutherans responded by saying the presence of Christ is not "in" the elements, but "over and around" the bread and the cup. Presbyterians answered the Lutherans by saying there's a spiritual presence of Christ, but not in the same way that Lutherans have described it.

Many Baptists responded by saying the supper is primarily a memorial looking back to the death of Christ. Quakers countered by saying "no" to all these, and do not celebrate the sacraments or ordinances. The primary differences between denominations continue to be over church organization, ordinances, and sacraments; or how we understand baptism: who dips or dunks, or whether a drop or a dab is enough water to qualify as a baptism. Whether we understand denominationalism from the vantage point of organizational structure, sociological movements, theological emphases, polity, or worship, there are huge differences among those who name the name of Christ.

A Sociological Perspective

Others have suggested the sociological window as the best perspective for understanding denominational life, observing that there are three major churches, the church in the East (Orthodox), the church at Rome (Roman Catholic), and the church in England (Anglican). Every other group, so it is maintained, is understood as a renewal sectarian group that has broken off from one of these. Lutherans broke from the church of Rome, Baptists broke from the church of England, and on and on. . . . The story is repeated.

But often the work of the Spirit seems to decline when these breakaway groups, these so-called purifying groups, these renewal movements become denominational structures themselves. When these movements go from "outcast sectarian groups" to "responsible denominations" within society, the emphasis seems to shift to concerns regarding structure, resulting in bureaucratic tendencies and often taking away from the work of the Spirit.

Jaroslav Pelikan has keenly observed that there is always a struggle between the work of structure, which is necessary to carry forward the work of Christianity, and the movement of the Spirit. Too much Spirit on one side or too much structure on the other can create error in one direction or the other.[2] It seems to me that the call for a Great Commission Resurgence in the SBC is something like that: a call to balance the structure with the renewing work of the Spirit. We have pointed to the beginning of denominationalism basically by going back to the seventeenth century. From that point we can see the proliferation of denominations, which grew out of and from within Protestantism through the movements of Puritanism

---

[2] See Jaroslav Pelikan, *Spirit Versus Structure: Luther and the Institutions of the Church* (New York: Harper & Row, 1968).

and Pietism, bringing about initiatives that rose from within these so-called renewal movements, all seemingly in search of a more pure and true form of NT Christianity.

Denominationalism through American Eyes

Denominationalism, however, like Evangelicalism—as most of us know it—is primarily an American phenomenon. This is not because America is the only place where denominations can grow and proliferate, but because the freedoms in America have enabled denominations to expand, flourish, and break off from those groups from which they were birthed. Now we find ourselves with so many denominations that it is almost impossible to keep up with them. Denominationalism, like Evangelicalism, is best understood as an American development.

Unfortunately—I say this carefully and with some dread—I believe this development has resulted more in the Americanization of Christianity than the Christianization of America. Because of this we need to think in a fresh way about denominations. We need to think anew about the structure that will be able to carry forth the Christian movement in the twenty-first century. Looking back to the time of the Revolutionary War in the eighteenth century, there were only three major denominations in the Colonies. Almost everyone was a Congregationalist, Presbyterian, or Episcopalian. About 75 percent of the population belonged to one of these three movements. But by 1850, less than 20 percent of the people belonged to one of these "big three." By this time, there were two new kids on the block: the Methodists and the Baptists. Particularly with growth in the South and in the Midwest, the Methodists and the Baptists outpaced other groups in numerical growth. The Methodists grew from a handful of people at the time of the Revolutionary War to becoming the largest denomination in this country by the Civil War.

This does not take into account ethnic groups and others who came along in the eighteenth, nineteenth, and twentieth centuries.

African-American churches were founded by George Lyle and Andrew Bryan, with the first such church established in Savannah, Georgia. The focus on freedom, pilgrimage, and hope characterized both their song and their sermon. From this initial work has come a great movement within the African-American churches as well as immigrant churches, many of which have remained largely non-English speaking even into the twenty-first century.

The charismatic movement of the twentieth century now has full sway among a growing sector of people. The songs that so many of us sing in praise and worship services can be traced back to the participatory worship emphasis among charismatics. This once-small group that was birthed at Azusa Street in 1906 has now spread worldwide. William Seymour could not have imagined what would happen with the Pentecostal and charismatic movements that began a century ago as sectarian outcast groups, looked down on by all other denominations. Now these groups, as previously mentioned, are the only ones in the country and perhaps in the world that are consistently growing—the Assemblies of God in particular.

The Birth of American Evangelicalism

The twentieth-century divisions, however, paved the way for the birth of Evangelicalism as we now know it. It is to the movement known as American Evangelicalism that we now turn our attention.

The Rise of Liberalism

The beginning of the twentieth century was characterized by social and cultural turmoil, massive immigration, urban growth, and a shift toward an industrialized economy. Every aspect of society and culture was influenced by these movements, even the religious world. People began to ask whether the Christian faith as it had been known, practiced, believed, and lived was still relevant in the midst of this changing cultural context. The Enlightenment and evolutionary thought that accompanied these movements resulted in the rise of Liberalism. Liberalism had a strong foothold in this country at the changing of the nineteenth to the twentieth century, largely brought about by these changes.

Influential shapers of Liberalism included Friedrich Schleiermacher, Horace Bushnell, and Walter Rauschenbusch. Schleiermacher with his book, *On Religion: Speeches to Its Cultured Despisers*, called for a way in which the Christian faith could be heard afresh in a culture influenced by the Enlightenment, attempting to adapt the Christian faith to this changing culture. Bushnell suggested that we needed to focus on nurture rather than conversion. Rauschenbusch, Baptist theologian in the early twentieth century, brought his emphasis on the social application and the social witness of the gospel, which began to substitute those things for the gospel itself, resulting in what has become known as the "social gospel."

These three influential shapers changed the Christian faith with their attempts to adapt it to the changing context of the culture and society at the beginning of the twentieth century. Their serious academic work was popularized by three great preachers, Harry Emerson Fosdick, Henry Ward Beecher, and Phillips Brooks, in key pulpits in the New York and Boston areas. Their sermons were echoed over and over again; they were masterful orators who had the ability to speak clearly, confidently, and prophetically. In 1922, Fosdick stood in his pulpit and suggested that it was time for the end of fundamentalism with a sermon titled, "Shall the Fundamentalists Win?" His answer was a resounding "no." He and others believed it was time for the triumph of Liberalism in the churches, a statement boldly confirmed in 1926 by the editors of *The Christian Century*.

These popularizers brought about changes in churches that could be characterized as the adaptation of faith to changing times. It was not just an attempt to make the Christian faith relevant, nor an attempt to bring it to where it could be heard afresh; instead, they were transforming the message of the Christian faith. The result was a lost connection with the great history of Christian doctrine, a disconnect with the "Great Tradition."

Their naturalistic perspectives about the world tended to dominate. These creative communicators brought skeptical views of the supernatural—particularly the reality of the miraculous—which elevated reason above revelation. This included the importance of experience over tradition. Now all these are characteristic of classical Liberalism, but we would be wrong to relegate these things to the last century, as we see aspects of them surfacing today.

Orthodoxy, Fundamentals, and Fundamentalism

Liberalism was challenged by orthodox Christians. The best response to Liberalism came from the great Presbyterian thinker, J. Gresham Machen. Machen suggested in his wonderful 1923 book that Liberalism was not a form of Christianity. He brilliantly contended that Christianity and Liberalism are different religions. Machen's work was masterful, articulate, and generally well received. It resulted in a revival of orthodox thinking. Many people found new ways to articulate their faith in the face of changing culture and the rise of Liberalism.

The claim that Liberalism is not a form of Christianity but rather another religion altogether found followers in the churches. Basically, Machen argued that Liberalism is empty, a position which was echoed by H. Richard Niebuhr, who poignantly insisted that Liberalism's basic message was: "A God without wrath brought men and women without sin into a kingdom without judgment through the ministry of Christ without an atoning cross." But Machen's response to liberalism was not the only one.

People in various regions of the country offered a more reactionary approach to Liberalism, resulting in a fiery fundamentalism. Different from the articulate, well-reasoned, orthodox approach of Machen, these reactionary approaches—best exemplified in the Southern fundamentalist J. Frank Norris, known as the "Texas tornado"—took no prisoners in advancing their movement. Fundamentalism developed from a defense of historical orthodoxy in The Fundamentals as they were so well articulated in the set of books by that name. These volumes offered reasoned and convincing biblical and theological arguments from a wide range of contributors including British thinkers such as J. Edwin Orr, Southern Baptists such as E. Y. Mullins, and some of the well-known Evangelical and fundamentalist leaders of the early twentieth century.

But the movement for an orthodox Christianity turned in a different direction when Norris and others redirected it from a commitment to the fundamentals to "fundamentalism," which changed the nature of the movement. Fundamentalism became reactionary, separatist, and legalistic, with a call for withdrawal from denominations. At this time, near the end of the nineteeth century and the beginning of the twentieth century, prophetic conferences came on the scene and called for commitment to what Norris and those who agreed with him believed to be foundational issues of the Christian faith, including the truthfulness of Scripture, the deity of Christ, the virgin birth, the substitutionary atonement, Christ's bodily resurrection, and belief in miracles. The list, however, became longer and longer as the fundamentalists had more influence in churches. Soon the list included commitment to dispensationalism, separatism, and withdrawal from denominations, which started the movement away from denominational entities and the important structures that had carried Christianity forward, particularly from the sixteenth through nineteenth centuries.

Fundamentalism became hard-lined, harsh, and isolationist, resulting in additional breaks and fragmentation. Splits in denominations started to take place across the country, particularly in the North among Presbyterians and Baptists. Numerous Presbyterian groups and hundreds, even thousands, of independent Baptist churches began to spring up across the country, as well as Bible churches and other nondenominational groups. New mission groups and Bible colleges were started, which brought new networks—informal networks that related to one another. These networks began to take the place of denominations. A need for some kind of structure became apparent, and so fundamentalism grew out of these controversies of the early twentieth century.

Twentieth-Century American (and British) Evangelicalism

Around the time of World War II (the 1930s and 1940s), many began to question whether fundamentalism had fallen off the tracks, as Liberalism had done. Several people came together around the leadership of Billy Graham, Harold Ockenga, and Carl F. H. Henry, all of whom called for renewed commitment to historical orthodoxy, or what was called "the new Evangelicalism," with connections to aspects of Revivalism, Pietism, Puritanism, and the Reformation.

In Henry's masterful 1947 work, *The Uneasy Conscience of Modern Fundamentalism*, he called for three primary changes within fundamentalism:

1. Christianity must not be anti-intellectual; it needs serious engagement with the Christian intellectual tradition, engaging the academy and the culture.

2. Christianity must not be only other worldly, nor may it focus only on this world either, for there must be a balance.

3. Henry responded to patterns of separatism within fundamentalism and called for Evangelicalism to be non-separatist and nonlegalistic.[3]

Ockenga, commenting on Henry's work, claimed that the fundamentalists had lost sight of the ability to do theological triage. They could no longer prioritize what was important as opposed as to what was preferential. Therefore, Ockenga said, fundamentalists could not distinguish the importance of the deity of Christ from the importance of opposition to playing cards. Building on the three pillars of

---

[3] See Carl F. H. Henry, *The Uneasy Conscience of Modern Fundamentalism* (Grand Rapids: Eerdmans, 1947).

Henry's argument in *The Uneasy Conscience of Modern Fundamentalism*, the new Evangelicalism appealed to a transdenominational, gospel-centered, historical orthodoxy, an appeal echoed in Britain by the likes of John Stott, J. I. Packer, and F. F. Bruce.

New Affinity Groups: Transdenominational Evangelical Networks

The early days of the National Association of Evangelicals, which began in 1942, pulled Evangelicals together into new networks, new alliances, and new ways of relating to one another, creating energy away from historical denominational entities. While people largely stayed within denominations, they related with one foot in the denomination and another foot planted outside the denomination. Most denominations, including the SBC, were quite divided over whether this new Evangelicalism was helpful or harmful.

As during the awakenings and the revivals, Evangelicalism primarily worked around denominational structures rather than through those structures, and created new entrepreneurial networks that were doing things differently from the way denominations had done them before. It therefore seems best to understand the development of historical Evangelicalism over the last 60 years as being carried out by people characterized not only by David Bebbington's fourfold description of traditional beliefs around the truthfulness of the Bible, the uniqueness of the gospel, the necessity of conversion, and the importance of service and missions, but also people who identify (at least in part) with these transdenominational movements, special-purpose groups (as Robert Wuthnow calls them), and connecting networks.[4] These new, interlocking networks, more than denominations, have formed and framed the center of Evangelicalism in this country over the past 60 years.

---

[4] See David W. Bebbington, *Evangelicalism in Modern Britain: A History from the 1730s to the 1980s* (London: Unwin Hyman, 1989).

Toward Restructuring

As Wuthnow emphasized in his book, *The Restructuring of American Religion*, this shift toward transdenominational movements is the biggest change in Christianity since the Reformation.[5] No longer do people identify with kindred spirits in vertical alignments such as Lutherans, Anglicans, Presbyterians, Methodists, or Baptists. Instead, they identify more around other connections and identifying markers such as Fundamentalists, Conservatives, Evangelicals, Moderates, and Liberals. Thus Liberal Anglicans and Liberal Methodists have much more in common than Liberal Anglicans and Conservative Anglicans; Evangelical Baptists and Evangelical Presbyterians more than Liberal Baptists and Evangelical Baptists. With this shift, we have the restructuring of American religion along horizontal lines rather than along vertical lines, which has changed the way that the structure of Christianity has been understood, especially when compared with the denominational developments of the past four centuries.

Wuthnow also has observed that the rise of special-purpose groups, sometimes called parachurch movements, has had a large impact on the shape of horizontal networks. Parachurch organizations, evangelistic and missionary agencies, relief and social organizations, publishers, broadcasters, schools, colleges, and seminaries have created new networks and coalitions. If you look at a directory of the National Association of Evangelicals, you will see that all these groups basically form the index or lineup of the NAE. These groups connect this loosely organized coalition called the Evangelical world.

The Influence of D. L. Moody and Billy Graham

But just as during the First Great Awakening, when George Whitefield made the first step in a transdenominational direction, so in the nineteenth century D. L. Moody popularized such movements. Moody was an entrepreneurial activist who wanted to connect the

---

[5] See Robert Wuthnow, *The Restructuring of American Religion* (Princeton: Princeton University Press, 1988).

dots in any direction he could to advance the gospel. These movements that Moody started were blessed under Billy Graham in the twentieth century, leading to expansion of these organizations. In this process, the organizations became more important than historical denominational structures. So with the rise of these special-purpose groups, the blessings of Billy Graham, the decline of liberalism, and the mainline denominations being untethered from their heritage, there developed new movements, not new denominations, into which Evangelicals poured their energy and their lives—parachurch groups such as Youth for Christ, World Vision, Young Life, Campus Crusade, Navigators, Prison Fellowship, *Christianity Today*, and thousands of others.

If I were to ask you, "What is the connection between Rick Warren, Chuck Colson, Carl F. H. Henry, Harold Lindsell, and Billy Graham?" the answer would probably not be obvious to some, but all had or have their membership in Southern Baptist churches. Yet hardly anyone thinks of them as Southern Baptists. Their identity comes from a parachurch group, a social network, or an organization, rather than a denomination. Historically, we identify Lutheranism with Martin Luther, Presbyterianism with John Knox, Anglicanism with Thomas Cranmer, Methodism with John Wesley, and the Baptist faith with William Carey. Christian leaders have normally connected with a denominational identity, but in the twentieth century, Christian leaders—at least in the Evangelical world—have been more often identified with a parachurch organization, or to use Wuthnow's term, "special interest group," which has changed the way we think about the importance of denominations.

Networks, Denominations, and a Theology of the Church

The Evangelical movement is largely understood as a grassroots kind of ecumenism that holds people together because of like beliefs and like structures. While Evangelical theologians have done a magnificent job focusing on the truthfulness of Scripture, hermeneutics, the doctrine of revelation, and the importance of the gospel, for the most part Evangelicals have not done a good job of articulating a theology of the church. That weakness has led to an ambiguous understanding of how churches relate to one another and how they relate to structures within and outside denominations, creating this uneasy marriage between the church and the parachurch movements. This observation is one of the reasons that many believe ecclesiology will be the doctrinal focus of the first decades of the twenty-first century.

Over the past 25 years there has been a slight shift. These networks have started to move away from parachurch organizations as a base, and more toward church structures. The shift started in California, largely with Calvary Chapel, which arose out of the Jesus movement. It then moved to the Willow Creek and Saddleback networks with Bill Hybels and Rick Warren. So that generation birthed the next generation with all kinds of new networks we know today as Acts 29, the Emergent Village, Desiring God, Nine Marks, the Gospel Coalition, Together for the Gospel, and Together for Adoption.

Now we are at the beginning decade of the twenty-first century, with major changes in the way people think about denominations and denominationalism. In 1955, when Will Herberg wrote his classic volume *Protestant Catholic Jew*, one of twenty-five churchgoing Americans tended over a lifetime to change denominations.[6] In 1985, one in three Americans during their lifetimes changed denominations. Today, in 2009, that number is about 60 percent, which means nearly everyone will make a denominational change in the twenty-first century. We have seen not only a change and decline in denominational loyalty, but also an increase in the number of people who identify more with a special-purpose group or parachurch group than with a denomination.

---

[6] See Will Herberg, *Protestant Catholic Jew* (New York: Doubleday, 1955).

Denominational Rivalry and Geographical Perspectives

These shifts have changed the way we perceive the importance of denominations, which results in additional challenges to the denominational diversity we have observed. The rivalry between denominations has changed. We find ourselves in a new, pluralistic context. Nevertheless, we cannot ignore the importance of geography, of place. New movements and groups have developed as the country moved westward over the past 100 years. One of the reasons that there seems to be conflict in almost every group and every denomination in America is that there is nowhere else for people to go. Thus, we see the rise of new, global opportunities. Certainly geography has shifted, but the generalizations about geographical presence and denominational influence still hold. Roman Catholics still have great sway in New England, Lutherans are most prevalent in the upper Midwest, Baptists are a majority in the South, and Dutch Reformed are represented throughout the Midwest.

Perhaps even more important than geographical regions are the kinds of cities or towns or places where people reside. Great differences in the understanding of denominational importance exist in metropolitan areas and cities versus those who reside in more rural areas. Suburban areas are where megachurches have tended to thrive. Surprisingly, more than 50 percent of churchgoing Americans attend fewer than 12 percent of the churches. The megachurches in the suburbs now shape large aspects of Christianity. They tend to be rather generic, which means that the denominational label means much less than it did in generations before.

Nancy Ammerman, a sociologist at Boston University, acknowledges this trend by pointing to the responses to denominationalism on the West Coast and in the Northeast, where only 32 percent of people respond positively to denominational identity, as opposed to 70 percent who do so in the South. The difference is even more exaggerated from rural to urban areas: 84 percent of people who live in rural areas still think that denominational identity is important, as opposed to less than half who reside in an urban or suburban setting.

One more important point regarding place: most churches can still be found in rural areas while most people live in urban and suburban areas, another reason for the decline of denominations. So, in addition to the influence of postmodernism and the other great changes and challenges around us, the shifts in population and perceptions regarding denominational importance are hard to calculate, particularly in metropolitan areas on the East and West coasts.[7]

From Mainline to Sideline

Most of the mainline denominations have sadly lost their way. Some have become disconnected from their heritage, and even more so from Scripture and the Great Christian Tradition. Some are not only postdenominational, but are on their way toward becoming post-Christian as their conversations focus around issues of inclusiveness and universalism, sexuality and inter-religious spirituality. In January 2009 the Gallup Poll issued results of a survey that it has taken every year since 1955. Over this time the poll has uncovered great changes. Sixty-seven percent of people surveyed in January 2009 said that religious identity or denominational identity was declining. Seventy-four percent of regular churchgoers agreed. Moreover, 28 percent of Americans said that denominational identity is "largely out of date." Compare that with 1959, where 69 percent of Americans said that denominational identity and religious influence were increasing, almost the opposite of the 67 percent who now say it is in decline.

Denominationalism and Evangelicalism: Questions About the Future

So what does this say about the future of denominationalism? While denominationalism is in decline, denominations still matter; certainly

---

[7] See Nancy Ammerman, ed., *Everyday Religion: Observing Modern Religious Lives* (New York: Oxford, 2006).

some sense of structure matters. I have appealed more than once in this chapter to Jaroslav Pelikan's important book on *Structure and Spirit*, where he maintains that Christianity needs structure in order to carry forward the Christian message. Yet, if we focus too much on structure we wind up on one side of the ditch, leaning toward bureaucracy. If we focus too much on the other side, with too much emphasis on the Spirit, we move toward an amorphous, shapeless kind of Christianity. So there must remain some place, some future for denominationalism or for structures, even as we recognize the importance of variety in an increasingly pluralistic context.

Denominational Conviction and Cooperation

Perhaps more important for the twenty-first century than the denominational future will be the importance of networks. Networks fit well the Wuthnow descriptions regarding groupings and structure. Networks now seem to be replacing denominations for many people, at least for the short term, and may be the most significant change in the religious landscape for the twenty-first century. I believe there will be a place for denominations, the SBC in particular, and denominations that thrive will remain connected by conviction to Scripture, the gospel, and their tradition, while working and exploring ways to partner with affinity groups and networks moving out of their insularity and seeking to understand better the changing global context around us. Learning to work afresh in cooperative ways will be important, with denominations no longer seeing themselves as rivals with either the networks or other denominations, looking instead for commonalities while working together with other special-interest groups. In this regard, I don't think I am naïve in thinking that the future of Southern Baptists can be very bright with such convictional grounding in Scripture and the gospel and with such a cooperative spirit and mind-set. Conviction and cooperation, boundaries and bridges, structure and the work of the Holy Spirit will all be necessary to move forward in a dynamic and constructive way in coming years. Tension among all these must be held together in balance without ignoring any or overemphasizing one to the neglect of the others.

A Global Perspective

We now find ourselves in this global context of the twenty-first century. It presents us with what I believe is a new opportunity in which we find great challenge and change. I want to suggest that there also is great opportunity for hopefulness. If we look around and all we see are the trends and signs such as secularism, the new atheism, the new liberalism, and fundamentalist reactions, we will likely be discouraged. When we hear talk of the decline of Christian America and an embattled Evangelicalism of young people characterized by a therapeutic deism, we can easily get pulled off track. But I would like to suggest that it is time for us to move from hand-wringing to hopefulness.

Without losing our heritage and the key distinctives that have shaped the Christian tradition, it is time for us to recognize that we no longer need to look solely to the Western Hemisphere for the future of the Christian faith. It is time for us to think more globally, even imperative to do so. In 1900, 80 percent of the Christians in the world lived in Europe and America. But in 2000, 60 percent of the Christians in the world were found in Asia, Africa, and Latin America, an unbelievable historical change. We must turn our attention away from our own intramural and denominational squabbles in this country in order to see what God is doing around the world through His Spirit.[8]

During the twentieth century, Africa was transformed from a continent that was 10 percent Christian in 1900 to 46 percent Christian in 2000. It is unbelievable to see what God is doing. There are now more Christians in Africa than there are citizens in the United States.

---

[8] See Philip Jenkins, *The Next Christendom: The Coming of Global Christianity* (New York: Oxford, 2002).

Over the last hundred years, Christianity in Africa has grown from 10 million professing believers to over 360 million. By 2025, the most conservative estimates are that if these trends continue, Africa will have over 630 million believers, Latin America will have 640 million, and Asia will have 500 million.[9]

At that point the typical Christian will be a woman living in a Nigerian or Brazilian village, as opposed to the typical Christian of 1900: a man living in a Midwestern town in the United States. What an incredible change in both the growth and the center of Christianity! Let us not miss the fact that the same kinds of directional influences are affecting us in America as well, for wherever denominations are growing here, they are growing largely among Asian-Americans, Hispanic-Americans, and African-Americans. Let us not miss this point: the look of SBC churches in particular must change. God's Spirit is moving around the globe, and it seems as if it is time for us to look in different ways with new eyes and fresh viewpoints in this country and around the world rather than with the old lenses we have employed in the past. While we continue to struggle with Enlightenment and post-Enlightenment issues, our brothers and sisters in Africa face the challenges of the demonic and intense persecution from Islam on a daily basis. As we look at them, their world seems more closely identified with apostolic Christianity than most anything you or I know from experience.

Toward Hopefulness and Renewal

But please hear this word: We must realize that our struggles are not against fellow Christ followers, but rather against the demonic, secularism, and unbelief. What is at stake if we do not take our eyes off the intramural squabbles that seem to characterize most denominations is not only a loss of the unity within the Christian movement but a loss of the mission focus of the Christian movement in

---

[9] Ibid.

the West. What is needed today among Southern Baptists and Evangelical groups is a fresh, committed, biblical orthodoxy, a historical Christianity, a faithful transgenerational and transcontinental and multiethnic movement that stands or falls on first-order issues.

Without forsaking our denominational distinctives, I am calling for a commitment to gospel commonalities that are more important than and precede our denominational distinctives. These include a commitment to the divine nature and authority of God's written Word, the deity and humanity of Jesus Christ, a heartfelt confession about the Holy Trinity, the uniqueness of the gospel message, the enabling work of God's Spirit, salvation by grace through faith alone, the importance of the church and the people of God who are both gathered and scattered, the hope of Christ's return, and the sacredness of life and family. In the twenty-first-century church we must learn to disagree graciously over our differences. We will likely not find ways to agree on a wide variety of secondary and tertiary issues. We must find ways to connect and re-create contexts of belonging for the multiple generations and ethnic groups within the body of Christ.

A Plea for Denominational Faithfulness

Still, we are drawn back to our opening question: What then do we do with denominations and denominational distinctives—especially the SBC? I still maintain that denominational structures can be helpful, guiding, informative, connecting, cohering, and even essential for us. If, for instance, you decide that worship on Saturday as the Sabbath is more important than worship on Sunday, then you'll be perhaps more at home worshiping with Adventists than Anglicans. If you decide that baptizing your infant children is more important than waiting for them to be baptized after a faith commitment as a mature young person or adult, then you will be more at home with Presbyterians than with Baptists. If you decide that going to war is not faithful to the biblical tradition, then you likely will find a place of belonging with Anabaptists or Mennonites. We still need to recognize that we have to find places of belonging around these common beliefs and practices because in our local expressions of Christianity we will still find it difficult to ignore these kinds of key secondary matters. Yet, we must be willing for those things truly to be secondary matters for the sake of a common mission to fulfill the Great Commission in this generation.

What is also needed for our day is a model of dynamic orthodoxy that must be reclaimed. The orthodox tradition must be recovered, one that is in conversation with the great history of the church, the great intellectual tradition that traces its way from Nicea to Chalcedon, from Augustine to Bernard, to Luther and Calvin, to Wesley, the pietists, and the revivals, resulting in what J. I. Packer and Thom Oden have called "the one faith," which has been believed by all people in all places at all times.

A recommitment to that kind of confessional integrity, I believe, will help us recover a call to the unity of the Christian faith in accord with the Nicene Affirmation that the church is one, holy, universal, and apostolic. All of us in this changing twenty-first-century world must recommit ourselves afresh to the oneness and the universality of the church. This recommitment must be supported by the right kind of virtues: a oneness that calls for humility and gentleness, patience, forbearance of one another, a love and diligence to preserve the unity of the Spirit in the bond of peace. I trust that God will help us to do so. Along with these things will be a kind of global perspective that includes a renewed dedication to racial reconciliation in this country, looking forward to a day in which the great multitude from every nation, all tribes and all people groups and tongues, shall stand before the Lamb as proclaimed and promised in Rev 7:9.

Trinitarian Christians, Gospel-Centered Missions, the Church, and the Future of Denominationalism

So do denominations still matter? Yes! I believe they do matter and they will continue to matter, but only if they remain connected to

Scripture and to the orthodox tradition. We need conviction and boundaries, but we also need a spirit of cooperation to build bridges. We need to understand that denominational heritages and distinctives do matter, but more importantly what is needed today is a fresh kind of transgenerational and transcontinental approach to the Christian faith. We need a new spirit of mutual respect and humility to serve together with those with whom we might have differences of conviction on less important matters. It is very possible to hold hands with brothers and sisters who disagree on secondary and tertiary matters of theology and work together for the common good to extend the work of the gospel and the kingdom of God on this earth. Our partnerships need to pull us out of our inward-focused insularity—particularly where we can work together in social action, cultural engagement, and matters involving the public square with Trinitarian Christians from across the board, and religious freedom, marriage, sexuality, and beginning and end-of-life issues. We can do evangelism and missions with gospel-centered people of various denominational stripes. Please, however, hear this: we will do congregational life with those with whom we find common beliefs, not only with those with whom we agree on primary matters of faith, but those with whom we find commonalities regarding polity as well. If this is true—which I believe it is—and if we can do more together than we can do alone, and if we need accountability and connections for our work—which I wholeheartedly believe—then denominational structures that reflect the attributes we have so described, and which connect the work of these congregations, will still serve us well in days ahead, and there can be a most hopeful future for the SBC.

We can trust God to bring a fresh wind of His Spirit, to bring renewal to our theological convictions, to our work of evangelism and missions, to revive our education and service so that we can relate to one another in love and humility, bringing about true fellowship and community, and, yes, to bring new life to Southern Baptists in particular and to other denominations as well. We pray not only for a new commitment to confessional, convictional, and courageous orthodoxy as modeled by many of the global church leaders, but also for a genuine orthopraxy that can be seen before a watching world, a world particularly in the West that stands on the verge of giving up on the Christian faith.

Will you join me in asking for God to grant to us a renewed commitment to the gospel, to the church, to the truthfulness of Scripture that will forge a consensus among Evangelicals and Southern Baptists, in particular, in bringing about genuine renewal and a renewed spirit of cooperation for the good of the churches and the people of God around the globe. Indeed, let today be a day in which we move from hand-wringing to hopefulness. Let's work together to advance the gospel and trust God to bring forth fruit from our labors resulting in renewal to churches, enabling partnerships with networks and structures, faithfulness to and for our denominations and denominational entities for the extension of God's kingdom on earth and for the eternal glory of our great God.

Sources

Ammerman, Nancy T., ed. *Everyday Religion: Observing Modern Religious Lives*. New York: Oxford, 2006.

Barrett, David, George Kurian, and Todd Johnson. *World Christian Encyclopedia. 2nd Edition*. New York: Oxford, 2001.

Bebbington, David W. *Evangelicalism in Modern Britain: A History from the 1730s to the 1980s*. London: Unwin Hyman, 1989.

Bloom, Harold. *The American Religion: The Emergence of the Post-Christian Nation*. New York: Simon & Schuster, 1992.

Dockery, David S. *Southern Baptist Consensus and Renewal: A Biblical, Historical, and Theological Proposal*. Nashville: B&H, 2008.

_____, editor. *Southern Baptists and Evangelicals*. Nashville: Broadman, 1993.

Dudley, Carl S., and David A. Roozen. *Faith Communities Today*. Hartford: Hartford Institute for Religion Research, 2001.

Dyrness, William A., and Veli-Matti Karkkainen. *Global Dictionary of Theology*. Downers Grove: InterVarsity, 2008.

Ebaugh, Helen Rose, ed. *Handbook of Religion and Social Institutions*. New York: Springer, 2006.

Ferguson, Sinclair, et al., eds. *New Dictionary of Theology*. Downers Grove: InterVarsity, 1988.

Finke, Roger, and Rodney Stark. *The Churching of America. 1776–1990: Winners and Losers in Our Religious Economy*. New Brunswick: Rutgers, 1992.

Garrett, James Leo, Jr. *Baptist Theology: A Four-Century Study*. Macon, GA: Mercer, 2009.

Gaustad, Edwin Scott, and Philip L. Barlow. *New Historical Atlas of Religion in America*. New York: Oxford, 2001.

Hamilton, Adam. *Christianity's Family Tree*. Nashville: Abingdon, 2007.

Hatch, Nathan. *The Democratization of American Christianity*. New Haven: Yale, 1989.

Haykin, Michael A. G., and Kenneth Stewart, eds. *The Emergence of Evangelicalism*. Nottingham: Apollos, 2008.

Henry, Carl F. H. *The Uneasy Conscience of Modern Fundamentalism*. Grand Rapids: Eerdmans, 1947.

Herberg, Will. *Protestant Catholic Jew*. New York: Doubleday, 1955.

Heyrman, Christine Leigh. *Southern Cross: The Beginnings of the Bible Belt*. New York: Knopf, 1997.

Jenkins, Philip. *The Next Christendom: The Coming of Global Christianity*. New York: Oxford, 2002.

Jones, Cheslyn, Geoffrey Wainwright, and Edward Yarnold. *The Study of Liturgy*. New York: Oxford, 1978.

Marty, Martin. *Pilgrims in Their Own Land: 500 Years of Religion in America*. New York: Penguin, 1985.

_____. *Righteous Empire: The Protestant Experience in America*. New York: Harper, 1972.

_____. *The Christian World: A Global History*. New York: Random House, 2007.

Mathews, Donald G. *Religion in the Old South*. Chicago: University of Chicago, 1977.

McGrath, Alister. *Evangelicalism and the Future of Christianity*. Downers Grove: InterVarsity, 1995.

Mead, Frank S., and Samuel Hill. *Handbook of Denominations in the United States*. 12th ed. Nashville: Abingdon, 2001.

Melton, J. Gordon. *Nelson's Guide to Denominations*. Nashville: Nelson, 2007.

Niebuhr, H. Richard. *The Kingdom of God in America*. New York: Harper & Brothers, 1937.

_____. *The Social Sources of Denominationalism*. New York: World, 1929.

Noll, Mark, et al. *Eerdmans Handbook to Christianity in America*. Grand Rapids: Eerdmans, 1983.

Noll, Mark A. *The Rise of Evangelicalism: The Age of Edwards, Whitefield, and the Wesleys*. Downers Grove: InterVarsity, 2003.

Packer, J. I., and Thomas C. Oden. *One Faith: The Evangelical Consensus*. Downers Grove: InterVarsity, 2004.

Partridge, Christopher, ed. *Dictionary of Contemporary Religion in the Western World*. Downers Grove: InterVarsity, 2002.

Pelikan, Jaroslav. *Spirit Versus Structure: Luther and the Institutions of the Church*. New York: Harper & Row. 1968.

Raschke, Carl. *The Next Reformation: Why Evangelicals Must Embrace Postmodernity*. Grand Rapids: Baker, 2004.

Reid, Daniel G., et al, eds. *Dictionary of Christianity in America*. Downers Grove: InterVarsity, 1990.

Rhodes, Ron. *The Complete Guide to Christian Denominations*. Eugene, OR: Harvest, 2005.

Richey, Russell E. *Denominationalism*. Nashville: Abingdon, 1977.

_____, and Robert Mullin, eds. *Reimagining Denominationalism*. New York: Oxford, 1994.

Sweeney, Douglas A. *The American Evangelical Story: A History of the Movement*. Grand Rapids: Baker, 2005.

Weber, Max. *The Sociology of Religion*. Boston: Beacon, 1963 [1922].

Wigger, John. *Taking Heaven By Storm: Methodism and the Rise of Popular Christianity in America*. New York: Oxford, 1998.

Wills, Gregory A. *A Democratic Religion: Freedom, Authority, and Church Discipline in the Baptist South: 1785–1900*. New York: Oxford, 1997.

Wuthnow, Robert. *America and the Challenges of Religious Diversity*. Princeton: Princeton University Press, 2005.

_____. *The Restructuring of American Religion*. Princeton: Princeton University Press, 1988.

Chapter 2

Denominationalism: Is There a Future?

ED STETZER, VICE PRESIDENT OF RESEARCH AND MINISTRY
DEVELOPMENT AND PRESIDENT OF LIFEWAY RESEARCH

Denominational Struggle

Denominations appear to have fallen on difficult times—including my own. Some denominations have been weakened by theological controversies over core Christian beliefs. Others have succumbed to classic liberalism. A handful of denominations, including the Southern Baptist Convention, have reaffirmed their commitment to theological orthodoxy. Even some conservative denominations have been going through difficult days. Statistically speaking, larger denominations (with the exception of a few Pentecostal ones) are generally on the membership decline.

Sensing this numerical decline, many church leaders believe the days of denominations are over. I have heard many pastors proclaim denominations to be more of a hindrance than a help to their mission.

The sense of loyalty that people in the past felt toward a denomination has in many cases declined, and in some cases disappeared.

Furthermore, some of the better-known churches in America today have no affiliation with a denomination. In the annual study by *Outreach Magazine* and LifeWay Research of the 100 largest churches in the United States for 2009, half of those churches considered themselves nondenominational. So many churches without denominational affiliation would have been surprising just 40 years ago. Much has changed regarding denominational identity in the past few decades.

A few decades ago, denominational meetings were some of the most widely attended places to connect and receive training. Now, events such as Catalyst, Exponential Conference, or those held by local churches receive more attendees than most sponsored by denominations. During the course of a year, I speak in conferences that are denominational in nature and nondenominational by design. At events such as the Catalyst Conference, I am often asked, "Why are you still in a denomination?" as if it is old-fashioned and out of style to belong to something like the Southern Baptist Convention. The answer to that question will become clear as I seek to answer the question: *Is there a future for denominationalism?*

This is a unique question for Southern Baptists, who are not a denomination in the normal sense of the word. The Southern Baptist Convention is a convention of churches, rather than a hierarchical denomination. Nevertheless, the founding documents of the convention explain it as a "body politic," with "said corporation being created for the purpose of eliciting, combining, and directing the energies of the Baptist *denomination* of Christians, for the propagation of the gospel, any law, usage, or custom to the contrary notwithstanding" (emphasis mine). Furthermore, most observers consider the Southern Baptist Convention a denomination from a sociological, if not ecclesiological, perspective. It is a different kind of denomination, and that deserves notice.

This question is being asked by more than just Southern Baptists. Throughout the Evangelical community, denominational loyalties appear waning among the membership. New church plants are regularly given nondescript names. Other denominations are feeling the effect of fewer members among their ranks as well.

Fifty years ago, one might have titled this chapter: "The Future of Denominationalism" under the assumption that (of course) denominations will continue to exist. But the very fact that another question seems more appropriate ("Denominationalism: Is There a Future?") signals a recognition that denominations are struggling.

LifeWay Research conducted a study of Protestant churchgoers who had attended more than one church as an adult. We explored the reasons that adults who have changed churches chose their current churches. The most important factors were the beliefs or doctrines of the church, the preaching, and the authenticity of members. Only half of these churchgoers indicated that denomination was important. Out of 19 possible factors, denomination ranked 13th in terms of the number of adults indicating it was important or extremely important. In the end, what the church says it believes and whether the members live out what they believe are far more important to churchgoers than denomination.

I have had the privilege of speaking at dozens of national meetings of denominations over the last two years. Leaders tell me they are struggling—with lower denominational loyalty and an unclear path for future impact. They are working hard to discern what the future holds.

When LifeWay Research polled Protestant pastors in 2010, the majority strongly agreed with the statement, "Personally, I consider it vital for me to be part of a denomination." Three-fourths of pastors agreed strongly or somewhat. The same proportion agreed strongly or somewhat with the statement, "Our congregation considers it vital for our congregation to be a part of a denomination." Despite the strong current life that pastors see in denominations, the majority see the importance waning. Twenty-eight percent of these pastors strongly agreed with the statement, "I believe the importance of being identified with a denomination will diminish over the next 10 years." An additional 34 percent somewhat agreed.

This last statement represents a pessimistic majority of Protestant pastors concerning the future of denominations. Only a couple subgroups of pastors differed significantly. Pastors aged 65 and older are less likely to agree that the importance of being identified with a denomination will diminish over the next ten years. Fifty-four percent of pastors aged 65 and older agreed with this statement, while 67 percent of pastors aged 55–64 agreed strongly or somewhat.

The strongest differences, however, are seen across responses of pastors of different size churches. Seventy-two percent of pastors of churches with 250 or more in average worship attendance agreed with the statement concerning the diminishing importance of denominations. This is compared with 64 percent of pastors in churches of 100–249 attendees, 62 percent of pastors in churches of 50–99 attendees, and 53 percent of pastors in churches of less than 50 attendees. (This not-yet-published study by LifeWay Research was conducted in March 2010.)

Denominations will face great challenges over the next few decades, and some people wonder whether the future of Evangelicalism lies in the independent church movement or in historical and traditional denominations such as the SBC.

Avoiding Two Faulty Assumptions

We must guard against two faulty assumptions when considering the future of denominations. First, it is a mistake to assume that denominations are necessary or even an integral part of the mission of God. This is not to say they are not, but lacking clear biblical commandment, we cannot assume that they should be. Second, it is a mistake to attempt to interpret the role of denominations in the life of local churches apart from the mission of God, since the *missio Dei* is the sum and substance of what God is doing in the world.

If we assume the need for denominations before the need has been proven, we commit a logical fallacy called "begging the question." We should not assume denominations are necessary without proof. Unfortunately, there is not sufficient space to make the argument within the purpose of this chapter. Instead, I will work from the framework of belief that a theological basis for denominational cooperation is both needed and possible to create.

Also, I will write from the position that denominations will, at least for now, continue to exist even if we do not consider them a necessity. Nevertheless, I will not assume that the present form of denominationalism will continue unchanged. As culture changes, we should expect that different forms of cooperation (and thus denominationalism) will emerge.

Addressing the second faulty assumption—attempting to interpret the role of denominations in the life of the local church apart from the *missio Dei*—is the key, in my opinion, to successfully navigating these waters of philosophical upheaval that have left many people wondering whether there is any place for such a structure. Until we are assured of the role of denominations within the framework of God's mission, we should assume them to be flexible, malleable, and possibly even temporary.

To neglect the *missio Dei* is to miss the point. The gospel has priority over the mechanism of a denominational channel. If denominations are to exist, and I believe they should, it will be to help churches fulfill the Great Commission and join God in His mission.

Recent history has taught us that many American denominations have lost even the basic capacity to retain their own membership. Reaching generations who are distant from the gospel and skeptical of religious bureaucracy seems to be out of their grasp for the moment. If denominations are to continue, it will largely depend on how their existence can be justified in relation to local churches and the *missio Dei*: can they enable the former, promote the latter, and be subject to both?

The Value of "Unnecessary" Denominations

I understand that denominationalism has a bad name in many circles. I suspect that a good number of people would like the answer to the chapter's title to be "no." Some might even say, "Let's hope not! And good riddance!" Some people view denominations as baggage from the past to be dropped in order to move forward to a more promising future.

But I think the bad connotations surrounding denominationalism are overblown. Do we have problems? Yes. Are there negative aspects of denominations? Yes. Are there weak and ineffective denominational leaders? Yes. But these negative aspects are a sign of our sin and human fallibility. They do not indicate an inherent problem with denominational affiliation.

I have seen denominations up close (particularly my own), and in all honesty they are not very impressive. They are not the answer to all the world's ills. Nor are they our last and only hope. They are not the savior of the world (only Jesus is), and I don't think they are the key to making known the mystery of the gospel (the church is). But, I do believe in the value of denominations. Having seen them up close, I know they can be a valuable partnership for churches on mission.

Many are impressed with the denomination—too many, in my opinion. It is their focus and passion. *But being consumed with the machine of the denomination distracts us from the mission of the church.* The goal is joining God on His mission, and denominations are merely a tool to that end. But we often turn tools into rules, and our focus becomes the machine instead of the mission. A denomination should exist to help us *live sent* rather than *maintain a structure*.

In my Bible study with Threads Media titled *Sent: Living the Missional Nature of the Church*, I used the illustration of a yo-yo to describe how a church should constantly be pushing outward into the mission.

> Think of it in terms of a yo-yo. When you swing a yo-yo around, two forces are at work simultaneously. The centrifugal force (technically "inertia") pushes the yo-yo outward, and at the same time, the centripetal force is exercised by the string, pulling the yo-yo inward. In the yo-yo, these forces are in balance at the same time.
>
> The church's challenge is similar. At any given moment, there is a centripetal force pulling us inward, tempting us to care most about ourselves, our comfort, and our development. This strong force is actually part of human nature, and it results in things like the Constantinian model of church. What makes it even more complicated is that the thicker the string, the greater the force pulling inward. So the more stuff we have—the more programs, buildings, and clergy we add—the greater the temptation to focus primarily on ourselves. When that happens, the church becomes little more than a spiritual department store, a kind of Wal-Mart for Jesus, providing religious goods and services to Christian consumers.

The same is true of denominations. Too many of those who are impressed with denominations are impressed with the thickness of the string. So we tend to look at it—to cherish the tool, the string— rather than to remember why it exists, which is to aid the church in advancing God's mission.

This is not to say that all have fallen into this trap. I served in New York and Pennsylvania where the average SBC denominational worker makes less than a full-time employee at Home Depot, and yet works for many more hours and for a much greater purpose. Even in places where the denominational structures are better funded, denominations are often led by people who are deeply committed. But we must also remember that it is our nature to get distracted from the mission and focus on the machine. Times such as this help refocus us and ask, "Is there a future and what might it be?"

Despite the struggles that denominations are facing today and will continue to face tomorrow, I believe that denominationalism does indeed have a future. There are several reasons why this is true.

Why There Is a Future for Denominations

Let me share a few reasons why denominations will be an integral part of the future of the church and its mission.

Denominations are inevitable.

Like-minded people will always find a way to associate with one another. Where independence certainly has its benefits, denominational affiliation has its benefits as well.

The Positive Side: Missional Cooperation

Denominations have been networking and partnering for decades, even centuries in some cases. From the Wesleyans' district partnerships, to the PCA's Mission to the World, to the Southern Baptist Cooperative Program, denominational churches have been working together for the sake of gospel influence longer than many newer movements. On top of that, the vast majority of world missions, church planting, and other forms of ministry are done through denominational partnerships.

Some level of cooperation between like-minded churches is both unavoidable and beneficial for those who want to make an impact in unreached areas of the world. A church gripped by the desire to make Christ known to the nations usually realizes it is unable to accomplish this task alone. We are watching as many independent churches begin to test the waters of cross-congregational partnerships and networks. I believe these networks are proto-denominations. Even though networks are increasing in prominence, when it comes to global missions, denominations tend to be the tools used by local churches to get the global work done. *Thus, my contention: denominations are inevitable in mission-focused churches and the best denominations may be understood as networked cooperative relationships for mission.*

The Negative Side: Tribal Self-Preservation

Denominationalism is unavoidable in a negative sense as well. Sometimes denominationalism leads to the perpetuation of a tribal, insular identity. One example is found in the Churches of Christ and the Christian Church from the 1800s. What began as a renewal movement determined to bring about ecumenical consensus and unity—essentially an anti-denominational movement—eventually became a narrowly focused nondenominational "denomination" that, in some cases, denied the possibility of salvation for those not in their rigorously defined theological camp. While some of the fundamentalist strains of the Restorationist group continue to dispute the idea that they are a denomination, the rest of the Evangelical world recognizes that part of the movement now evidences that an insular, tribal denominationalism has often been the result of an anti-denominational mind-set.

Denominationalism seems to be unavoidable. It exists whether propelled by a missional cooperation for the gospel or by a need to maintain tribal identity in an ever-changing culture. Although denominations are seemingly imperfect, I believe there is a positive reason for their existence: partnering with like-minded Christians for the propagation of the gospel. Interconnection with other congregations and ministries should be the heart of denominational participation. Although I'm not thoroughly impressed with denominations, I am committed to mine and to the need for others when (and only when) the focus for their existence is gospel cooperation. Cooperation for the gospel accomplishes more within denominational frameworks than independence without them.

What are some other reasons there is a future for denominations? Let's look ahead to the mind-set of the younger generation.

Younger Evangelicals are looking for rootedness in a fragmented society.

A variety of recent movements among young people demonstrates the need for rootedness and history. A mistake of the Church Growth Movement in the 1970s and 1980s was perpetuating the idea that only new and novel methods were effective in reaching the next generation. In our exchange of older traditions for newer methodologies, we unintentionally cut ourselves off from a rich legacy of faith.

Today's younger generation yearns for a sense of rootedness. In an age of fragmented societal identities, establishing a connection with the past has become synonymous with purpose and meaning.

We are seeing this passion in a number of current movements: the "Young, Restless, Reformed," the Emerging Church, the New Monasticism, and Robert Webber's "Ancient-Future" movement. Note how important this is to Jim Belcher's "Deep Church" efforts. He wrote, "The vast majority of people are confused by the debate" between the leaders of traditional Evangelicalism and Emergent leaders . "After all, don't they want the same thing—a deeper, more robust Evangelical church that profoundly affects people and the world?" In his book, Belcher expands on the idea of a "third way" that is rooted in history and contextualized in ministry.

These are sometimes overlapping, sometimes distinct, and sometimes competing movements. But each has been informed and fueled by a resurgent yearning for historical lineage and religious heritage. Many leaders of the Baby Boomers untied their churches from tradition and charted their own courses; many of the Boomers' children have spent the past few decades looking back wistfully to the shore. Denominations have not done a good job of making the case, but they can provide history and legacy to a generation longing for stability.

Even the incessant worship wars give evidence of this yearning among churches to engage contemporary currents. The musical artists at Sojourn Church in Louisville recently released an album returning to the hymns of Isaac Watts with a "new sound." The David Crowder Band often offers an old hymn redux on CDs. Chris Tomlin uncovered the earliest verses of "Amazing Grace" and reminded us of stanzas that are not in most of our hymnals.

The need to trace our spiritual lineage and Christian heritage drives us to shine a light on how we have arrived where we are. Historian and futurist Leonard Sweet offers the metaphor of a swing—its physics depend on interdependent motions of leaning back and pressing forward. Denominations can tell inspiring stories of pioneering and progress. They offer a rich sense of theological and ecclesiological legacy that the independent church simply cannot provide.

Churches in denominations have confessional systems that ground them in orthodoxy.

Nondenominational churches are pioneering the brave, sometimes confused, new world of American spirituality. But internal conflict and external pressure can inflict irreparable damage on a nondenominational church. And where will an independent congregation turn for help? When a denominational church is in crisis, it has a relational network, it has experience, and it has a support system on which to draw.

Denominations and their leaders have weathered many storms over decades and even centuries. Denominations have more experience at handling conflict, engaging in mission, and fighting through crisis. While none of these resources guarantee the survival of a member church, they do increase the possibilities. For our youth-obsessed Evangelicalism, this is a hard truth to hear. But where some see age, decay, and obsolescence in denominations, you may find longevity, maturity, and wisdom.

Evangelical denominations often are bastions of orthodoxy, while independent congregations more easily shift in their theology, sometimes quickly. Many (although not all) of the major nondenominational institutions have moved left theologically in the past several decades. Illustrations of this shift range from Fuller Seminary, to the YMCA, to many large nondenominational churches.

Of course, while some denominations have moved to the left in their theology, denominations with clear faith statements are more likely to maintain orthodoxy. Confessional anchors have kept denominations such as the Assemblies of God, Missouri Synod Lutherans, and the Evangelical Free Church from drifting. I find that some of today's most articulate Evangelical theologians are connected to those denominations. Today, denominations appear to have become the collective standard-bearers of orthodoxy.

What Kind of Denominationalism Is Desirable?

Up to this point, I have given reasons why denominationalism will continue to exist. So the answer to the question, "Denominationalism: Is There a Future?" is a "yes." But I'd like to go a little further than just speaking about *why* denominations will persist. We also need to ask ourselves, "What kind of denominations *should* exist? What kind of denominationalism is desirable?"

Let me reiterate that I do not have an unwavering allegiance to denominationalism. I work in a denomination that is at times dysfunctional and frail—like me. There are times when I grow weary of denominational foolishness and its drama. Working independently is, at times, tempting. In some ways, it would be easier for me to operate independent of the bureaucracy, red tape, and letters to my office castigating me for stepping outside someone else's comfort zone.

So I am not *for* denominations in the sense that I think they are God's answer for the world. No, only the local church is charged by Christ to storm the gates of hell. But a denominational structure can have value as a tool for the church in her mission. So, having established that there is a future for denominations, the question is, "What kind of denominationalism do we want for the future?"

We want to see denominations that are missional as opposed to tribal.

Denominations should be made up of churches that look outward rather than inward and help other churches do the same. There are times when it is important to take a look inside and see what problems exist. In the Christian life, we affirm the value of healthy introspection. Christians who never peer into the recesses of their own hearts and never ask God to root out their sins have too low a view of sin and too high a view of themselves.

But excessive introspection can cause spiritual paralysis. Becoming overly consumed with one's own status can make a person ineffective for the kingdom of God. Excessive introspection turns the Christian inward rather than outward toward the mission.

The goal and purpose of introspection must be to focus us again on God's global mission. As Timothy George pointed out at the Baptist Identity conference in 2006, there is something narcissistic about spending too much time debating and talking about Baptist identity. We must be careful to keep the mission in view instead of a perverse self-preservation. Introspection as an end, rather than a means, is done for ego's sake rather than for perpetuating a missional impulse. Evaluating a denomination's missional effectiveness guards us from tribalism. Introspection must be done only in order to be more effective in reaching *outside* ourselves.

Denominations should value self-sacrifice above self-preservation. Institutionalization drives its members to protect their unique brand rather than take risks to expand their influence. A tribal denomination full of tribal-minded churches will promote a tribal and inadequate gospel. When tribalism takes root, denominations deliver a message of "come and join us" rather than "go and live for Christ." We focus on preserving who "we are" rather than proclaiming who "He is."

With such a message, we create religious consumers looking for localized results within small boundaries, when Christ has come for the whole world. A missional denomination is made up of churches and Christians who are willing to make tough decisions at great personal cost to be on mission. A missional denomination is a place to focus as much on the giving we can do as the receiving we enjoy.

We want to see denominations based on confessional consensus.

I believe strongly in the importance of confessions of faith. My denomination is working to become more ethnically diverse, partner together with biblically faithful contemporary, traditional, and Emerging churches, and work through questions of our future. But in all our demographic variety, we must maintain a strong confessional consensus in order to complete the mission of God.

No denomination or fellowship of churches can effectively work together long term without a confessional statement. It enables the members to embrace biblically faithful but culturally diverse churches because we stand together around the biblical essentials. A denominational confession is a statement of biblical truths around which our churches partner. It serves at least five purposes, and each is essential. Let me use the Baptist Faith and Message as an example.

First, it is a statement for the denomination. I cannot tell you what every Southern Baptist believes, but I can tell you what the Southern Baptist Convention as a whole believes. That is the value of a faith statement—it says, "This *we* believe!" with an emphasis on the "we." Some Baptists may act in racist ways, but Southern Baptists have come together to acknowledge that racism is a sin. Some Baptists may believe traditional worship is a command, but our faith statement welcomes diverse types of worship expression. A statement of faith gives us enough agreement to work together knowing that we share a common theology.

Second, it is a standard for denominational agencies. Confessional statements give direction about who may serve at a denominational agency, whether a professional employee or a missionary. Churches do this every day—they make sure their staff believes what they believe. The standard of a confession promotes trust—the churches are assured that their missionaries (whom they may never meet) and the churches they plant are adhering to the collaborative statement adopted by the churches.

Third, it is a source for local churches. There is no mandate that a local church adopt the SBC confessional statement. Nevertheless, the SBC's confessional statement can be a tool that aids local churches. First, it can help a local church that wants to affiliate. Before they choose to cooperate, they know our standard. As churches are started, they may wish to look to the denominational confessional statement as a guide. Established churches have a tool they can use to state their general doctrinal beliefs as well as a source for teaching theology.

Fourth, it is a sentry against moving left. Our doctrinal statement says that Southern Baptists believe in certain things—the authority of Scripture, the deity of Christ, the sanctity of life, the standard of marriage, and much more. These statements define who we are and shield us from moving to the "theological left" by defining the theological boundaries of what it means to be Southern Baptist. Young or old leaders outside those bounds may be believers, but we think they are outside our best understanding of biblical truth.

Fifth, it is a shield against excessive distinction. A faith statement also shields a denomination from overemphasis on certain rules or distinctions. It defines an often-overlooked boundary—that which creates excessive distinction and unnecessary division between churches. Some will say we must dress a certain way, have a certain name, or use certain programs, but tertiary issues are not what define us. If the confession does not include it, it is not SBC doctrine. It may be a distinctive to a local church, an association, or a state convention, but it is not an SBC belief.

Confessional statements are always controversial. That is part of their nature—they draw boundaries on the left and the right. Because they serve such a great purpose, there is great wisdom in updating a faith statement, but it is such a major task it should be done infrequently.

A confession does need updating because culture changes. For example, who would have known in 1963 that homosexuality would be an accepted cultural reality by the year 2000? Or, thank God, that He has allowed us to see the sin of racism more clearly than we did in 1963. It is impossible to know what issues will need to be addressed in the future, but we can be sure that new issues will arise and old issues will need to be revisited.

Again, I do not know what every Southern Baptist believes. Nobody can. But I can tell you what Southern Baptists believe because we adopted a confession to inform the world, inform the churches, inform those on the left and right, and affirm to the Lord where we stand biblically and culturally. That faith statement can also help us in measuring ministry. As our churches become more diverse culturally and methodologically, we can measure innovations by the standard we have agreed on—a set of doctrinal principles that hold firm while our methods remain fluid within those doctrinal parameters.

I am the beneficiary of doctrinal consensus bound up in our confession of faith. Denominations in the future will stay tethered to confessional identity. But we also hope that denominations will allow freedom in areas not addressed in the confession, specifically our churches' diverse approaches to ministry. As I have taught and written, there are some things for which we contend (Jude 3) and others for which we contextualize (1 Cor 9:22–23). And that brings us to the third aspect we hope will be true of future denominationalism.

We want to see denominations that value methodological diversity.

Confessions are important but do not answer all the methodological questions that churches will face. Holding a common confession as a denomination gives us the confidence to trust those within the confessional community who differ methodologically from us. One of the signs that tribalism has replaced a missional identity is when we think that the denomination would be much better off if everyone operated "just like our church."

The inability to serve with churches of differing methodologies is one of the greatest hindrances to cooperation today. It is a hindrance originating often with those to the right of the confessional standard. Some will object with a "straw man" argument of a church on the extreme fringe of methodology. It is a tired argument that exposes an insular attitude.

Southern Baptists cooperate because of common doctrine, not uniform methodology. God forbid that we should apply the domestic standard some have of a uniform methodology to our foreign missionaries. It would only mean the outsourcing of a bygone era of Americana.

True cooperation can be maximized when those who pushed out many contemporary church pastors during the last two decades stand up at the SBC and say, "We were wrong—you shared our confession, but we mocked you from our pulpits until you left—and then we quietly changed our churches to look like yours did in 1987." It will further advance when my contemporary church friends will stand up and say, "We were wrong for demeaning the work of legacy/traditional churches on our blogs when your members were witnessing to my neighbors." We need mutual repentance and common appreciation for real partnership.

Some denominations specialize in doing everything the same way. Think of some of the mainline denominations who use a common liturgy and whose services all look alike. Some of these denominations take pride in the fact that there is so much doctrinal diversity within their churches. They value a monolithic methodology and a diverse doctrine. That's a problematic course.

I believe it should be the other way around. Denominations that are effective for the kingdom of God unite in doctrine and diversify in methods. We are to seek a confessional consensus, not a methodological one. We can work on a common mission for the glory of God and not require all churches to look the same.

It is a difficult shift for Southern Baptists who once operated as part of a monolithic culture in the South. Southern Baptist churches had a programmatic identity that was based on doctrinal consensus *and* common methods. We were a franchise-based denomination where churches operated the same in Alabama, Nebraska, and Oregon (if you could find one in Oregon). But in a fast-changing world that has turned multicultural, global, and urban, we can no longer stand united by programs. Our Bible, our confession, and a common mission must be the common bonds.

We are seeing some progress. Southern Baptists are not just talking about methodological diversity, but are practicing it. The illustrations often come in our annual meetings when we look at who preaches at the pastors conference and what churches are highlighted by the North American Mission Board's report. I am glad to see the platform widen and the reports remain gracious to those of a methodological variety all sharing a passion for a confessional consensus.

The denomination of the future must avoid the pitfalls of demanding methodological uniformity and instead look to unity around God's global mission. We need to include rather than exclude those who would have preferred a different future, who hoped the denomination would move more to their desired theological agenda—but we need to include them as they agree to cooperate with others around a common confession.

Example: Expository Preaching

Let me give an example that should elicit a response from some theologically minded Southern Baptist readers. I think most in Southern Baptist leadership share a commitment to text-driven preaching. But it is a mistake for theologically driven Southern Baptists to draw a line in the sand and refuse to partner with people who do not practice verse-by-verse expository preaching. Dogmatic rhetoric on the subject is divisive and unhelpful. Why? Because we have a commitment to unite around our doctrinal consensus—the Baptist Faith and Message 2000. And it does not specify any form of preaching as biblically prescriptive.

If you believe that verse-by-verse expository preaching is the only biblical form, I can respect that position. In fact, I preach expository messages most of the time. But when it is more helpful for the setting or need, I will utilize other forms of preaching such as doctrinal sermons or using multiple passages. Sometimes I even preach topically. (Insert your gasp of horror!) Of course, I always want the Bible to set the agenda of any sermon I present, as should every preacher.

Now, I should be able to make a case for why I think expository preaching is the most biblically faithful way. It is a case that should be made by persuasion with the Scripture (first) and our common confession (second) as a basis for thought. But I do not feel the need to demand complete uniformity in this matter or its inclusion in the confession of faith. I should be able to convince others of my point of view (in a charitable way that brings honor to Christ, I hope). But I will not attack those who do things differently.

Regarding other methodological issues, we should be able to utilize persuasion with our brothers and sisters. We should not resort to enshrining our methodological preferences into policy. Demanding uniformity in a matter of preference will decimate cooperation in matters of the mission.

Using policy to enforce preferred methodology (or, for that matter, theological issues that go beyond the denominational confession) distracts us from the mission. Instead, we should start utilizing persuasion to bring people to our point of view. By maintaining our baseline commitment through the Baptist Faith and Message, we can find value in the varied methodologies while cooperating for the Great Commission. The circle of Southern Baptist cooperation must line up with the circle of our confession, or else everyone (and every agency) does what is right in his (or her) own eyes—the result is a confused and ultimately divided convention.

In politics, we often hear about the need for a party to have a "bigger tent." For the SBC, we simply need an "honest tent," one that clearly displays the boundaries of cooperation and partnership. Obviously, that includes the bulk of our churches: a wonderful family of small, rural, and traditional. But, if our confession is to have any integrity, we need to welcome young missional Calvinists who preach verse-by-verse, contemporary church pastors who have most of their counseling sessions in coffee shops, and even the Emerging Church leaders who affirm our confession to be a part of the cooperation while they also move forward with other methodologies that are biblically faithful.

Pushing Forward to the Mission

In addition to always being challenged by the danger of theological compromise from the left, we might want to consider that the SBC also faces a challenge from those to the "right" of the BFM2000. I am glad people more conservative than our confession are part of the family. But I would like to see them stop pulling us theologically to the right and instead push us toward the mission. Those to the right of the BFM2000 should not seek to push out those who do not share their narrower frame of reference. Establishing new standards on secondary and tertiary issues must never determine cooperating relationships when a confessional consensus has been created.

More specifically, if an SBC leader says that he or she cannot be in the same denomination with a contemporary church leader because of his or her personal convictions (more like preferences), then he or she is the one who needs to leave the convention. Why? Because that person has established a more narrow standard than the Baptist Faith and Message 2000 (BFM2000). If Emerging Church leaders affirm the BFM2000, then they are within the confessional consensus.

If those to the right cannot cooperate with people who might not line up with them on every jot and tittle of their personal theology, they have moved outside the realm of Baptist Faith and Message cooperation and are operating under the independent Baptist mindset. It is their right, but they must not be allowed to undermine the confessional consensus that allows for methodological diversity.

Should we discuss the theological implications of methods? Absolutely. But we must not allow secondary issues to control the conversation. Nor should we preach against things that should be left to the conscience of individual churches. Instead, we should use persuasion like brothers in Christ rather than policy like corporate executives. To callously exclude those who disagree with you methodologically is to invite a level of arrogance that will bring ruin on us all.

I fear that the SBC is facing the danger of becoming like Machen's "Warrior Children," referring to the title of a lecture from John Frame in which he pointed out that the movement begun by J. Gresham Machen, which took a strong stand against liberalism in the Presbyterian tradition, eventually led to the splintering of denominations over less-important issues such as eschatology, Christian liberty, and worship style.

Frame wrote, "Once the Machenites found themselves in a 'true Presbyterian church' they were unable to moderate their martial impulses. Being in a church without liberals to fight, they turned on one another." The harsh reality is that these Fundamentalists ate their young.

Of course, there are hills worth dying on. Truth should indeed come before friendship. But Scripture condemns a contentious spirit, promotes unity in the body of Christ, and refuses to make every disagreement a test of orthodoxy. If we die on every hill, no one will be left to proclaim the good news of the gospel.

If Southern Baptists are not careful, now that we are in a denomination without liberals to fight, we will turn on each other. Fifty years from now, what will historians write about us, that we were warrior children of the Conservative Resurgence, splintering into dozens of subgroups? I pray we are remembered as warriors for the Great Commission, spreading the gospel to the nations.

Southern Baptists are at our best when healthy discourse leads to unity of direction for the Great Commission. We are at our worst when we threaten to swing policies around like baseball bats at Al Capone's diner. The BFM2000 is a sufficient guide to know what

Southern Baptists believe. There is room within it for our various views of soteriology, pneumatology, eschatology, and missiology.

Some in our denomination would like to move the convention in more Reformed directions, others favor more Revivalist traditions, and still others want to limit practices of certain spiritual gifts. No matter how sincere these beliefs, our partnership for the gospel must trump the differing of opinions we hold within our confessional orthodoxy.

The boundaries of the BFM2000 are gracious for a reason: to allow the greatest range of partnership possible for the propagation of the biblical message of Christ alone for salvation to the greatest number of people to be receivers of it. As we operate within the unity of our confession, I suggest we return to gentlemanly persuasion and a humble apologetics in the realm of our methodologies while celebrating God's salvation of souls, no matter if it be from Paul's planting or Apollos' watering.

We want to see denominations that assist local churches, not vice versa.

We must remember that denominations are begun for missional reasons and that denominations should continue for missional reasons. The denomination exists to help churches carry out the Great Commission. When we get this backwards, self-preservation becomes the goal.

The denomination is subservient to the church. The denomination exists to support the mission of the churches, not to perpetuate a temporary organization. The church carries forth God's eternal purpose and the denomination assists the churches to do so better, together.

By affirming that the denomination exists to assist churches in carrying out their mission, we are also affirming that the denomination's role is not to carry out the mission for the churches. Let me give you an example of this, beginning with an illustration. There are some churches with members who will not serve in the children's ministry or nursery care. But they realize that children's ministry is important. They understand the need to have someone in the nursery; they just don't want to be the ones who serve in that way. So they hire some workers to come in and keep the babies every week. They pay someone to serve so they can sit in the pew. By doing so, they exclude part of God's mission for the church and they become religious consumers focused on self-satisfaction.

In the same way, there is a mind-set in many of our churches that the denomination should send missionaries and plant churches. The churches can sit back in the pews and give an annual missions offering to our patron saints of Annie Armstrong and Lottie Moon. They give equal weight to Great Commission work and funding missions efforts. But God's mission is not solely a work-for-hire basis to a denomination. If the denomination tells churches to "pay, pray, and get out of the way," the end result will be churches that are unengaged, outsourcing what God has called them to do.

An urban spiritual legend persists that says denominations exist to plant churches and call out missionaries. It is wholly untrue. Local churches are responsible for church planting and missionary sending. Our SBC mission boards exist to help churches in their ongoing mission efforts— from the corners of the churches' own backyards to the far corners of the earth. The church is on a mission with the denomination in the role of servant to the churches.

This means the denomination is accountable to the local churches. There is no Baptist pontiff in Nashville, Atlanta, Louisville, Winston-Salem, or Fort Worth, or in any state convention office or mission agency headquarters. The heart of the Southern Baptist Convention is in its 50,000 congregations. Denominational leaders are not the boss, but the servants of the Southern Baptist churches. If the local churches believe we can be more efficient or more effective, then the denominational structures ultimately must bow to the wishes of the churches they serve. We believe that God grants authority to local churches and that in issues of cooperation, the churches—not the denominational leaders—decide how that cooperation is to go forward.

Conclusion

Yes—I believe there is a future to denominationalism. I was raised in a Roman Catholic setting. After God saved me, I became convinced of believer's baptism and the perseverance of the saints. Doctrinally, I became a Baptist. I am a *Southern* Baptist because of our cooperative efforts. I am a Baptist by conviction and a Southern Baptist for cooperation. So, I am staying in our denomination for five reasons.

I believe what we believe. The Southern Baptist Convention has a faith statement with which I agree. One of the great things about being in a denomination with a faith statement is that I'm not likely to show up at church on Sunday and find out that our doctrine has changed.

Churches that belong to denominations are the primary agents of global evangelization. On the foreign mission fields, "faith" missionaries struggle with spending part of their time at home raising money for the work. But you will find denominational workers in the field year round. With funding secured, denominational missionaries can focus all their energies on expanding gospel influence where Christ is not yet known.

Diverse leadership environments stretch me. I am a contemporary church pastor. That's all I have ever known. But I'm encouraged by the challenge I receive when meeting with godly pastors who dress and sing differently than I do. I need to be around cultures and faith expressions other than mine. In my case, I need to be reminded that God is bigger than jeans and guitar-driven worship.

Because God led me to be in the SBC. Sometimes being in a denomination isn't easy. While not every biblical Christian is called to be part of a denomination, I am. For me, this is where God has led and, thus, what He expects of me.

Denominational affiliation is not just about me. A denomination is not just a place to get something; it is a place to give and serve. Here I can contribute to the higher good of God's kingdom on earth. My gifts, passions, and experiences have greater influence through a worldwide denominational network. Through my denomination, I can give away resources to people I will never meet to reach places I will never go and give the gospel to the lost who are beyond my reach. It is a system where you can find what you need and give as much as you want to give. The key to cooperation is to both give and receive.

I am by no means starry eyed about denominationalism, but I believe wholeheartedly in partnership. In my denomination, we give to cooperative missions efforts on a voluntary basis. The churches I planted always gave 10 percent of their finances to that common effort (the Cooperative Program)—not because my denomination was perfect, but simply because we still believed in it.

If, one day, my denomination loses its focus, that can change. If some have their way, it would narrow parameters further and churches like the ones I started would not be welcome because they are not traditional, cessationist churches that practice closed communion. If others had their way, it would move to the left and I could not stay because of the affirmations of unbiblical positions on universalism, sexuality, or the nature of biblical inspiration.

But for now, I find strength in my denomination. It is not a prison, but a home. It is a home that has matured me and sent me out on mission. It allows me to share particular theological convictions, practice expressions of ministry relevant to my community, and serve a common mission with my brothers and sisters in Christ. And I believe it is a place of good stewardship. In His wisdom, God has allowed for the cooperation of churches in networks and denominations so that the greatest number of people in our darkened world can be most effectively reached with the one thing that brings true unity: the gospel.[1]

---

[1] This chapter was originally presented as the lecture "Denominationalism: Is There a Future?" for the Union University Conference: "Southern Baptists and the Future of Evangelicalism," Jackson, TN, October 6, 2009. The lecture is revised and expanded here. A smaller and less denomination-specific version of this chapter was published in *Christianity Today*, May 2010.

Chapter 3

Denominationalism and the Changing Religious Landscape

D. MICHAEL LINDSAY, ASSISTANT PROFESSOR
OF SOCIOLOGY, RICE UNIVERSITY

In 1988, Robert Wuthnow wrote a landmark book titled *The Restructuring of American Religion*. In it, the Princeton sociologist traced the development of religion in America—more specifically, Christianity in America—from World War II until the mid-1980s. Twenty years have passed since the book's publication, and we now see that many of Wuthnow's prescient analyses have come to pass. As predicted, sharp disagreements between denominations—such as battles between Presbyterians and Episcopalians—that formerly consumed the attention of religious leaders have abated. Wuthnow argued that in their place the principal dividing line would be between religious conservatives and religious liberals. New alliances and divisions in the American religious community now resemble larger partisan divisions and political factions. Indeed, we have seen a striking rapprochement between conservative Catholics and conservative Protestants to such a degree that Evangelical historians such as Mark Noll can legitimately ask in a recent book title, *Is the Reformation Over?*[1] It is not without irony that Noll left the Wheaton College faculty a few years ago for the University of Notre Dame. His academic journey as a scholar reflects wider trends whereby conservative Catholics and Protestants share institutional affiliations, work together in common cause, and find great synergy between their respective priorities and visions for society. In fact, the University of Notre Dame has become one of the most amenable institutional homes for committed Evangelicals to conduct top-flight academic research.[2]

As I argue in my book, *Faith in the Halls of Power*, American Evangelicalism owes a great deal to Notre Dame and other Catholic institutions for the movement's rising intellectual respectability, political clout, and cultural influence. From Harvard to Hollywood, conservative Catholics and conservative Evangelicals have found common ground as cobelligerents, building on a concept originally articulated by Francis Schaeffer.[3] As Wuthnow determined, from the 1960s to the 1980s, religious conservatives largely worked together in joint opposition to religious liberals, and vice-versa. The National Council of Churches (NCC) and the National Association of Evangelicals (NAE) rarely worked together and often had very negative views of the other group. Religious conservatives worried about liberals' indifference to the traditional teachings of orthodox Christianity while religious liberals fretted over conservatives' insensitivity to the plight of marginalized groups such as the gay and lesbian community. Most of these disputes occurred at relatively high levels as supradenominational entities (such as the NCC and the NAE) tried to position themselves within the cultural milieu.

---

[1] See Mark Noll and Carolyn Nystrom, *Is the Reformation Over? An Evangelical Assessment of Contemporary Roman Catholicism* (Grand Rapids: Eerdmans, 2005).

[2] See D. Michael Lindsay, *Faith in the Halls of Power: How Evangelicals Joined the American Elite* (New York: Oxford, 2007).

[3] See Barry Hankins, *Francis Schaeffer and the Shaping of Evangelical America* (Grand Rapids: Eerdmans, 2008); also, Francis Schaeffer, *How Should We Then Live?: The Rise and Decline of Western Thought and Culture* (Old Tappan, NJ: Revell, 1976).

Today, however, the major religious dividing line is not between conservatives and liberals. It is between those who are connected to faith communities and those who are not, between believers of all stripes and nonbelievers. Of course this has been the primary dividing line for the church for centuries—between the saved and the unsaved. Yet ever since Constantine's conversion, there has been a tacit—if not explicit—endorsement of Christianity in the institutional structures of the West. From the fifth through the twentieth centuries, a nascent Christian ethos increasingly permeated the public square of Western civilization, influencing everything from education to government to the economy.[4]

A number of findings have emerged in the last ten years that are cause for significant attention regarding this split. Consider five sets of numbers. The first is 6/6/16. In 1947, when Gallup measured religious affiliation among the American general public, they found that only 6 percent of adults were religiously unaffiliated. The majority of Americans were Protestant, about 20 percent were Catholic, 5 percent were Jewish, and a smattering of other groups made up the rest (The Gallup Poll 1947). When Will Herberg wrote his classic book on American religion in 1956, *Protestant-Catholic-Jew*, the title was a good summation of the religious mosaic.

Ten years ago, George Gallup and I coauthored a book called *Surveying the Religious Landscape: Trends in U.S. Beliefs.* In that work, we noted that measures of religious affiliation had been remarkably stable for nearly fifty years, starting with the 1947 poll and continuing until the late 1990s. In a 1998 survey, Gallup found that the religiously unaffiliated population was still 6 percent of American adults.[5] But something significant has happened over the last ten

---

[4] See Robert Wuthnow, *America and the Challenges of Religious Diversity* (Princeton: Princeton University Press, 2005); also Rodney Stark, *For the Glory of God: How Monotheism led to Reformations, Science, Witch-Hunts, and the End of Slavery* (Princeton: Princeton University Press, 2003).

[5] See George Gallup and D. Michael Lindsay, *Surveying the Religious Landscape: Trends in U.S. Beliefs* (Harrisburg, PA: Moorehouse, 1999).

years. In 2008, the *Pew Forum on Religion and Public Life* released a landmark study involving 35,000 respondents, and they found a dramatic change. The religiously unaffiliated population had grown to 16 percent—ten percentage points in just ten years. The General Social Survey and a number of other studies have subsequently confirmed that finding (American Religious Identification Survey 2009; General Social Survey 2008). Somewhere between 13 percent and 18 percent of the adult population in this country currently claims to have no religious affiliation. That is, they are not members of a local house of worship. When you ask them for their religious identity, they reply, "None." These religious "Nones" are growing in this country, and if that continues, it will have enormous implications for the American religious landscape.

Nevertheless, one important thing to keep in mind is that American religion, and American Christianity in particular, is remarkably durable. Pundits have predicted the end of faith for decades. The cover of *Time* magazine once asked, "Is God Dead?" (*Time* 1966). Just as social scientists reached consensus about the ever-increasing secularization of American society in the 1970s, there was a resurgence of faith expression in American politics—Jimmy Carter was elected president and Christians mobilized on a range of policy issues including abortion, human trafficking, and international religious freedom.

That leads to the second set of numbers: 56/16. Fifty-six percent of Americans who are affiliated with a religious tradition say that religion is "very important" to their lives. But so do 16 percent of unaffiliated Americans (*Pew Forum on Religion and Public Life* 2008). There are a few ways to interpret this finding. It could be a reiteration of the distinction between religion and spirituality, suggesting that even among those who do not want to associate with a local house of worship or claim a specific religious identity, there is a hunger for spiritual growth and development. Nevertheless, we tend to make a little too much of that distinction. After all, these respondents did not say "spirituality" was very important to their lives; they said "religion" was very important. Perhaps a better way of understanding this is through the growing anti-institutionalism we see in nearly every sector of our society. People today do not want to be categorized or identified with major institutions, and this invariably affects the religious sector as well.[6]

Americans increasingly do not like institutions—whether it be Congress, public education, or organized religion. Regarding confidence in organized religion, three numbers are key to remember: 65/60/52. In 1979, 65 percent of Americans said they had a "great deal" or "quite a lot" of confidence in organized religion. In 1998, 60 percent of Americans said the same thing. In 2009, when Gallup asked Americans, the confidence level had dropped to 52 percent. The good news is that organized religion fares better than other institutions. Only 38 percent of Americans say they have similar levels of confidence in public schools. Only 22 percent have this kind of confidence in banks; HMOs, Congress, and big business are ranked even lower.[7]

The remarkable thing is that we are highly dependent on institutions. They make life easier for all of us. In *The Social Construction of Reality*, Peter Berger and Thomas Luckmann adapted the philosophical thinking of Alfred Schutz and other phenomenologists to explain how people make sense of their lives.[8] We rely a great deal on institutions to simplify things. When a professor enters a classroom to teach students, he is unconsciously relying on the norms and conventions of the institution of higher education to justify why he stands at the front of the room, why his attire is more formal than the students', and why his assessment of a student's work matters more to her than that of a fellow student. The professor does not scrutinize these assumptions, and neither do the students. We have been socialized

---

[6] See Mark Chaves, "Secularization as Declining Religious Authority," *Social Forces* 72 (1994), 749–74.

[7] See Lydia Saad, "Americans' Confidence in Military Up, Banks Down," Gallup Poll 2009.

[8] See Peter L. Berger and Thomas Luckmann, *The Social Construction of Reality: A Treatise in the Sociology of Knowledge* (Garden City, NJ: Anchor, 1966).

into the expectations of spatial configuration, role hierarchy, and self-presentation in such a way that we take them for granted. That is how institutions exert the most power. Michel Foucault and Steven Lukes are social thinkers who have written a great deal about the exercise of power; they have convincingly argued that power is most potent when it is accepted without question.[9] Institutions have that effect on us; they facilitate the way we can take things for granted.

The concept of "institution" is very expansive. It can refer to a single organization, such as Union University, or it can represent a group of organizations such as "Christian colleges and universities." At the same time, institutions can cut across organizational boundaries. Just as marriage is an institution, so also are academic disciplines and schools of thought. Institutions organize and orient every moment of our lives. Post-Soviet Russia is an example of what happens when institutions fail. When the Soviet Union collapsed, so also did the principles of its planned economy, welfare state, and nearly every public service that people had come to depend on. We do not realize how much we depend on these institutional structures until they are dismantled. Even simple things such as being paid on time by our employers or not having to pay bribes to get our kids into good classes at school are things we take for granted because of institutional structures in our society. So did the people of Moscow until the breakup of the Soviet Union.[10]

Sometimes institutions save our lives. In a landmark study, Julia Wrigley and Joanna Dreby found that the death rate for infants in home-based childcare is seven times that of childcare centers.[11] In centers, infants are almost completely protected against violent

---

[9] See Steven Lukes, *Power: A Radical View* (New York: Palgrave Macmillan, 2005); also, Michael Foucault, *Power/Knowledge: Selected Interviews and Other Writings, 1972–1977* (Brighton: Harvester, 1980).

[10] See Theodore P. Gerger, "When Public Institutions Fail: Coping with Dysfunctional Government in Post-Society Russia," *Contexts* 3 (2003): 20–28.

[11] See Julia Wrigley and Joanna Dreby, "Fatalities and the Organization of U.S. Child Care 1985–2003," *American Sociological Review* 70 (2005): 729–57.

death, but in home-based care, infants are far more vulnerable to death from assault or shaking. Not only are workers in childcare centers screened more carefully and supervised more regularly than people who provide care in their homes, but they also have structural supports that dramatically decrease the odds that a child will die in their care.

In home care, some fatal injuries result from the anger of family members of the childcare workers. In one instance, a family day-care provider went to take a shower, leaving her boyfriend with the 13-month-old boy in her care. When the baby would not stop crying, the boyfriend put his hand over the baby's mouth for two or three minutes, smothering him. In another family day-care case, the caregiver's husband became angry when a 13-month-old girl threw cereal at him. She began crying, so he put his hand over her nose and mouth and then threw her into a crib. The child died, and the husband was charged with first-degree murder. In childcare centers, when kids become difficult and the worker's patience wears thin, there is almost always another person to whom the worker can hand the child, and the presence of other caregivers minimizes the likelihood that the worker will do something drastic when angry.

What does this have to do with denominations and the changing religious landscape? For one, it reminds us that institutions matter. Regardless of public opinion, Americans need institutions, and Christianity has come to depend on the structure and support provided by denominations. This is not to say that what has worked in the past will continue to work in the future, but it does suggest that denominations are important players in the field of American religion.

In some ways, Southern Baptists have been ahead of the curve, reinventing the focus of the Foreign Mission Board from countries to people groups and expanding the target audience of the Baptist Sunday School Board to the wider Evangelical world with LifeWay Christian Resources. In other ways, however, Southern Baptists are the final holdouts on a previous era's denominationalism, which is not good. Southern Baptist churches no longer give to denominational entities like they once did, and the average person sitting in the pew of a Southern Baptist church likely has far less interest in denominational affairs than was the case in his grandfather's generation.

The next set of numbers are positive 16 and negative 19. Mark Chaves of Duke University has shown in his National Congregations Study that the typical American congregation's average spending has increased 16 percent over the last 10 years using inflation-adjusted dollars. Its average income has increased slightly more. But the average giving of congregations to their denominations—through special missions offerings and annual budgetary allocations—has declined by 19 percent (National Congregations Studies 2006–2007 and 1998). Congregations are spending a higher proportion of their money to meet the ever-increasing costs of running a congregation. So even though congregations are taking in more money and spending more money, they are dedicating less in funds to their sponsoring denominations. Instead, a greater proportion of their funds are subsidizing internal operations—church programs, ministers' salaries, and operational expenses.

Southern Baptists are more entrepreneurial and more decentralized than many other religious traditions, which will help them find new ways to respond to these shifting tides. Presbyterians and Lutherans may not fare as well. Nevertheless, Baptist institutions will have to apply their entrepreneurial genius to find new constituent groups to serve and consider institutional aims that appeal to wider segments of our society if they are to survive the changes underway.

When I was researching for *Faith in the Halls of Power*, I found many committed Christians who had very little knowledge of denominational life. Thirty percent of them did not come from a churched background, and nearly 60 percent of them had a "born-again" experience after age seventeen. This is highly unusual in the context of church demographics. Typically, if people are going to come to faith in Christ, it happens before they graduate from high school. In fact, the figure among the people I studied is nearly nine times greater than that of average churchgoers (Lindsay 2007). Of course, my study population is not a group of typical churchgoers; they are top leaders in business, government, and culture. As such, they are different in many ways from average Americans, but they are still faithful Christ followers. Yet on the whole, they know very little about their own denominations and often could not articulate the differences between Baptists and Catholics, much less between Baptists and Methodists.

I thought this could be an artifact of age; younger leaders—like younger Americans—simply do not know their denominational heritage. But then I interviewed Art Linkletter who was 93 at the time. When I asked him about his faith tradition within Christianity, he replied, "I'm a floating Christian." I pressed him about this, and he continued, "Well . . . I'm just a little, frankly . . . burned out." Linkletter, like many leaders I interviewed, thinks that denominations focus too much time on administrative and internal affairs and not enough on reaching people outside the church or meeting their needs. As a result, these leaders care very little about denominational concerns, and as a result, they invest little time and energy in denominational affairs.

The last set of numbers is 59/52. Among the elite group of Evangelicals who were the focus of my book, 59 percent had changed denominational affiliations at least once. Many of them switched multiple times. To the extent that these leaders are involved in denominational activities, it is usually by serving on the board of a denominational college or university or seminary. They are relatively disconnected from their pastors. In fact, many of them are quite distant from their pastors, and I found that both parties play a role in this division.

From the minister's perspective, top business leaders rarely participate in local church life. Odds are they are not serving on the board of deacons, and if they are, they are not very active. Travel is a major factor. Senior business executives are gone much of the time. They cannot commit to weekly board meetings because they are not in the same place every week. This is also why they rarely teach Sunday school or serve in congregational leadership positions. This is extremely frustrating for most pastors. They may have someone in their congregation who is a proven leader, and yet he will not serve in any leadership position at the church. This flies in the face of what ministers learn at seminary. The basic framework for growing a church is to recruit people not involved in the life of the church and bring them into the congregation. The next goal is to exhort the people who are only nominally involved to a place of deeper commitment.

The problem is that the leaders I interviewed see this as a very insular approach. It is all about building a tighter community within the church. Instead, they want to engage in bigger issues beyond the church's walls. That is why they get excited when they find a pastor who wants to start a new health clinic for undocumented workers in a poor neighborhood, or to begin a new ministry for young people that involves mission work in Africa or the inner city.

Both approaches to ministry—focusing on the flock and scanning the horizon for new opportunities (and threats) are the responsibility of a shepherd. Church leaders need to see the value in both activities and find ways to join forces with those who are wired differently than they are. Sometimes, it also requires walking some distance in the other person's shoes. Out of 360 top leaders I interviewed, only one reported that his minister visited him in his place of work. That visit made an indelible impression on the business leader; he was able to recall what his pastor was wearing, what they talked about, and which colleagues and workers he introduced to his minister. Most remarkably, that encounter had taken place 20 years earlier. The leaders I interviewed long for their pastors to get to know their worlds better.

These kinds of issues might explain why 59 percent of the leaders I interviewed switch denominations. They do not feel connected to their pastors, may have only tangential connections with their churches, and as a result feel distant from their sponsoring denominations. My sense is that this is very different from 50 years ago, but

Art Linkletter's comments suggest that it is not merely the result of generational differences. This affects leaders of all ages.

Despite this finding, most of the leaders I interviewed are interested in religious activities. Fifty-two percent of them are actively involved in some type of faith-based small group. Whereas many of them are lukewarm about supporting their local churches and their denominations, they are noticeably committed to small-group Bible studies, fellowship circles, and accountability groups. Of course, these are smaller, and the participants select which groups they join. As a result, these groups are not very diverse—socioeconomically, politically, or culturally. But then again, neither are many churches.[12] What is appealing about these small groups is that they meet felt needs, including community, friendship, and Christian discipleship. Some small groups provide Bible study and facilitate deep personal reflection. Others do not. But nearly all of them create relationships that people can rely on in good and bad times.

Nearly all of the institutions that are thriving today have relational components. Growth is not necessarily a good thing, as evidenced by the public's concern about the increasing size of the federal government, but growth is a useful indicator, especially when it emerges out of willing participation. Consider the tremendous growth of online networks such as Facebook and LinkedIn. These represent institutions, but they are nimble institutions—more like networks than bureaucracies. In the religious realm, how is it that the Willow Creek Association has more than 12,000 congregations, making it larger than most denominations in this country including the Evangelical Lutheran Church in America and the Episcopal Church in the United States?

The Willow Creek Association provides what many denominations used to provide—quality continuing education programs and a platform through which ideas can be shared and professional

---

[12] See Michael O. Emerson and Christian Smith, *Divided by Faith: Evangelical Religion and the Problem of Race in America* (New York: Oxford, 2000).

connections can be made. Certain denominations, such as the Southern Baptist Convention, do a much better job than others at facilitating connections and providing resources. But much more work needs to be done.

It should now be clear that institutions are vitally important and that if we see denominations more like flexible networks instead of stolid bureaucracies, we can find examples of institutions that people sign up for every single day. Here are three cultural currents that underscore the need for denominations in American religious life.

First, institutions provide accountability, which increases levels of trust. A few years ago, I first encountered the research that I mentioned earlier about childcare centers and childcare work taking place in people's homes. I have a six-year-old daughter, and I have to say that I am now less inclined than I once was to support a childcare service out of somebody's home. That is not to say that I would never do it, but if given the choice and all things being equal, I will opt for the setting with more institutional oversight. I used to think that as long as I had confidence in the person who was taking care of the child—that he or she was loving, responsible, and competent—then all would be well. But there came a time that I was at my wit's end when our baby would not stop crying. It had been going on for hours. I was tired and frustrated, and suddenly I could understand how someone could shake a baby out of anger.

Institutions provide vital buffers against our worst instincts. Churches need denominations because they can provide institutional ballast when churches or pastors need help in weathering certain kinds of storms. The Southern Baptist model of ecclesial life provides less accountability and oversight than the ecclesiology of Roman Catholicism. That is why Southern Baptist institutions are not as massive as those of the Catholic Church. But the SBC still provides forms of accountability, which can inspire more trust and confidence among churchgoers and the general public.

Second, denominations exercise convening power, which is the ability to bring disparate people together, such as introducing one college president to another or one pastor to a missions executive. In essence, convening power is what flows through social networks. It allows leaders to marshal resources, to share information, and to deflect criticism. The power of a leader has to match his moment in history. Being a fierce warrior was an invaluable resource for a leader in the early medieval period, an era when conquest and military power were the primary currency of status and respect. Throughout much of Colonial America, theological education and scholarly erudition gave ministers significant clout and moral authority.

Today, the most powerful actors are people and groups who can bring individuals together and use their skills of persuasion to advocate for a certain course of action. Convening power is the currency of influence today. The bully pulpit of the American presidency is often used to convene groups for policy discussions and political maneuvering. Like all forms of power, the power to convene typically resides in a position or a group, not in the hands of a single individual. That is why institutions such as the World Economic Forum or the Aspen Institute are able to draw people together in ways that individual leaders such as Bill Clinton or George W. Bush cannot. Once convened, these meetings provide social space for interaction among peers where they can discuss ideas that can then be carried out by the organizations they run. Convening power is a potent resource for a group on the move. Of course, convening power is necessary but not sufficient for accomplishing goals. For that, decision-making power is also required. Nevertheless, denominations can exercise remarkable convening power, if deployed in the right ways.

Third, the institutional gravitas provided by denominations is especially needed in the current era because of the increasing complexity of getting things done in a globally connected, highly diversified world. Institutions continue to be formed every single day. They are nimbler and closer to the ground than institutions established a hundred years ago, but businesses and nonprofits recognize that institutional structures are required for long-term, systemic influence. We may complain about bureaucracies, but as Max Weber has shown us, they provide four useful tools for accomplishing organizational goals and retaining talented people. Simply stated, these four aspects of bureaucracy are rules, roles, records, and rewards, all of which are needed to deal with complexity and uncertainty in a global environment.[13]

Denominations can lay out ground rules for cooperation among churches and for mission activities. Without such guidelines, powerful personalities can take over the process, squashing dissent and alternative ideas in the process.

Denominations can also structure important roles occupied by people within their own organizations and in related entities. For example, the very structure of the Southern Baptist Convention's entities, which separates the functions of Christian education from Christian mission, has been replicated in thousands of SBC churches that employ one person devoted to the church's educational endeavors and another person devoted to missions priorities. Bureaucracies can help organize the work that people and organizations want to accomplish. That can be frustrating to an entrepreneur who wants to combine activities or rearrange responsibilities, but it can ensure that certain essential functions are carried out even as people transition from one job to another.

Denominations also help maintain records, which are vital today. In essence, our society has transferred the responsibility of institutional memory from individuals to organizational archives. That is a very good thing in this day and age. We keep track of so many measurable outcomes that there is no way one individual or even a group of individuals could keep track of all of them. Institutional records also help maintain a degree of objectivity, which is one of the main benefits of bureaucracy. We need impartial adjudicators when decisions have to be made under uncertain conditions. Bureaucracies help us structure the mechanisms to make those decisions.

---

[13] See Max Weber, *Economy and Society*, edited by Guenther Roth and Claus Wittich (Berkeley: University of California Press, 1947 [1978]).

Finally, bureaucratic denominations—when living up to their potential—reward people for good performance. The things that denominations reward become benchmarks for individual churches. If the SBC recognizes churches that have the most baptisms in a single year, member churches pay attention. Rewards have a way of reorienting our behavior in useful ways. They clarify what is important and identify metrics by which to evaluate our own progress.

So despite some of the statistics referenced earlier, institutions matter, and denominations have important roles to play in the American religious landscape. The Evangelical community tends to think mostly in terms of the individual. This individualistic thinking has some merits, but there is also a great need to think institutionally. That is how to ensure lasting influence in a society that is dominated by large institutions. Gone are the days when Evangelicals could be content with changing only one person's heart at a time. The issues the church will have to face in the coming years are too great; the demographic shifts currently underway are too significant to fall back into a simplistic individualism that is incapable of facing the challenges that lie ahead.

One of my favorite examples of how individual leaders can take advantage of their institutional authority involves Horst Schulze. I first met Horst five years ago while researching *Faith in the Halls of Power*. For 20 years, he served as president of Ritz-Carlton Hotels and Resorts. He was tapped for the job in the early 1980s after a successful career as an executive at Hyatt Hotels. When Ritz-Carlton's investors approached him, he said he would take the job on one condition: he wanted the power to build the new organization's culture. Because he had proven himself at Hyatt, the investors trusted Horst Schulze and gave him free rein to mold the institution as he saw fit. He used that occasion to pull out a paper that he had written as a 15-year-old boy in school. Horst attended hospitality trade school in his native Germany. He used to walk to and from school every day, and one week his teacher assigned a paper that required him to write a manifesto for the hospitality industry. As a 15-year-old, he was not sure what to say, but then he heard a sermon and the idea struck him.

His pastor preached a message on Sunday from Genesis where he explained what it means for humans to be made in God's image. Suddenly, Horst realized something within the hospitality industry that had always made him uneasy, but he had not had the words to explain it. One of the major messages of his trade school—which specialized in training workers for European luxury hotels—was that there is a difference between the hotel's clientele and its staff. It was not just a difference of roles; it was also an existential difference.

Students were taught that they were not worth the same as the customers they served. The hotels constantly reinforced this second-class citizenship mind-set by requiring, for example, housekeepers to acknowledge a guest when passing in the hallway, but then for house-keepers to look down, so as not to intrude on the personal space of the guest. For Schulze, this did not jive with his impression of the Bible's main message—that all people are made in God's image and that because of the love God has shown the world in Christ, his fol-lowers ought to love others as brothers and sisters. Do unto others as we would have done unto ourselves.

The paper that Schulze wrote earned the only "A" he received in school, so he knew he was on to something. His manifesto declared, "The hospitality industry ought to reimagine itself as being made up of ladies and gentlemen serving ladies and gentlemen." That became the organizational motto of Ritz-Carlton Hotels and Resorts. Dish-washers, housekeepers, bellmen, and staff at the front desk—all of them were to conduct themselves, and indeed see themselves, as ladies and gentlemen serving ladies and gentlemen.

The idea was brilliant. Ritz-Carlton was a workplace of incred-ible employee morale; the customers sensed something different, and they became loyal to the brand. Ritz-Carlton was awarded the cov-eted Malcolm Baldrige Award twice under Schulze's leadership. All of the hotel's competitors would come to the corporate headquarters in Atlanta trying to learn the company's secrets. Schulze told me, "They came to study us and how we did it. They peeled down the onion, and in the end, they saw a bunch of Christians . . . [operating an organization] with absolute sincerity . . . based on true Christian values" like all people made in the image of God and following the Golden Rule.

The amazing thing about institutions is that they outlive individuals. Schulze retired from Ritz-Carlton several years ago. A few months back, I stayed in one of its hotels while speaking at a conference. On my last evening, the manager sent a note, which I imagine he sends to every guest on their last evening at the hotel. He thanked me for staying there and invited me back. The letter concluded with a signature line that read "the ladies and gentlemen of Ritz-Carlton."

Institutions can be enormous resources in creating a more just, righteous, and peaceful society. The challenge that denominations face today is essentially the challenge of every institution in a changing society, especially religious institutions. It is to pool the resources and talent at their disposal not just to advance the aim of their individual organization, but to advance God's work of redeeming the very structures of our society by creating contexts that allow for human flourishing and by working together for the common good.

Sources

American Identification Survey. http://www.americanreligionsurvey-aris.org/, accessed 2009.

Anderson, William E. "The State of Giving in the Southern Baptist Convention: Third Report of the SBC Funding Study Committee to the Executive Committee of the Southern Baptist Convention (2003)." *Baptist 2 Baptist*. http://baptisttobaptist.net/b2barticle.asp?ID=293, retrieved February 11, 2010.

Berger, Peter L., and Thomas Luckmann. *The Social Construction of Reality: A Treatise in the Sociology of Knowledge*. Garden City, NY: Anchor Books, 1966.

Chaves, Mark. "Secularization as Declining Religious Authority." *Social Forces* 72 (1994): 749–74.

Emerson, Michael O., and Christian Smith. *Divided by Faith: Evangelical Religion and the Problem of Race in America*. New York: Oxford University Press, 2000.

Foucault, Michel. *Power/Knowledge: Selected Interviews and Other Writings, 1972–1977*. Brighton: Harvester, 1980.

Gallup, George, and D. Michael Lindsay. *Surveying the Religious Landscape: Trends in U.S. Beliefs*. Harrisburg, PA: Moorehouse, 1999.

Gallup Poll. http://www.gallup.com/home.aspx, 1947.

General Social Survey. http://www.norc.org/GSS+Website/, 2008.

Gerger, Theodore P. "When Public Institutions Fail: Coping with Dysfunctional Government in Post-Soviet Russia." *Contexts* 3 (2003): 20–28.

Hankins, Barry. *Francis Schaeffer and the Shaping of Evangelical America*. Grand Rapids: Eerdmans, 2008.

Lindsay, D. Michael. *Faith in the Halls of Power: How Evangelicals Joined the American Elite*. New York: Oxford University Press, 2007.

_____. "Evangelicals in the Power Elite: Elite Cohesion Advancing a Movement." *American Sociological Review* 73 (2008): 60–83.

Lukes, Steven. *Power: A Radical View*. 2nd ed. New York: Palgrave Macmillan, 2005.

National Congregations Studies. http://www.soc.duke.edu/natcong/, 2006–7, 1990.

Noll, Mark A., and Carolyn Nystrom. *Is the Reformation Over? An Evangelical Assessment of Contemporary Roman Catholicism*. Grand Rapids: Baker Academic, 2005.

Pew Forum on Religion & Public Life. *U.S. Religious Landscape Survey: Religious Affiliation: Diverse and Dynamic*. Washington, DC: Pew Forum on Religion & Public Life (2008). http://religions.pewforum.org/pdf/report-religious-landscape-study-full.pdf. Retrieved February 11, 2010.

Saad, Lydia. "Americans' Confidence in Military Up, Banks Down." Princeton, NJ: The 2009 Gallup Poll. http://www.gallup.com/poll/121214/americans-confidence-military-banks-down.aspx. Retrieved February 11, 2010.

Schaeffer, Francis A. *How Should We Then Live? The Rise and Decline of Western Thought and Culture*. Old Tappan, NJ: Revell, 1976.

Stark, Rodney. *For the Glory of God: How Monotheism Led to Reformations, Science, Witch-Hunts, and the End of Slavery*. Princeton: Princeton University Press, 2003.

"Theology: Toward a Hidden God." *Time*, April 8, 1966.

Weber, Max. *Economy and Society*. Edited by Guenther Roth and Claus Wittich. Berkeley: University of California, 1947, 1978.

Wrigley, Julia, and Joanna Dreby. "Fatalities and the Organization of U.S. Child Care 1985–2003." *American Sociological Review* 70 (2005): 729–57.

Wuthnow, Robert. *The Restructuring of American Religion: Society and Faith Since World War II*. Princeton: Princeton University Press, 1988.

_____. *America and the Challenges of Religious Diversity*. Princeton: Princeton University Press, 2005.

Chapter 4

The Faith, My Faith, and the Church's Faith

TIMOTHY GEORGE, DEAN, BEESON DIVINITY SCHOOL

Dear friends, although I was eager to write you about our common salvation, I found it necessary to write and exhort you to contend for the faith that was delivered to the saints once for all.

Jude 3 (HCSB)

Faith is used in the NT in two senses, which in the history of theology have been designated by two Latin expressions: *fides quae,* "the faith *that* we believe," and *fides qua,* "the faith *by which* we believe." In Jude, reference is made to *the* faith that was once for all entrusted to the saints. Jude is one of those small books near the end of our NT squeezed in between 3 John, which is even smaller, and Revelation, which is much bigger. We do not hear a lot about Jude. It is easy to skip over this little book with only one chapter and twenty-four verses.

The significance of Jude cannot be tied to its length or its bulk, but Jude is an important book because it was written at a time of great crisis in the life of the early church—a crisis that came both from without and from within. Christians were really beginning to feel the effects of harassment and persecution, as we read in the book of Acts in some of the early accounts of Christians facing hostility from the governing authorities. But when Jude was written—we do not know exactly when that was, perhaps toward the end of the first century— Christians were facing more sustained hostility, open violence, and persecution from the environing culture, from the Roman Empire. Perhaps Jude was written following the persecutions unleashed by that sadistic pyromaniac, Emperor Nero. When you visit Rome today you see the Coliseum. The Coliseum was originally a swimming pool for Nero's great palace on the hill above. In one of his banquets, Nero had Christians in Rome rounded up and tied to poles and set on fire so that as people came to dine, they passed these burning Christians—living lampposts—on the way to the banquet. In those days, human life was cheap and none more so than that of Christians and slaves. Jude was written in that kind of environment, when discipleship was costly, and the cross more than a metaphor.

In that environment, Jude wrote to these believers and said, I wanted to write to you about something else. I wanted to write to you about our common salvation. I wanted to write to you about the wonderful, glorious fact that we have been delivered from darkness and placed into light through the grace of our Lord Jesus Christ. What could be more important, more wonderful, more glorious than that—our salvation in Christ? But Jude says that there was indeed something more important. There was something more urgent and more pressing, something that I just had to write to you about. Jude knew that the Holy Spirit was only going to give him 24 verses. Jude is not like the prophet Isaiah—he had 66 chapters! Jude just had 24 verses and he could not say everything so he had to prioritize the message that God gave him to deliver. He boiled it down to what was urgent: I *had* to write to you.

What is this thing that motivates Jude? I *had* to write and urge you to contend . . . for *fides quae*, the faith *that* we confess. Now what is *the* faith? Well, *the* faith is the essential content of the Christian *kerugma*, the Christian message—the proclamation of Jesus Christ as Lord of lords and King of kings; the Way, the Truth, and the Life. *The* faith is what it is we have to say and tell the world about what God has once and for all done in Jesus Christ. This phrase is used a number of times in the NT, not only here in Jude 3, but also in 2 Tim 4:7 where Paul says, "I have fought the good fight, I have finished the race, and I have kept *the* faith." Or, in Eph 4:5, where we are admonished to hold forth one Lord, one faith, and one baptism. Again, in 1 Cor 16:13, Paul writes to the saints at Corinth and encourages them to stand firm in *the* faith. Now, *the* faith as it is used here in the singular and particular sense is what came to be summarized and passed on to successive generations of Christians as the Apostles' Creed and later the Nicene Creed of the early church.

Why do we need creeds in the first place? I know it is popular in a lot of circles to talk about "no creed but the Bible." But sometimes that phrase, "no creed but the Bible," is just a pretext for neither creed nor the Bible. There is a sense in which "no creed but the Bible" is a good phrase if we mean "no creedalism, only the Bible" because we do not want to elevate any humanly constructed statement, however venerable or wonderful it may be, to a level equal with or much less above the written Word of God in Holy Scripture. Nor do we hold any humanly constructed statement of faith to be beyond reform, beyond revision, beyond restatement. We always must subject our statements of faith and the creeds of the church to the written Word of God. The Bible is the *norma normans*, the norming norm, to which all our beliefs and our practices must be held accountable. Nor do we want the state, the government, the civil authority, to be writing creeds and imposing them on God's people. This is a violation of religious liberty.

So, in those three senses I have just mentioned—no creed that is above the Bible, no creed that is irrevisable, and no creed that is imposed by civil sanction—it is right to protect against the abuse of creeds. But what you are really talking about is not creeds but creedalism. I say, God give us creeds, but save us from creedalism! This is what Jude is writing about. *The* faith, once for all entrusted to the saints. That word "entrusted," or as the KJV and HCSB translate "delivered," to the saints is itself a very interesting word. It is the word for handing on, handing down, from one generation to another, or you may think of it in terms of a race. We have a relay and one person gives the baton to another runner and he carries it toward the finish line. That is the idea, and this word *traditor* in Latin is very close to another word, one that sounds similar in English to traitor. There is a fine line between being one who *hands on* the faith intact, a *traditor*, and one who *betrays* the faith, a traitor. They are very close words etymologically and semantically. We must be cautious, those of us who have been charged with preaching and teaching the Word of God, that in our efforts to pass it on we do not betray it.

In the early centuries when the Roman authorities came to a Christian town or village, their first request was, "Give us the books." They did not care so much about the church buildings and the rest of the things the Christians had. But the books—by which they meant, of course, the Bible, the Word of God, the Holy Scriptures—were important. Their theory was that if they could destroy the Bible, they could destroy the faith. If they could burn the books, they could obliterate the Christian message. They were on to something.

Why do we need creeds? We have the Bible, after all. Why do we need these humanly constructed statements of faith, the creeds and confessions of the church, to proclaim *the* faith, once for all entrusted, passed on? When our children were very small, my wife and our family lived for one year in Switzerland, surely one of the most beautiful places on earth. Switzerland is famous for its gorgeous Alps that stretch into the heights of the sky above the clouds. We would often take family trips over those Alps and into the valleys between. We would drive along those hairpin curves, as dangerous as it was, especially in a car that did not work very well, with two children screaming in the back seat!

One time we set out in our old Mitsubishi, and I noticed as I drove along that there were guardrails on either side of those narrow roads across the Alps. Someone had put them carefully in place so that those of us trying to get over the mountain would not be tempted to wander one way or the other; to swerve to the right or to the left into a ravine meant sudden death. Our confessions of faith are like those guardrails. When you are traveling dangerous mountain roads, you are glad someone has put those guardrails in place. Now you do not want to confuse the guardrails with the road and start driving up there on the guardrails—then danger is really imminent! Stay on the road. The road is Jesus Christ. He said: "I am the Way (the Road), the Truth and the Life" (John 14:6). But we need guardrails as we are tempted this way and that in the history of the church, guardrails to keep us on the road guided by the light that is the Holy Scriptures: "Thy Word is a lamp unto my feet, and a light unto my path" (Ps 119:105 KJV).

Let us examine the first part of the title to this chapter: *the* faith and *my* faith. Just as there are two expressions, *fides quae* and *fides qua*—the faith *that* we believe and the faith *by which* we believe—so too there are two words in Latin for faith, and they figured prominently in the debates of the Reformation. One word is *assensus*. You can tell what it means just by the way that it sounds in English. *Assensus*—to assent to, to agree with, to say yes to. It is a part of the faith *that* we confess. Let us not downgrade this kind of faith. It is a part of the objective content and deposit of faith that is true for everybody everywhere. This is what *the* faith means. Does a tree that falls in the forest make a sound whether you are there to hear it or not? Did Pluto revolve around the sun before it was "discovered" 80 years ago?

There is an objective content, a deposit of faith given by God as a part of the divine revelation of himself in Jesus Christ and in the Holy Scriptures. That is *assensus*. Say yes to that. Assent to this content is absolutely necessary, but it is not sufficient. There is another word, *fiducia*, and we have a word in English, fiduciary, related to that as well. Fiduciary is a word that has to do with holding something in trust for someone else. It involves a personal commitment you make yourself, and this is a word that Martin Luther used to describe saving, believing faith, personal trust, letting loose of yourself. In German, it is *Gelassenheit*. We do not have a good English equivalent for the beautiful German word, *gelassen*, to let loose of yourself, let go of yourself, stop depending on yourself, and throw yourself wildly into the arms of Jesus Christ. That is faith. That is saving faith. That is *fiducial* faith. That is when *the* faith becomes *my* faith.

In the early years of the Reformation, Thomas Bilney came to Cambridge, England. He was a scholar, and was interested in studying the classics, the great texts of antiquity. It was just at the time when Desiderius Erasmus translated the Bible into Latin based on the critical edition of the NT in Greek that he had published at Basel in 1516. When Bilney came to Cambridge, Erasmus had been there just a few years before, working on his Latin translation. Bilney was particularly interested in reading it because it was not in the old medieval Vulgate Latin but was all spruced up in Ciceronian Latin, and he loved that, the challenge of it, the excitement of it. But as he began to read this Bible just for the sheer literary joy and pleasure of taking in the beauty of the Latin language, he came across a verse, 1 Tim 1:15, in which Paul says, "I give unto you that which is a true and faithful statement." Well, the old Latin translation would have been *fidelis sermo*, a faithful word, a true word, but in the new Erasmian translation, that word "faithful" was rendered *certa*, believable, credible, assured. When Bilney read that word and the text that followed where Paul says, "Christ Jesus came into the world to save sinners," it struck him in his heart that the verse was meant for him. He was a sinner and Christ Jesus had come into the world to save him, even him. He says that when reading that verse, "Immediately I felt a marvellous comfort and quietness, insomuch that my bruised bones lept for joy." That is when *the* faith becomes *my* faith.

David Bebbington, an eminent Scottish historian of Evangelicalism, has talked about the four great traits, characteristics of Evangelicalism: the Bible—we believe the Bible is the Word of God. We are committed to the understanding of Jesus and His atoning work on the cross, the mission of the church—he uses the word "activism"—we go into the world in Jesus' name to share His good news to everybody everywhere. All of this is related, Bebbington says, to another characteristic which is the new birth, which is being converted, turned around, changed—to use a little more theological language, "regenerated"—by the power of the Holy Spirit. As long as *the* faith remains detached, divorced, distant, as long as *the* faith is simply a system of doctrine codified in a systematic theology, as long as *the* faith is kept at arm's length, then we are like Nicodemus who came to Jesus by night and said to Him, "Teacher, we know you are a rabbi sent from God. No man can do these things you are doing except God be with him." Jesus said to Him, "Nicodemus, you must be born again. Born from above, born anew." That is the message that Evangelicals have proclaimed to the world. This is why we *are* Evangelicals. We proclaim this message in all its fullness to those who need to know that Jesus Christ has come into the world. Just like Thomas Bilney. He became a believer because he read that one verse of Scripture and his life was changed. It cost him something, for in 1531 he was burned alive at the stake in the city of Norwich. He became one of the first martyrs of the English Reformation. So the question I want to ask you today is this: Has *the* faith become your faith? Is *the* faith *my* faith? Can you say as we sing sometimes, "Oh happy day that fixed my choice on thee my Savior and my God"? Is that true for you? "When Jesus washed my sins away, Oh happy day."[1]

I have discussed *the* faith and *my* faith. I want to spend a few minutes now on the *church's* faith. In the history of theology, *the* faith

---

[1] "O Happy Day," in *Worship and Rejoice* (Carol Stream, IL: Hope Publishing Company, 2001), 368. Words: Philip Doddridge (1702–51); Ref. *Wesleyan Sacred Harp* (1854); Music: Attr. Edward F. Rimbault (1816–76).

and *my* faith taken in isolation from one another have led to some dead ends that we must avoid at all costs. *The* faith without *my* faith will issue in an arid scholasticism, a joyless rationalism, a dead orthodoxy. It has done so and it will do so. On the other hand, *my* faith without *the* faith ends up in a sloppy sentimentalism and a groundless subjectivism, and this is at the root of so much of the theology that has corroded the church of Jesus Christ for the last 150 years. When I was a student at Harvard, I used to walk across what we called The Yard, the quadrangle in the center of the campus, on my way to the library. Every day I walked past Emerson Hall. Emerson Hall was constructed to house the philosophy department in the early part of the twentieth century. William James, who was the great founder of psychology of religion and an advocate of the philosophy of pragmatism, was appointed to a committee to come up with a saying, a legend, that would be carved in stone across the portal of Emerson Hall. His committee came up with a pre-Socratic maxim, "Man is the measure of all things." But, unbeknown to William James, Harvard President Charles W. Eliot overrode the committee's recommendation. When it was unveiled, instead of that pre-Socratic maxim, "Man is the measure of all things," people looked up astonished, and William James most of all, to read a verse from Psalm 8: "What is man that thou art mindful of him?" The church's faith is a faith that is rooted in the objectivity of God's revelation in Jesus Christ and in the Holy Scriptures.

Why do I call it the *church's* faith? Well, because ecclesiology is the new frontier of Evangelical theology in the twenty-first century. We have wrestled with many issues in recent decades, and there are still many to be considered in the life of the Evangelical church today. But in the future, I do not think anything is going to be more urgent than the question of the church. What is the church? How are we as faithful, believing Christians to relate the church and the gospel?

A few years ago my wife Denise and I edited a collection of documents called *Baptist Confessions, Covenants, and Catechisms*. When you say "Baptist catechisms" to many people today, it's like talking about a pregnant pope or a married bachelor—it is an oxymoron. Yet confessions of faith had a tremendous place and catechisms a formative role in the shaping of generations of God's people, including Baptists. We forget that Charles Haddon Spurgeon published a Baptist catechism, and that the first item published by what is now LifeWay Christian Resources (originally the Baptist Sunday School Board) was a Baptist catechism written by John A. Broadus. We need to go back to these documents and recover something of what they tell us, not just about *my* faith or *the* faith in an abstract sense, but the *church's* faith.

Now, what is the church? The church is local, it is congregational, it is particular, it is covenantal. Yes, but the church in the NT is also universal, it is ecumenical; it is the one, holy, catholic, and apostolic church. As the Baptist Faith and Message says, "The church is the company of all the redeemed of all the ages." Thus the church has both a local and a universal dimension, both a congregational and an associational form, both a covenantal and an ecumenical thrust, always and ever grounded on our confession in the one God who is forever Father, Son, and Holy Spirit. The *church's* faith is meant to be sung as well as said, prayed as well as proclaimed. I think we need a revival in singing the great hymns of the faith, such as "The Church's One Foundation";[2] "O For a Thousand Tongues to Sing";[3] and "And Can It Be That I Should Gain." Listen to these words. Listen to this theology. Listen to this faith, the *church's* faith. "And can it be that I should gain an interest in the Savior's blood? Died he for me, who caused his pain. For me, who him to death pursued. Amazing love, how can it be, that thou, my God, shouldst die for me?"[4] Or the

---

[2] "The Church's One Foundation," in *Worship and Rejoice Hymnal* (Carol Stream, IL: Hope, 2001), 544.

[3] "O for a Thousand Tongues to Sing," *The Baptist Hymnal* (Nashville: Convention Press, 1991), 216. Words: Charles Wesley (1707–88); Music: Carl G. Gläser, (1784–1829); arr. Lowell Mason, (1792–1872).

[4] "And Can It Be," in *Worship and Rejoice Hymnal*, 366.

hymn we sing at the beginning of every semester at Beeson Divinity School, our school hymn.

> "For All the Saints"
> For all the saints who from their labors rest,
> who thee by faith before the world confessed,
> thy name, O Jesus, be forever blest.
> Alleluia! Alleluia![5]

Well, "Drop-kick me Jesus through the Goalpost of Glory" will just not cut it! Now, I am not against everything that is recent. One of our favorite hymns at Beeson Divinity School was written within the last 20 years, and you know it too, "In Christ Alone."[6] It does not have to be old to be good, but it ought to be good to be sung and used in the worship of God. We have to sing our faith. We ought to pray our faith, not just preach it and teach it. Yes, but it also needs to be mainstreamed into our devotional life and our prayer life. And one more thing I want to write about the church's faith: it is a public faith. It is a faith that we cannot keep to ourselves.

This is a time of great anniversaries—Calvin's birthday 500 years ago, in 1509; the beginning of the modern Baptist movement 400 years ago in Amsterdam, in 1609—but there is another anniversary that has not been talked about very much, and we ought to remember it. It is 1934, 75 years ago, when a group of committed Christians, pastors and laity, gathered at a little German town called Barmen, near Düsseldorf. There in the face of the onslaught of what would become the reign of terror of the Third Reich under Adolf Hitler, they issued a declaration of conscience, the Barmen Declaration.[7] This took place after Hitler had come to power and before the "German Christians" had Nazified the church and taken over

---

[5] "For All the Saints," in *Worship and Rejoice*, 529.

[6] "In Christ Alone," released in 2007, Words and Music by Stuart Townsend.

[7] The "Theological Declaration of Barmen" was written by Karl Barth and the confessing church in Nazi Germany in opposition to Adolf Hitler's national church. Its central doctrines concern the sin of idolatry and the lordship of Christ, and may be found at http://www.sacred-texts.com/chr/barmen.html.

so many of its offices and prerogatives, and when the Aryan paragraph, as they called it, had excluded Jews from the common life of people in Germany—the forerunner to sending them to concentration camps. In 1934, the camp at Dachau had already been built. All this was in the air. Catholicism as a national movement in Germany was sidelined and compromised to some extent by the Concordat the pope had entered into with Hitler. Protestantism and its reigning liberal theology were undermining the witness of the church. In this time of great crisis these Christians gathered and issued the Barmen Declaration, which said: "Jesus Christ, as he is testified to us in the Holy Scripture is the one Word of God whom we are to hear, whom we are to trust, whom we are to obey in life and in death."[8] Those who signed that statement, those who drafted it, soon found themselves excluded. Karl Barth, one of the drafters, lost his professorship at the University of Bonn and was sent into exile. Another, Martin Niemöller, was placed in a concentration camp and became Hitler's private prisoner. Again and again he was interviewed by Hitler, and on one of those occasions he said to Hitler, "You can imprison me and you can torture me and you can kill me, but Herr Hitler, one day you will give an account to one who is the King of kings and the Lord of lords." Where did he get a faith like that? It was not because he was depending on his own private emotions, not because he had simply studied theology in a scholastic and academic way, but rather because *the* faith had become *his* faith and it was the *church's* faith. This is what we need in our world today.

At the end of World War II, Albert Einstein wrote a letter to Martin Niemöller, and this is what he said:

> Having always been an ardent partisan of freedom, I turned to
> the Universities, as soon as the revolution broke out in Germany,
> to find the Universities took refuge in silence. I then turned to
> the editors of powerful newspapers, who, but lately in flowing
> articles, had claimed to be the faithful champions of liberty.

---

[8] Ibid.

These men, as well as the Universities, were reduced to silence in a few weeks. I then addressed myself to the authors individually, to those who passed themselves off as the intellectual guides of Germany, and among whom many had frequently discussed the question of freedom and its place in modern life. They are in their turn very dumb. Only the church opposed the fight which Hitler was waging against liberty. Till then I had no interest in the Church, but now I feel great admiration and am truly attracted to the Church which had the persistent courage to fight for spiritual truth and moral freedom. I feel obliged to confess that I now admire what I used to consider of little value.[9]

Einstein was driven from Germany because he was a Jew, but it was the church of Jesus Christ, the church's faith put forward in a tumultuous time, that impressed the greatest scientist of the modern world.

Now, you say we are not living in Nazi Germany today, and thank God that is true. But we are living in perilous times. We are living in times not altogether unlike those in which Jude wrote his little epistle, at the end of the first century, when the church of Jesus Christ was beset by hostility from without, and by corrosion from within. Now as never before, we need to declare *the* faith—the faith entrusted to us, the faith of which we are trustees, *the* faith—once for all, delivered to the saints—which must become *my* faith—alive, real, personal, fiducial, *my* faith—and which must come together in our standing with humility before God and others but courageously with the help of the Holy Spirit, to say to all the world that this is the *church's* faith.

I end this essay with prayer:

Dear Heavenly Father,

We thank you for the way in which you have blessed our lives beyond measure. Your love is infinite, your grace is immeasurable. And we thank you and we praise you that you have saved us in Jesus Christ and you

---

[9] Ernst C. Helmreich, *The German Churches Under Hitler: Background, Struggle and Epilogue* (Detroit: Wayne State University Press, 1979), 345.

have called us to follow him into this your broken, fragile and so beloved world. Now help us we pray to be faithful in these days, these difficult days, to know how we ought to relate to one another as believers in the body of Christ, to know how we ought to proclaim your message with clarity and also charity. In Jesus' Name,

Amen.

Evangelicals and Southern Baptists:
Identity, Beliefs, and Ministry

Chapter 5

The Future of Evangelicalism
(and Southern Baptists)

Duane Litfin, President Emeritus, Wheaton College

The title *Southern Baptists, Evangelicals, and the Future of Denominationalism* inevitably suggests three subtopics: first, Southern Baptists; second, Evangelicals; and third, the future of denominationalism. But of course all of these converge into a single topic, which I suspect is the real subject of this book: "Whither the SBC?" In other words, where is the Southern Baptist Convention heading; or, perhaps more to the point, where should it be heading?

This is an important question. You can hear it in the title of David Dockery's latest book: *Southern Baptist Identity: An Evangelical Denomination Faces the Future*. "Who are we Southern Baptists and where are we going?" the title seems to ask. The SBC once again, it strikes me as an outsider, finds itself wrestling with its identity, its calling, its future.

This is scarcely a new question, of course. Many of us watched, up close and personal, though from the outside, what the SBC has endured over the last three decades or so. With no little pain the SBC made some difficult decisions about what it was going to be, and what it wasn't going to be. You asked some hard questions and you gave some difficult answers, and you're living with those answers today.

The problem is, these sorts of questions never stay answered. The environment around us, both individually and corporately, keeps changing. Often it keeps buffeting us, all the more so in this generation. It's constantly raising new questions for us, questions we cannot avoid. It does not pose the same questions the SBC attempted to answer over the last quarter century; it poses the new question of what it means to live out your previous answers in the kaleidoscopic environment of the twenty-first century. It is a vital question for us all. But since we're talking here about the SBC's answer to that question, I'd like to see whether I can offer some help. I'll let you be the judge of whether I manage to do so.

My assigned contribution to this discussion focuses on "The Future of Evangelicalism." This topic requires me to do a bit of prognostication, so I must begin by qualifying everything I say with the acknowledgment that I am no prophet. There is much I do not know about the SBC. There is even more I do not know about the future, and especially the future of Evangelicalism. So I must be careful to avoid pontification. I want to speak to you from what I do know, and then let you decide whether it's of any use to you. I will turn first to the topics of denominationalism and Evangelicalism. Then I will conclude by turning to some modest suggestions about the future of the Southern Baptist Convention.

Let me touch briefly on the first of our subtopics: the future of denominationalism. The subject is complex, and I do not have a great deal to say about it. I must leave the substantive analyses to people who spend their lives studying such things. But here at least is some common wisdom about the subject.

Denominationalism appears to be in decline, a development that is often attributed to generational changes. Working in a collegiate environment as I do, I have come to believe these generational changes are real.

I have been reading several books about this current generation, the so-called Millennials. I'm not usually much impressed by these generational labels—every few years it seems someone comes up with a new one to sell some more books. But I think the notion of the Millennial generation makes some sense. It rings true with the students I see every day.

One of the books I read recently focused on the so-called Net-Gen, that generation of young people who have never known life without the Internet. Most of us here lived the bulk of our lives without the Internet. Today we have adapted to it and we use it effectively, but we don't swim in its waters the way this generation does. For many of these young people, for better or worse, the Internet serves in large measure as their social space, and this may be influencing everything about them, including perhaps even the physical wiring of their brains. They have spent their lives immersed in this virtual, digital world, and they may be wired differently from previous generations. What does it all mean, for their relationships, for their learning, for their ways of handling life? The answer is, We do not know. But the people who are studying this generation seem to think they see in this generation a resistance to hierarchy, a retreat from organizations, different norms of organizational behavior, and diminished organizational loyalties.

If this proves to be the case, what does this bode for denominations? Former House Speaker Tip O'Neill used to say, "All politics is local." We may be entering a period when all church is local as well. The farther we move from the local level, the less the coming generations may be interested.

This is not all bad. In my estimation there are some denominational tendencies, and not a few denominations themselves, that leave much to be desired. Up to a point, moving away from undue denominationalism may be taking us closer to a biblical pattern. To be sure, this can be taken to extremes. Many of us have seen George Barna's book, *Revolution*, where he argues that in the U.S. today there is not only a retreat from denominationalism but even a retreat from the local church. According to Barna, even the local church becomes dispensable; it can quite nicely be replaced by small fellowship groups. We need not question that this phenomenon is on the increase, not least, perhaps, because some of the marketing approaches championed earlier in his career by Barna himself have so dumbed down many churches as to render them anemic and without substance. But to the extent Barna is right, this development will prove disastrous. The biblical answer to weak churches is not to pronounce them dispensable; the answer to weak churches is strong churches, a point that appears to be lost on many today.

Nonetheless there are real changes taking place in this business of how we do denominationalism in America, and these changes have implications for the SBC. I will return to this point briefly at the end.

I want to move now to the subject I've been called here to address: Evangelicalism. But even here I do not wish to speak as one having authority. I must be careful because there are people who study Evangelicalism in a rigorous, in-depth way, and as a pressurized college president that is not one of my options. I come to this conversation as a participant, not a scholar-researcher. What you will hear is from one who is immersed in Evangelicalism. But that also means that if ever the metaphor of the "forest and the trees" applies, it's here. I live with my nose pressed up against the trees of American Evangelicalism, so I may be missing the forest. But for what it's worth, let me offer my take on the topic of Evangelicalism and its future.

What's more, for good or ill, mine will inevitably be a Wheaton's-eye view of Evangelicalism. There may be debates—have been, probably still are—within the SBC about whether Southern Baptists belong within Evangelicalism. We lived for almost a decade in Memphis, and one of my good friends there was Adrian Rogers. Adrian would always make a point of it: "We are not Evangelicals," he would say. "We are Baptists." For all I know, that distinction may still be stressed by some within the SBC. But no one ever debates whether Wheaton College is an Evangelical institution.

For most of the twentieth century the city of Wheaton served as a geographic center for this thing we think of as American Evangelicalism, and Wheaton College was often tagged as its flagship institution. There is good reason for that. Consider what took root in the vicinity of Wheaton during the twentieth century—the Evangelical mission agencies, publishers, churches, *Christianity Today*, one organization after another. Why did all these Evangelical institutions cluster in Wheaton? It was because Wheaton College was already there, reaching back to 1860. The institution was strong and thriving by the time our twentieth-century version of Evangelicalism emerged in the 1930s and 40s. All these Evangelical organizations gathered in Wheaton because they were congealing, so to speak, around Wheaton College.

Today, many of these organizations have departed, mainly for economic reasons; Wheaton is an expensive place to live. A sort of Evangelical Diaspora has taken place, away from Wheaton toward locales such as Colorado Springs. But my concern today is not for that Diaspora, which has for the most part been a good thing. My concern is the degree to which this Diaspora has become a useful metaphor for the theological spread of the movement itself.

Let me offer up a quick theological survey (see Figure 5.1). We can use it as a shorthand way of thinking about our topic. It's pretty basic stuff, but it will give you a Wheaton's-eye view of how Evangelicalism has unfolded during the past century and a half.

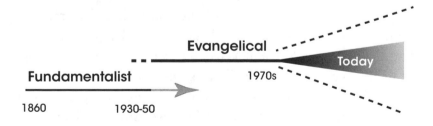

Figure 5.1: Theological Survey

Wheaton College was founded in 1860, and during the early period of its history it was part of what during the 1920s came to be called fundamentalism. Wheaton was there in the midst of what we think of as American fundamentalism, right up until the emergence of what would become Evangelicalism.

Twentieth-century Evangelicalism emerged during the 1930s and 40s, but by the time it entered the 1950s and 60s, the movement had come into its own. It had become highly generative, producing a wide variety of organizations, institutions, and publications. Some time during this period Wheaton College shifted over to the Evangelical line on the diagram. It was largely a demographic shift, and certainly a shift in tone, but what it wasn't was a theological shift. If you reach back to the mid-twentieth century, everyone was quite vocal about the fact there was no theological shift taking place—Evangelicals believed essentially the same thing fundamentalists believed. The Evangelical line on our diagram was probably less millenarian than the fundamentalist line, but for the most part the shift took place in areas other than theology. Evangelicals sought to demonstrate a different spirit. They evinced a developing irenicism, a toning down of polemics, and a reaction against the anti-intellectualism of their predecessors. Evangelicals wanted to break out of the circled wagons of fundamentalism. They wanted to embrace their intellectual task and engage the culture, believing that God had given them a mind and hands as well as a spirit. In many ways a new day had dawned.

It was during this period that Wheaton College became a flagship institution of the Evangelical movement. Theologically it was what it had been before, but Wheaton shifted in terms of its spirit and its openness to intellectual engagement with the world. It was a time when Evangelicalism was still fairly tightly drawn theologically and fairly well defined, but not because some elite had decided, "Let's delineate Evangelicalism this way." It was something that simply gelled out of the early decades of the twentieth century and came into its own. It had its leading lights, voices who were giving it shape, but there existed a widespread unity of theological focus. If you had asked "What does 'Evangelical' mean?" during this period, you would have received some fairly clear and unified answers.

Already by the late 1950s and into the 1960s, however, this question was becoming harder to answer. There emerged a need to pin some things down. This can be seen by the appearance of a series of books edited by Carl F. H. Henry in a Contemporary Evangelical Thought series. These books consisted of collected chapters written by dozens of authors from across a variety of traditions, but their titles are instructive: *Contemporary Evangelical Thought* (1957), *Revelation and the Bible* (1958), *Basic Christian Doctrines* (1962), *Christian Faith and Modern Theology* (1964), *Jesus of Nazareth: Savior and Lord* (1966), *Fundamentals of the Faith* (1969). The purpose of these books was to anchor a movement that was beginning to require some anchoring. Evangelicals needed to pin some things down.

But it was not to be. The developing sprawl might be slowed, but it could not be stopped. As we moved into the 1970s the process continued. It was highlighted for me by the publication of Harold Lindsell's book, *The Battle for the Bible*, in 1975. There was indeed a battle for the Bible going on during this period, a battle which has not ceased. But the truth is, Lindsell's book and the underlying challenges it was dealing with, were not so much about a battle for the Bible as a battle for the term "Evangelical." The essential question Lindsell was asking—and attempting to answer—was, Must you believe in biblical inerrancy to be an Evangelical? Or, Can you legitimately be an Evangelical and not hold to inerrancy? Some were saying yes, while Lindsell and others were saying no. But it was essentially a definitional question at stake. It was in many ways a battle over the semantic boundaries of this term "Evangelical."

This discussion was indicative of the broadening that was taking place in the Evangelical movement, and there was no way officially to resolve the issue. You cannot legislate a binding definition for a term such as "Evangelical." Nor can you turn it into a technical term. Technical terms have formal, tight definitions; they are part of the jargon of every specialty. Beyond that, most of our definitions are determined by usage. Language is constantly changing. Like a massive sand dune, it's always on the move, undulating, evolving. Thus our terms seldom remain static. This was the case with "Evangelical."

The usage of this term was already changing, mirroring the movement it was intended to denote. You can observe during this period the Evangelical movement trying to maintain some boundaries, with the debates often centering on the issues surrounding the trustworthiness of Scripture. Hence the1978 International Council on Biblical Inerrancy, and then the *Chicago Statement* which came out of that, and a whole series of other efforts to keep things nailed down. Those of us who lived through this period were inhabiting a movement that was worried about its own boundaries. Who are we, we were asking, and what are we about?

That tendency toward sprawl, toward a loss of definition, has continued. Like all such movements, Evangelicalism has no ability to prevent this from happening. It cannot police itself, as the SBC did some years back. The SBC saw its own sprawl taking place and decided to do something about it. I have no brief to make about how it was done; I watched as an outsider—again, up close and personal, since I was living in Dallas through much of it and knew some of the people directly involved—and it seems to me that there was a needless amount of blood spilled in the process. But my point is that you stood up and said, "This is who we are, and this is who we are not." You had the capacity to police your own boundaries. But Evangelicalism possesses no such ability. At any given time the movement simply is what it is, and the semantics of the term simply are what they are. To be sure, the Evangelical Theological Society periodically sees the need to police itself, but notice that it's only ETS that is being policed, not the movement itself. ETS may be able to maintain its own boundaries—and it struggles even to do that—but Evangelicalism as a movement cannot.

Such broadening seems to me virtually inevitable. It has continued from that earlier period until today, and if we peer out into the future, I suspect there are reasons to think the process will only persist.

One reason for this is that the issues Evangelicalism is dealing with today are more complex than they were in its heyday, when things were still fairly well-defined. For example, go back and reread the 30-year-old *Chicago Statement on Biblical Inerrancy*. Today it sounds almost quaint. Back then all sides were working from a fundamentally similar set of epistemological assumptions. Today that common epistemological framework has evaporated, certainly in the culture as a whole and even among those who still wish to claim the label "Evangelical." The debate over whether the Bible includes errors is charming in the assumptions it makes about the nature of truth and error. But today, the fissures being explored in that debate, fissures in the superstructure of our thought, have spread to the hermeneutical and epistemological foundations we used to hold in common. Back then there existed a sort of working critical realism which, in one form or another, informed people on all sides of the Evangelical community. Today the cancer has metastasized, so to speak, to the vital organs. The farther we have come, the less unity we can find among Evangelicals on these underlying hermeneutical and epistemological issues. This, it seems to me, can only further the movement's loss of definition.

Other developments during this period have also encouraged the sprawl. Evangelicalism rose to a position of cultural influence during the middle of the twentieth century. From its marginalized, defensive posture in the 1920s and 30s when Modernism was riding high, Evangelicalism rose up on its hind legs and began moving. It prospered in its numbers, its outreach, its organizations, and its influence. By the 1970s, *Time* magazine published its cover story on "The Year of the Evangelicals." Jimmy Carter drew attention for being "born again" and Evangelicals began to flex some muscle. Religious movements such as the Moral Majority began exerting political clout. What was popularly called Evangelicalism had developed some considerable weight and began to throw it around. The result was the pushback, often against an undifferentiated Religious Right, which we have witnessed ever since.

Moreover, it was during this same period, when in some ways Evangelicals seemed to be riding high, that we experienced another phenomenon: an unseemly parade of high-profile Evangelical scandals. We will leave the names mercifully unmentioned, but suffice it to say, every time we experienced another one, we Evangelicals would collectively cringe and cry out, "Oh Lord, protect us from ourselves." But the scandals just seemed to keep coming. When matched with our perceived moralism and self-righteousness, it all combined to provide powerful ammunition to Evangelicalism's opponents. We were falling into the very trap the apostle Paul had warned against (Titus 2:8).

All this was bad enough, but I fear the problem ran deeper than even a series of public scandals. Our underlying problem may be that we Evangelicals have allowed ourselves to be coopted by what I will call "Americanism." I recall a commentator on 1 Corinthians making the point that the problem with the church in Corinth was that there was too much Corinth in the church and not enough church in Corinth. I confess that I sometimes wonder whether we American Evangelicals do not suffer a similar malady.

Many of us will remember former Vice President Dan Quayle's remark about Murphy Brown. As I recall, it was just a few lines in a public speech about the negative example set by having Candace Bergen's character become a mother without a husband. For these comments Quayle was savaged by the media. To this day he remains the butt of public jokes for having offered that criticism.

Somewhere around that time I attended a National Prayer Breakfast where Mother Teresa was the main speaker. She stood up at that breakfast and, with the president of the United States sitting beside her, proceeded to stick her finger in America's face and say, "Mr. President, you must stop this holocaust of innocent babies. The abortion industry is the greatest evil of our day. America, if you don't want your babies, give them to me." It was a prophetic word delivered to the heart of American culture. Afterward, I watched the media response. They treated Mother Teresa with kid gloves. They scarcely touched her.

What was the difference between these two cultural responses? It was of course the contrast in the moral credibility of these individuals. It is no doubt unfair to Quayle to say it, but his public image is that of a comfortable, affluent, superficial, moralistic scold. By contrast, Mother Teresa had behind her a lifetime of sacrificial care for others. I had all sorts of theological issues with Mother Teresa, but only the most cynical of observers—such as Christopher Hitchens— could gainsay the level of self-sacrifice that marked her life. It was a life that granted her a moral credibility Dan Quayle did not possess.

I lay this contrast on the table to make this point: I think American Evangelicalism looks to our culture a lot more like Dan Quayle than Mother Teresa. Then we wonder why the culture seems so unwilling to hear us, why our voice is so easily dismissed in the cultural dialog.

For all these reasons I think the Evangelical sprawl will continue. The Evangelical movement has lost its headway. At our best, the above analysis does Evangelicalism a disservice. But why is it that we Evangelicals so often seem not to be at our best? We aspire to more, but how often do we achieve it? I'm reminded of the golfer who remarked that he played his normal game about 10 percent of the time. I'm afraid our normal game in recent decades has led not only to a loss of cultural credibility, but a loss of direction. To be sure, given the right issues to react against, we can still generate a lot of votes. But does the movement retain sufficient focus to provide our generation credible leadership?

What, after all, is an Evangelical today? The best we seem able to do is adopt David Bebbington's minimalist fourfold description of an Evangelical stance: Biblicism, cruci-centrism, conversionism, and activism. These abstractions are sound as far as they go, but they seem thin compared with the robust discussions of, say, the Contemporary Evangelical Thought series of a half century ago. Try gaining any Evangelical consensus around those volumes today. The farther we move back along our diagram, the less satisfactory such a minimalist definition as Bebbington's would have seemed. But not today. It's probably the best we're going to do.

Today we observe the valiant, but also rather poignant, spectacle of one of Evangelicalism's leading lights, D. A. Carson, offering his sobering analysis: *Evangelicalism: What Is It and Is It Worth Keeping?*[1] This title I fear says it all. Professor Carson attempts to answer his questions by providing the movement some needed definition and then arguing that, yes, Evangelicalism is worth keeping. I do hope he is successful. But we must acknowledge this: the sheer fact that there exists a need for such a book, addressing such a rude question, cannot be a good sign.[2]

So what does all this mean for the SBC? Here are three observations, offered strictly on a "for-what-they're-worth" basis.

First, I think Baptist polity may in some ways be well positioned for the decline of denominationalism. Your resistance to hierarchical structures, your strong emphasis on the autonomy of the local church, the localism that's built into Baptist polity—these seem to me to be working for you in our current environment. It appears to me that even if denominationalism is in decline, there may be ways in which the SBC, unlike the more hierarchical denominations, can hold on to some of the genuine benefits of denominational life without the baggage of some of its liabilities. You may see more and more of the ways in which the SBC is seeing itself, its churches, and its internal organizations playing down their Southern Baptist identity, without severing that affiliation or leaving it behind. You need not be ashamed of that affiliation, but you aren't thrusting it into people's faces. This may turn out to be a useful strategy: maintain the strengths of what you can do when you work together while also avoiding the sorts of things this generation—the one you are seeking to engage—finds less

---

[1] D. A. Carson, *Evangelicalism: What Is It and Is It Worth Keeping?* (Wheaton: Crossway, 2010).

[2] On the other hand, see J. I. Packer's attempt to provide his own far richer and fuller definition of what it means to be Evangelical, in his "Reflection and Response," in *J. I. Packer and the Evangelical Future: The Impact of His Life and Thought*, ed. by Timothy George (Grand Rapids: Baker, 2009), 171–85. If the Evangelical movement can rise to the summons Packer provides here, its future may prove to be far brighter than the one I am projecting.

meaningful. It appears the SBC may be exceptionally well positioned to strike this balance out into the future.

Second, I think these developments will force the SBC to become less insular.

The Southern Baptist Convention has long enjoyed the luxury of insularity. You have your own churches, schools, colleges, universities, publishers, Sunday school material, mission agencies, even your own style. You could remain isolated because you had the full complement of what you ostensibly needed within your own boundaries. In fact, I could recite some striking anecdotes of that insularity from my own experience.

But during the latter half of the twentieth century it seems to me that this insularity was breaking down. There were certainly those voices who wanted to keep the SBC insular, and you may have some of them left within the SBC today. But others have become determined to join the broader Evangelical world. The result is that many have broken out of the SBC mold, so to speak. And I want to commend you for that.

The Southern Baptist Convention has joined the broader Evangelical world. You can see it in your publishing houses, you can see it in your churches, and you can see it not least in one of the groups with which I've been closely involved: the Council for Christian Colleges and Universities (CCCU). If you reach back even 20 or 30 years ago, there were almost no Southern Baptist schools in this mix of more than a hundred institutions. Today there are, with David Dockery and Union University among the leaders, an increasing number of SBC members. This is a promising sign for the future. Those SBC leaders who have been moving in this direction all along were prescient, I think, not least because an insular stance will be more and more difficult to maintain in the decades ahead.

As an outsider, I would say it's a good thing you are reaching out. I would encourage you to participate everywhere you can, with whomever you can, in whatever way you can, without compromising the truth. We all need to work at maintaining an irenic spirit.

You can learn from others by working closely with them. Believe it or not, you will in some ways be better for it. But equally so, you can exert a positive influence if you're part of that broader conversation. On behalf of the rest of the Evangelical world, I would say we need you. I've seen it in the CCCU. We need the Southern Baptist Convention—you and the people you represent—sitting at the table, participants in the conversation. If nothing else, it will provide you wonderful opportunities to defeat unattractive stereotypes. Insularity will be less available to you in the years ahead, and you can make a virtue of this necessity by taking every opportunity to participate in the broader Evangelical conversation.

Third, I would urge you not to depend overmuch on Evangelicalism as a movement. Do not put too many eggs in its basket. I say that not because I'm willing or ready to write off Evangelicalism; that would be premature. I believe the National Association of Evangelicals is stronger than it was just a few years ago, and *Christianity Today* remains an important organ. What's more, the Evangelical Theological Society makes an important contribution without which we would be worse off. I value the label "Evangelical" and I still use it, both for myself and for Wheaton College.

But if I'm honest, I must say that, to some extent and in some ways, that term also works against what we are trying to do at Wheaton. The Evangelical sprawl I discussed above, which in many ways could happen only through a loss of content, means that Evangelicalism is broader now than is Wheaton College. There are things taking place within Evangelicalism, and voices espousing ideas within Evangelicalism, that are not for Wheaton. But then someone will inevitably say, "Well, what about so-and-so, or such-and-such? That's coming from an Evangelical, and Wheaton is an Evangelical institution. Why shouldn't that be included at Wheaton?" In this way the term "Evangelical," now much broadened in its usage, begins to work against us and can sometimes take us in unwanted directions.

So I would say the same thing to you. I do not think you and the SBC should distance yourselves from Evangelicalism. You are an Evangelical group: Don't fight it, plunge in and participate, we need you there. Just don't put too much weight on it. Do not entertain undue expectations about what this means. Movements, terms, labels: they come and go. We should not expect them to serve us indefinitely. As for you—or for that matter, for any of us—we must keep ourselves grounded in something much less ephemeral: not a movement or a label, but God's truth.

It would be a colossal mistake to say, "Whatever the semantic boundaries of the term 'Evangelical' become—well, I suppose that's who I am, or who we are." We must be anchored in something deeper. I would say for you what I say for myself, and for Wheaton College: Keep yourselves biblically grounded. Stay Christ-centered, gospel-centered, Word-centered. This is what will keep you useful to the Lord. If you do this, and you do it as a part of the larger Evangelical movement, the Lord may use the SBC to help keep American Evangelicalism relevant deep into the twenty-first century.

Chapter 6

The Care for Souls: Reconsidering Pastoral Ministry in Southern Baptist and Evangelical Contexts

RAY VAN NESTE, ASSOCIATE PROFESSOR OF CHRISTIAN
STUDIES AND DIRECTOR OF THE RYAN CENTER
FOR BIBLICAL STUDIES, UNION UNIVERSITY

Other authors in this book are dealing with the larger issues of the role of denominations and our interactions. My task is a bit smaller, taking up one important issue—pastoral ministry—and asking how we should move ahead in the future and what role denominations and interactions with broader Evangelicalism have on this issue.

I find it interesting that almost 100 years ago, W. J. McGlothlin, a professor at The Southern Baptist Theological Seminary, was asking this same question. In his book, *Vital Ministry*, McGlothlin stated, "One of the most perplexing problems that confronts the young minister of to-day in America is that of the relation of himself and his church to other churches and denominations."[1] As much as things change, they stay the same. The professor went on to say, "Ours is apparently an age of transition."[2] So, too, is our age.

Statement of the Problem

We do live in a transitional time, and we do well to consider how we should approach the future as regards pastoral ministry. Other authors have talked about how in denominational life a shift occurred from seeing the denomination as a resource for the churches to seeing the churches as franchises of the denomination. Some of the current move away from denominationalism is a reaction against this—and that is good. We need to regain the priority of the local church. In so doing we need to think carefully about the nature of pastoral ministry.

For the sake of time, let me go ahead and state what the title of my chapter already suggests. If pastoral ministry is going to thrive in our churches we need to regain an understanding of the centrality of the oversight of souls. In fact, I will argue that the heart of pastoral ministry is this attentive care of souls. For many in our day, management is considered the central aspect of pastoral ministry. For many others, preaching is the most fundamental aspect of pastoral ministry. The renewed emphasis on substantive preaching in many quarters is to be celebrated, but preaching is not the heart of pastoral ministry; rather, preaching is an outflow of oversight. We do not guard souls in order to preach. Rather we preach as one means of guarding souls.

Our central task is not managing good programs, drawing large crowds, or even delivering powerful messages. Our central task is shepherding souls as they depart the City of Destruction and hazard their way toward the Celestial City.

It is so easy to forget this or to miss it altogether. When we do, all else is skewed. Ministry to masses can overshadow the needs of

---

[1] W. J. McGlothlin, *A Vital Ministry* (New York: Fleming-Revell, 1913), 171.
[2] Ibid., 172.

individuals, programs can replace people, and sermons can become lightweight pep talks or, even when soundly biblical, they can end up abstract lectures which fail to provide real guidance for people as they struggle with sin, self, and Satan.

Put simply, our current setting will, if given half a chance, suck all the personal pastoral care and concern out of our ministries, and replace it with slick professionalism which is efficient but impersonal and lacking in spiritual power.

This lack is being noticed and is showing up in the growing number of books on the discontent of believers with church. One such book is Julia Duin's *Quitting Church*. Based on wide and varied interviews, Duin discussed several reasons why otherwise mature believers were deeply disaffected with the church. Among those reasons was the lack of pastoral care. She wrote, "My research suggested that people simply were not being pastored. Often ministers are out of touch with what's happening on the ground."[3]

She cited difficulties people had getting in touch with their pastors or finding care and guidance for their souls. People often felt they were just supposed to attend mass meetings, fill their cog in the machine, and not expect anything more. They did not feel shepherded, or that anyone was engaging their day-to-day world.

In her work Duin interviewed Eugene Peterson, who perhaps as much as anyone in our day has thought and written profoundly on the importance of shepherding God's flock. Duin wrote about her interview:

> It's the job of pastors, he added, to know about their sheep and not dump the job on a subordinate. "People deserve to have their name known," he said. "They deserve to have somebody who is a spiritual guide and a preacher and pastor to them and who has had a cup of coffee in the kitchen. There is so much alienation, so much loneliness around us. Classically, that is what

---

[3] Julia Duin, *Quitting Church: Why the Faithful Are Fleeing and What to Do About It* (Grand Rapids: Baker, 2009), 22–23.

a pastor does. We've lost that. Of course some people think I'm out to lunch because we don't do that in America. We do something big and influential and cost-efficient. Well, a pastoral life is not cost-efficient, I'll tell you. You don't spend three hours in a nursing home and come away feeling like you've been cost-efficient."[4]

Calvin Miller has written winsomely on this issue in his book, O *Shepherd, Where Art Thou?* He states, "Most often when people do leave the church they are leaving because they feel the church failed to minister to them in a time of need. Yet pastors are often more stimulated to make their church grow than to take care of its members in their needy times. No one ever gets his or her picture in an Evangelical magazine simply because they visited the sick."[5]

Of course people are not free to give up on the church just because they are dissatisfied, but we would do well to hear the complaints that are being given to see what substance they have. Duin's research, for example, traced the lack of connectedness so many people feel, even in places where good sermons are being given. Good preaching is essential. It is just not all that is needed. Larry Crabb has provocatively written:

> Perhaps it is time to screw up our courage and attack the sacred cow: we must admit that simply knowing the contents of the Bible is not a sure route to spiritual growth. There is an awful assumption in evangelical circles that if we can just get the Word of God into people's heads, then the Spirit of God will apply it to their hearts. That assumption is awful, not because the Spirit never does what the assumption supposes, but because it has excused pastors and leaders from the responsibility to tangle with people's lives. Many remain safely hidden behind pulpits, hopelessly out of touch with the struggles of their congregations,

---

[4] Ibid., 126.
[5] Calvin Miller, O *Shepherd, Where Art Thou?* (Nashville: B&H, 2006), 42.

proclaiming the Scriptures with a pompous accuracy that touches no one.[6]

Now that is a tough statement. It may be overstated, but there is truth here. It is too easy to remain aloof from our people, failing to get our hands dirty in the day-to-day business of applying the truths we preach. This reality has been understood and addressed through the history of the church, and we need to consider this once again.

If we are in earnest about the salvation of souls, we must labor in the teaching of the Word and in the careful oversight of the souls of our flock. These two activities cannot rightly be divorced. John Angell James, in his classic book on pastoral ministry, *An Earnest Ministry*, stated, "Good preaching and good shepherding are quite compatible with each other, and he who is in earnest will combine both."[7]

Careful oversight may not make us famous, since people cannot download our oversight to their iPods, but our preaching cannot be what it ought to be without this care for individual souls.

In this talk I want to look again at the Scriptures and the witness of the church through the ages to discern what the heart of pastoral ministry should be. We need to look to the past in order to give perspective to our contemporary conversations. If we only listen to ourselves and our contemporaries we can fool ourselves into thinking a certain idea is the only way to think, when in fact we may be the first people in history to think this way. By thinking along with the best minds of previous generations we can be, as C. S. Lewis put it, rescued from "the great cataract of nonsense that pours from the press and the microphone" of our own age.[8]

If you look through the history of the church you find that the importance of the oversight of souls is not a Baptist distinctive. It is not even limited to Evangelicalism. It is truly part of the Great

---

[6] Larry Crabb, *Inside Out* (Colorado Springs: Navpress, 1988), 160.

[7] John Angell James, *An Earnest Ministry: The Want of Our Times* (Carlisle, PA: Banner of Truth), 149.

[8] C. S. Lewis, "Learning in War-Time," in *The Weight of Glory: And Other Addresses* (San Francisco: Harper Collins, 1980), 58–59.

Tradition. It is thus fitting that we notice it at this conference. This is an issue where Christians can and should unite.

I cannot here cover all the relevant scriptural texts or historical affirmations. I will focus on some key texts, and then in the discussion of these texts use selected quotes from across the range (chronologically and ecclesiastically) of church history. We could discuss the texts without these quotes but I am using them to demonstrate that this reading of Scripture is not unique but is the common voice of the church.

Scriptural Texts on Pastoral Ministry

We are not at a loss for texts on this topic, although it seems they are not referenced enough. When thinking of the pastor's role we ought first look to Jesus Himself, the "great Shepherd of the sheep" (Heb 13:20). In John 10:11–15 (HCSB), Jesus describes Himself as the true shepherd, and in so doing gives us a picture of what true under-shepherds should be as well:

> I am the good shepherd. The good shepherd lays down his life
> for the sheep. The hired man, since he is not the shepherd and
> doesn't own the sheep, leaves them and runs away when he sees
> a wolf coming. The wolf then snatches and scatters them. This
> happens because he is a hired man and doesn't care about the
> sheep. I am the good shepherd. I know My own sheep, and they
> know Me, as the Father knows Me, and I know the Father. I lay
> down My life for the sheep.

Undoubtedly one reason the term "pastor" or "shepherd" is used in the NT is to connect with the work and example of Jesus as the Great Shepherd. Notice first of all the care given to the sheep. The true under-shepherd must be one who does not run at the approach of danger. Rather, he is one who stands at his post defending the sheep, even giving his life if necessary. In the fourth century John Chrysostom applied this passage to pastoral ministry, stating, "A great thing, beloved, a great thing is the role of leader in the Church. It is one that requires much wisdom, and as great courage as Christ's words indicate: namely, sufficient to lay down one's life for the sheep; sufficient never to leave them unprotected and exposed to danger; and sufficient to stand firm against the attack of the wolf."[9]

Notice also that Jesus explicitly says He knows His sheep. There is no way to guard the sheep if you do not know them.

Alexander Maclaren, commenting on this passage, wrote:

> Individualising care and tender knowledge of each are marks of
> the true shepherd. To call by name implies this and more. To
> a stranger all sheep are alike; the shepherd knows them apart.
> It is a beautiful picture of loving intimacy, lowliness, care, and
> confidence, and one which every teacher should ponder. Contrast
> this with the Pharisees' treatment of the blind man.[10]

More on this later.[11]

Next, we look at perhaps the key text in this discussion, Heb 13:17 (HCSB), "Obey your leaders and submit to them, for they keep watch over your souls as those who will give an account, so that they can do this with joy and not with grief, for that would be unprofitable for you."

Notice that this passage posits significant authority in the pastors (and it is not really softened by translating "obey" as "be persuaded by"). Notice also, though, that this authority is directly tied to the work of watching over souls. Pastors have authority in the church

---

[9] John Chrysostom, "Homily 60," in *Saint John Chrysostom: Commentary on Saint John the Apostle and Evangelist (Homilies 48–88)*, vol. 41 of *The Fathers of the Church: A New Translation*, ed. Roy Joseph Deferrari (New York: Fathers of the Church, 1959), 133.

[10] Alexander Maclaren, *The Gospel of St. John*, Bible Class Expositions (London: Hodder and Stoughton, 1893), 106.

[11] After studying this passage in my pastoral ministry class, one student wrote: "This passage is an encouragement to me as one who feels called to preach the Word of God. If I become a pastor, I must love the sheep like Jesus did. I must be willing to die for my flock and guard my flock from wolves. I must be willing to encourage and rebuke my flock and always do what is for their eternal good. I must set an example for them in everything so that their faith may not be shaken by my poor leadership. What an enormous responsibility awaits me. May I never take it lightly."

precisely because they are to be guarding souls. And, then, Scripture makes the important point that pastors are to engage the work of this oversight in a manner shaped by the realization that God will call them to account. Here we are given a clear statement about what God expects of pastors and for what He will hold us accountable on the final day. No mention is made of drawing crowds, erecting buildings, or managing programs. Those things may be fine, but what matters is the oversight of souls.

Now, what is meant here by "keep watch over [your] souls"? The term is used elsewhere with the sense of watchfulness, staying awake, guarding, and protecting. We are to keep watch over our congregations, protecting them and guiding them by providing clear biblical teaching and personally rebuking and encouraging. As John Owen in the seventeenth century wrote:

> And the apostle compriseth herein the whole duty of the pastoral office. . . . The work and design of these rulers [pastors] is solely to take care of your souls, by all means to preserve them from evil, sin, backsliding; to instruct them and feed them; to promote their faith and obedience; that they may be led safely to eternal rest. For this end is their office appointed and herein do they labour continually.[12]

This idea is why Martin Bucer, leader of the Reformation in Strasbourg in the sixteenth century, titled his treatise on pastoral ministry, *Concerning the True Care of Souls*. It is striking also that he refers to a pastor as *Seelsorger*, a "carer of souls."[13]

This will require personal knowledge of the sheep. It will not be accomplished merely by sermons fired at random. We again must be like the Good Shepherd who pursues the wandering sheep. This task cannot be fulfilled in the pulpit alone. It requires us to commit

---

[12] John Owen, *The Works of John Owen*, ed. William H. Goold (London: Johnstone and Hunter, 1855), 465.

[13] Martin Bucer, *Concerning the True Care of Souls*, trans. Peter Beale (Carlisle, PA: Banner of Truth, 2009), vii.

to following up with our people. At the church where I serve, we commit to our people, saying, "We will love you enough to chase you down should you ever wander away. You can choose to break your connection with us but you will not just slip away and be forgotten."

John Erskine, an eighteenth-century Scottish Presbyterian, wrote:

> Sermons, like arrows shot at a venture, seldom hit the mark when we do not know the character of our hearers; and, in many instances, our knowledge of their character must be imperfect if we contract no familiarity with them.[14]

Similarly, Charles Brown, in Scotland in the nineteenth century, also wrote:

> After a long ministry I do not hesitate to express my belief, that . . . the best preaching will lose much of its power without the systematic visiting of the flock at their homes. Not only must the minister remain thus a stranger, to a large extent, to their condition and necessities, and so have to preach to them very much at random, but he shall fail of securing that kindly esteem and affectionate confidence at their hands, without which, however he may win their mere respect by his pulpit ministrations, his preaching will probably fail to a great extent of its grand use and end. As the people will most surely bid that minister right welcome to their homes whose voice they hear with joy on the Sabbaths, so will they return with fresh and ever-growing joy to the church, to listen to *his* voice whom they have found the sympathizing friend and counselor of their loved families.[15]

A similar point was made by a nineteenth-century New England Congregationalist, Silas Aiken:

---

[14] John Erskine, "Difficulties of the Pastoral Office," in *The Christian Pastor's Manual* 1826, ed. John Brown (1826, 1991; repr., Morgan, PA: Soli Deo Gloria, 2003), 191–92. Erskine goes on to comment on how difficult this is with a large congregation.

[15] Charles J. Brown, *The Ministry: Addresses to Students of Divinity* (Carlisle, PA: Banner of Truth, 2006), 84.

A particular oversight and care of the flock . . . is involved in the idea of the pastoral work . . . and can no more be pushed aside or ignored, than any other part. . . . The man who assumes the sacred office, and, in the neglect of the personal inspection and private instruction of the souls committed to his care, thinks to discharge his obligations by his pulpit labors, is sadly derelict in duty. He sets aside the scriptural model, and sets up a standard of his own devising instead.[16]

This is what is in view when the NT refers to pastors as "over-seers." This does not refer to "management" in our business model, but to the task of overseeing souls, watching out for the flock, fighting off wolves, and pursuing wandering sheep.

This theme is also found in Peter's exhortation to pastors in 1 Pet 5:1–4 (HCSB):

Therefore, as a fellow elder and witness to the sufferings of the Messiah and also a participant in the glory about to be revealed, I exhort the elders among you: Shepherd God's flock among you, not overseeing out of compulsion but freely, according to God's will; not for the money but eagerly; not lording it over those entrusted to you, but being examples to the flock. And when the chief Shepherd appears, you will receive the unfading crown of glory.

Here we are told to "shepherd" and to "exercise oversight." These two activities cannot be fully covered by preaching. Certainly preaching is an important element, but shepherding in these contexts would also conjure up the image of guarding, pursuing, and personal care.

These themes also show up in Paul's farewell address to the Ephesian elders in Acts 20:18–21,28 (HCSB):

And when they came to him, he said to them: "You know, from the first day I set foot in Asia, how I was with you the whole

---

[16] Silas Aiken, "On Pastoral Duties," *The Congregational Quarterly* 8 (January 1866): 30.

time—serving the Lord with all humility, with tears, and with the trials that came to me through the plots of the Jews—and that I did not shrink back from proclaiming to you anything that was profitable or from teaching it to you in public and from house to house. I testified to both Jews and Greeks about repentance toward God and faith in our Lord Jesus. . . . Be on guard for yourselves and for all the flock that the Holy Spirit has appointed you to as overseers, to shepherd the church of God, which He purchased with His own blood.

This passage is significant as Paul's summary of his ministry. Some at this point might find yourselves saying, "But the apostles in Acts 6 said their priority was to be the ministry of the Word and prayer. How does this fit with what you are saying?" This passage shows how it fits very well. Paul shows here that his "ministry of the Word" involved not only public proclamation but also proclamation "from house to house." If we would follow the apostolic pattern we must give public and private instruction. As we spend time with our people we speak truth to them in the midst of everyday life as well as preaching it on Sunday. In our own day when people so easily think of a rigid divide between the sacred and the secular, this everyday, private ministry is so important in showing that what is discussed in church is really supposed to be lived out in daily life.

This is also affirmed in the *Westminster Directory of Public Worship* (1645), which says, "It is the duty of the minister not only to teach the people committed to his charge in public, but privately; and particularly to admonish, exhort, reprove, and comfort them, upon all seasonable occasions, so far as his time, strength, and personal safety will permit."[17]

---

[17] "Concerning Visitation of the Sick," in *The Directory for the Public Worship of God, Agreed Upon by the Assembly of Divines at Westminster* 1645 (1845; repr., New York: Robert Kennedy, 1880), 32.

Also in this time period, Richard Baxter wrote, "I fear most those ministers who preach well, and who are unsuited to the private nurture of their members."[18]

This sort of ministry grows out of real care and affection for our people. This is simply not a task that can be done with our hearts carefully tucked away. I have often heard young pastors counseled not to get too close to their church members. They are encouraged to keep a "professional" or even "prophetic" distance. In one case the advice was that getting too close would make it too difficult to deliver rebuke when needed. This advice is not only unhelpful, it is downright ungodly! Rebuke ought not be delivered if it is too easy. It is the wounds of a friend that are faithful, not the cool correction of a hired hand.

Such distance is not the biblical model. Notice what Paul said in 1 Thess 2:1,7–12,19–20:

> For you yourselves know, brothers, that our visit with you was not without result. . . . Although we could have been a burden as Christ's apostles, instead we were gentle among you, as a nursing mother nurtures her own children. We cared so much for you that we were pleased to share with you not only the gospel of God but also our own lives, because you had become dear to us. For you remember our labor and hardship, brothers. Working night and day so that we would not burden any of you, we preached God's gospel to you. You are witnesses, and so is God, of how devoutly, righteously, and blamelessly we conducted ourselves with you believers. As you know, like a father with his own children, we encouraged, comforted, and implored each one of you to walk worthy of God, who calls you into His own kingdom and glory. . . . For who is our hope or joy or crown of boasting in the presence of our Lord Jesus at His coming? Is it not you? For you are our glory and joy!

---

[18] Richard Baxter, *The Reformed Pastor* (1656), rev. ed., ed. James M. Houston (Portland, OR: Multnomah, 1982), 7.

Does this sound like a man who has been careful not to get his affections wrapped up with his people? Of course not! The only way we will work "night and day" is if our people become "dear to us." This sort of affection will only grow as you get to know them, walk with them, share in their joys and sorrows, and permit them to walk alongside you, sharing your joys and griefs as well. Then we will treat them like gentle mothers and concerned fathers.

The great Reformer, Martin Luther, is known for being fiery and even rough. Yet notice how he speaks of love for the congregation:

> Men who hold the office of the ministry should have the heart
> of a mother toward the church; for if they have no such heart,
> they soon become lazy and disgusted, and suffering, in particular,
> will find them unwilling. . . . Unless your heart toward the sheep
> is like that of a mother toward her children—a mother, who
> walks through fire to save her children—you will not be fit to
> be a preacher. Labor, work, unthankfulness, hatred, envy, and
> all kinds of sufferings will meet you in this office. If, then, the
> mother heart, the great love, is not there to drive the preachers,
> the sheep will be poorly served.[19]

Moving forward one century, to the seventeenth, Samuel Rutherford is a powerful example of deep affection for one's congregation. Having been torn away from his people and exiled for his devotion to the gospel, Rutherford wrote letters to his people exhorting, counseling, challenging, and teaching them. The collection of these letters is now considered a spiritual classic. In one letter he addressed his congregation as a whole:

> Dearly beloved and longed-for in the Lord, my crown and my
> joy in the day of Christ, Grace be to you, and peace from God
> our Father, and from our Lord Jesus Christ.

---

[19] Martin Luther, "Ministers," in *What Luther Says: A Practical In-Home Anthology for the Active Christian*, ed. Ewald M. Plass (1959; repr., Saint Louis: Concordia, 1994), 932.

I long exceedingly to know if the oft-spoken-of match betwixt you and Christ holdeth, and if ye follow on to know the Lord. My day-thoughts and my night-thoughts are of you; while ye sleep I am afraid of your souls, that they be off the rock. Next to my Lord Jesus and this fallen kirk, ye have the greatest share of my sorrow, and also of my joy; ye are the matter of the tears, care, fear, and daily prayers of an oppressed prisoner of Christ. As I am in bonds for my high and lofty One, my royal and princely Master, my Lord Jesus; so I am in bonds for you. . . . What could I want, if my ministry among you should make a marriage between the little bride in those bounds and the Bridegroom? Oh, how rich a prisoner were I, if I could obtain of my Lord (before whom I stand for you) the salvation of you all! Oh, what a prey had I gotten, to have you catched in Christ's net! Oh, then I had cast out my Lord's lines and His net with a rich gain! Oh then, well-wared pained breast, and sore back, and crazed body, in speaking early and late to you! . . . My witness is above; your heaven would be two heavens to me, and the salvation of you all as two salvations to me. I would subscribe a suspension, and a fristing of my heaven for many hundred years (according to God's good pleasure), if ye were sure in the upper lodging, in our Father's house, before me.[20]

This is a pastor's heart!

When we have this sort of affection for our people we will be able to say of our churches the sort of thing we find the apostle Paul saying, "For now we live, if you are standing fast in the Lord" (1 Thess 3:8 ESV). This also explains Paul's description of his pastoral aims in Col 1:24–29 (ESV, emphasis added):

Now I rejoice in my sufferings for your sake, and in my flesh I am filling up what is lacking in Christ's afflictions for the sake of his body, that is, the church, of which I became a minister according to the stewardship from God that was given to me for

---

[20] "Letter 225," *Letters of Samuel Rutherford*, 5th ed. (Edinburgh: Oliphant Anderson & Ferrier, n.d.), 438–39.

you, to make the word of God fully known, the mystery hidden
for ages and generations but now revealed to his saints. To them
God chose to make known how great among the Gentiles are
the riches of the glory of this mystery, which is Christ in you, the
hope of glory. Him we proclaim, *warning everyone* and *teaching
everyone* with all wisdom, that we may *present everyone mature
in Christ*. For this I toil, struggling with all his energy that he
powerfully works within me.

Part of what is striking in this passage is the emphasis on individuals. Paul sought to warn and teach each member with the goal of
presenting each one mature in Christ. This aim should animate our
ministries. Too often today leaders are content with seeing maturity
or even attendance in a "significant percentage" of the membership.
But this is not Paul's aim. We are to labor and suffer to see that *each
one* attains maturity in Christ. John Calvin wrote, "The office of a true
and faithful minister is not only publicly to teach the people over
whom he is ordained to pastor, but, so far as may be, to admonish,
exhort, rebuke, and console each one in particular."[21]

One of the early Baptist confessions of faith includes the following affirmation:

> That the members of every church or congregation ought to
> know one another, so they may perform all the duties of love to
> one another, both spiritually and physically (Matt 18:15; 1 Thess
> 5:14; 1 Cor 12:25). And especially the elders ought to know the
> whole flock over which the Holy Spirit has made them overseers
> (Acts 20:28; 1 Pet 5:2–3). Therefore a church ought not to
> consist of such a multitude that each member cannot have
> individual knowledge of one another.[22]

---

[21] John Calvin, "Visitation of the Sick," in *John Calvin: Tracts and Letters*, vol. 2,
ed. by H. Beveridge (1849; repr., Carlisle, PA: Banner of Truth, 2009), 127.

[22] "A Declaration of Faith of English People Remaining at Amsterdam in
Holland" (1611), in *Baptist Confessions of Faith*, rev. ed., ed. by William L. Lumpkin
(Valley Forge, PA: Judson Press, 1959), 121.

Furthermore, Henry Scougal (1650–78), prominent Scottish pastor and theologian who profoundly influenced both Whitefield and the Wesleys, wrote:

> But certainly the greatest and most difficult work of a minister is in applying himself particularly to the various persons under his charge; to acquaint himself with their behavior and the temper of their souls; to redress what is amiss and prevent their future miscarriages. Without this private work, his other endeavors will do little good. . . . Now this supposes a great deal of care, to acquaint ourselves with the humors and conversation of our people; and the name of "watchmen" that is given to us implies no less.[23]

Baxter, considered by some to be the consummate pastor, wrote eloquently on this subject in *The Reformed Pastor*. Here are some pertinent samples that sum up the argument to this point:

> But our second concern must also be for *individuals* in the church. We need therefore to know every person that belongs to our charge. For how can we take heed to them unless we know them? We should know completely those in our flock. As a careful shepherd looks after every individual sheep, or as a good schoolmaster looks after every individual student, or as a good doctor knows each of his patients—in these ways we should know them. Christ Himself, the great and good Shepherd, takes care of every individual. . . . We, too, must give an account of our watch over the souls of all that are bound to obey us (Heb 13:7). Many more passages of Scripture assure us that it is our duty to take heed to every individual person that is in our flock. And many passages in the ancient church council do plainly tell us that it was also the practice in those days to do likewise. In one passage, Ignatius says, "Let assemblies be often gathered; inquire into all by name, despise not servant-men or maidens." So you

---

[23] "On the Importance and Difficulty of the Ministerial Function," in *The Works of the Rev. Henry Scougal* (1765), reprint, ed. Don Kistler (Morgan, PA: Soli Deo Gloria, 2002), 241, 252.

see it was then taken as a duty to look upon every member of
the flock by name, even if it should be the meanest servant-man
or maid. . . . A faithful pastor should have his eyes on them all.
He should labor to know each person's natural temperament,
their situations, and the context of their affairs in the world. A
pastor should be aware of the company they live with and deal
with, so that he may know where their temptations lie. Thus he
knows speedily, prudently, and diligently how to help them.[24]

In summing up his book, Baxter gives 20 points on the benefits of
attending to each individual in the congregation. In this context he
makes these statements:

But when a minister does not know his own people, he is not
able to really minister to them. By means of such personal
ministry we come to be better acquainted with each one's
spiritual state. Then we know better how to watch over them
and relate to them. . . . They should see us not as simply
necessary for their emergency situations. They should see
themselves as disciples or scholars who are being taught by
their pastors through personal advice and given help for their
salvation.[25]

Now some at this point may say, "Fine, but I have not seen much
Baptist representation in your historical quotes." Well, here are a few
to show the solidarity of Baptists with this stream of thought.

P. H. Mell was a messenger at the founding of the SBC who went
on to serve as its president, 14 or more years. Mell was known as a
powerful, doctrinal preacher. His biographer records this account of
his ministry:

Very much of his power as a preacher lay in the way he had of
getting close to his people. His custom was to visit *all* of them,
and so anxious were they not to miss the expected pleasure that
he made engagements ahead often as far as three months. The

---

[24] Baxter, 71–72, 76.
[25] Ibid, 107–8.

humblest householder was glad to entertain "Brother Mell," and the same ease of manner characterized him whether he sat at the bountiful board of the rich, or broth the plain bread and partook of the cup of milk from the pine table of the poorest. . . . If a poor man was harassed with debt, broken hearted over a willful child, or bowed down with bereavement, he never felt his load to be quite so heavy after he had talked it over with "Brother Mell."[26]

Moving to a Baptist in the Northeast, Hezekiah Harvey was a prolific Baptist pastor and professor at Hamilton Theological Seminary. In his treatise on pastoral ministry, he wrote:

The care of souls is the radical idea of the pastor's office. He is a shepherd to whom a flock has been committed to guide, to feed, to defend; and the divine command enjoins: "Take heed to *all* the flock, over the which the Holy Ghost hath made you overseers" (Acts 20:28). He is to be the personal religious guide, the confidential Christian friend, of his charge. Our Lord, in his description of the Good Shepherd, said, "The sheep hear his voice; and he calleth his own sheep by name, and leadeth them out. And when he putteth forth his own sheep, he goeth before them, and the sheep follow him; for they know his voice" (John 10:3–4). Each member of his flock is a soul entrusted to his care by the Lord; and if true to his trust, he is one of those who "watch for souls as they must give account." Paul, when in Ephesus, taught not only publicly, but "from house to house"; and in his farewell charge to the elders of that city he said, "Watch, and remember that, by the space of three years, I ceased not to warn every man night and day with tears" (Acts 20:31).[27]

---

[26] P. H. Mell Jr., *The Life of Patrick Hues Mell* (Harrisonburg, VA: Gano Books, 1991), 61–62.

[27] Hezekiah Harvey, *The Pastor: His Qualifications and Duties* (Philadelphia: American Baptist Publication Society, 1879), 78.

Then there is Charles Bray Williams, who was founding NT professor at Southwestern Baptist Theological Seminary, president of Mercer, and professor at Union University where he published his translation of the NT. Throughout this work he was also a pastor. His daughter, Charlotte Williams Sprawls, has written a biographical sketch of her father in which she recollects his ministry in his 80s when he was pastoring a 700+ member church. She wrote, "[he] believed strongly in a pastor's knowing personally every member in his church, and he had a very active plan of visitation of every family in their home every few weeks."[28] That is quite a testimony for a man at that age and church of that size.

Lastly, I could point to W. A. Criswell, who in his guidebook for pastors writes:

> The shepherd tending his flock, the pastor living in love and encouragement among his people, is the picture the New Testament presents of this God-called servant. . . . Prayer, even fervent prayer, is not enough, nor is prayer plus incessant Bible study enough. We must live with our people, minister to our people, encourage, and guide our people. . . . If the pastor would really succeed in his work, let him minister to the needs of his people. . . . The pastor who knows, loves, visits, and ministers to his flock has a place in their hearts sacred forever. . . . The example of the great pastors of the world is always one of personal contact with the people. The pulpit is the throne of the preacher, but the throne is not stable unless it rests on the affections of the people. To win the affections of the people, you must visit with them and know them and talk to them and let them talk to you. The man with whom you have wisely and tenderly conversed on vital, personal religion cannot turn a cold,

---

[28] Charlotte Williams Sprawls, *Charles Bray Williams: Greek Scholar, Professor, Writer, Pastor and Preacher, 1896–1952; Translator of "The New Testament in the Language of the People"* (Graceville, FL: Florida Baptist Historical Society, 2007), 12.

critical ear toward you on the Lord's Day, nor does he. The man who visits has the love of the people.[29]

Conclusion

The oversight of souls is the heart of pastoral ministry. From this effort of caring for souls comes preaching, visiting, counseling, and everything else a pastor does. We preach in order to guard and guide souls. We pray for them that they might hate sin, love God, be encouraged, and persevere. We visit and counsel so that we might point them in the way of truth and overcome the snares of sin. And, while there are various reasons why we pursue personal holiness, one reason is the fear of harming our dear people.

Brothers, let us shepherd God's sheep. He bought them with His own blood! Is there anything more valuable, more worthy of our attention? His saving of them was not haphazard or random. Neither should our care of them be.

On the final day we will be called to give an account before God Himself, and He will not inquire of our buildings, programs, and such. He has told us ahead of time that He will examine how we cared for the souls of those entrusted to our care. Let us consider this soberly and pursue our ministries accordingly. This will likely have radical implications for what we do and how we do it. Let us pursue this goal relentlessly since it is the clear command of our Master, the Great Shepherd of the Sheep. Let us imitate Him that we might please Him and know His pleasure in our lives.

Fellow pastors, we have been entrusted with a group of people who are feeble and frail, who still struggle with sin and get frightened and overwhelmed. Our task is to guide them faithfully on to heaven, fighting off the wolves, warning of snares, even chasing out false sheep.

---

[29] W. A. Criswell, *Criswell's Guidebook for Pastors* (Nashville: Broadman Press, 1980), 273–75.

Horatius Bonar, that wonderful Scottish pastor, ardent evangelist, and hymn writer, said it well:

> To this extent the office of the elder and the minister is the same. The design of both is *the oversight of souls*. . . . Oh! Remember, then, that it is for the care of souls that you have been now ordained; it is for souls that you are to labour, and watch, and pray; and it is for souls that you are to give an account when the great Shepherd shall appear.[30]

May we be found faithful in this task.

---

[30] Horatius Bonar, "The Union Between Christ and Believers, and the Union of Believers One With Another: A Discourse," *The Scottish Christian Herald* 2 (Jan.– Dec. 1840): 748.

Chapter 7

Awakenings and Their Impact on Baptists and Evangelicals: Sorting Out the Myths in the History of Missions and Evangelism

JERRY N. TIDWELL, SENIOR VICE PRESIDENT
FOR UNIVERSITY RELATIONS, UNION UNIVERSITY

If you have traveled to Israel you have probably seen the Dead Sea. It is 47 miles long and varies in width from two to 10 miles (although it is getting smaller each day). It rests at 1300 feet below sea level. It has no outlets, and the salt content is approximately 25 percent; normal sea water is 6 percent. Nothing lives in the Dead Sea because of the high salt and mineral content, thus its name.[1] But the irony is that in the northern part of Israel is the Sea of Galilee, which is the "life" of Israel, its water supply. Water from Mount Hermon flows into the Sea of Galilee, which has an outlet called the Jordan River, which carries that cool, life-giving water along to the Dead Sea. Nevertheless, the

---

[1] Harry Thomas Frank, *Discovering the Biblical World* (Maplewood, NJ: Hammond Incorporated, 1975), 27.

Sea of Galilee cannot give life to the Dead Sea because of the absence of outlets for the Dead Sea. It receives, but does not give. This is a model for how Baptists and Evangelicals have been at our best over the last 400 years when we have been passionate and consumed with allowing God's Spirit to flow not only to us, but through us.

This chapter is going to focus on the times in the last 400 years when we have allowed God to work through us to change our world. I will confess that I walked into this area of study thinking that I was somewhat of an expert on awakenings, missions, and evangelism because I have read what I needed for whatever sermon or study I was doing. That's called tunnel vision at best, and egocentric at worst. I'm sure none of you would ever do that. Going into study with presuppositions may not be unusual, but it did lead me to present my work in the form of "myths related to the awakenings and their impact on us and the way we carry out the Great Commission."

I thought I would simply do a historical overview of the awakenings and then share their impact on Baptists, missions, and evangelism. But I discovered something that many of you already know: not only do pastors occasionally disagree, but historians disagree even more! That led me to take a different approach, one that I hope you will appreciate. In sharing the fruits of my study, I want to present my findings by sharing these common "myths" about corporate revival and the awakenings. I might add that if you look carefully at the impact of the awakenings, you may think (as I did) that "awakening" may not even be the best word to describe these events. A study of the awakenings, if nothing else, will point out that these events were not marked by a *spiritual enlightenment* on the part of man, but an *infusion* of God's presence on individual or corporate believers.[2]

---

[2] Iain H. Murray, *Revival and Revivalism: The Making and Marring of American Evangelicalism* (Edinburgh: The Banner of Truth Trust, 1994), xviii.

Myth # 1 "There Is Agreement on the Number and Dates of the Awakenings"

There is perfect agreement as long as you read one historian at a time! Typically, the awakenings have been broken down as follows:

First Great Awakening: 1730–55

Second Great Awakening: 1790–1840

Third Great Awakening: 1850–90

Fourth Great Awakening: 1960–80

While there is little doubt about the dates of the last two awakenings, I found the dates of the first two to be in question. If you read accounts of revival, there seems to be one long awakening that started in the United Kingdom around 1735 and started almost simultaneously in Colonial America. The awakening waned in the United Kingdom as it ignited and spread in the American Colonies. When the awakening started in this country, it reached a plateau in some areas, but reignited in others. Rather than being "one large moment" of awakening, it would be better characterized as many regional moments of infusion of God's anointing on a gathered body of believers.[3]

The Great Awakening was marked by famous moments such as Jonathan Edwards' sermon, "Sinners in the Hands of an Angry God," on July 8, 1741. With the names of Edwards, John and Charles Wesley, George Whitefield, and others, men such as Andrew Fuller often get overlooked since he was not noted at the beginning of the awakening. And here's where the dating comes into play. Fuller, or "Fullerism," was the zenith of the revival, but his efforts were evident mostly after 1780 with his work titled *The Gospel Worthy of All Acceptation*. With the dating above, this places him outside the traditional boundaries of the awakenings.

Fuller was an intimidating presence, broad-shouldered, and was a wrestler as a youth. While he wrote against and rejected

---

[3] Ibid., 391–424.

hyper-Calvinism, he did not reject Calvinism outright. (One interesting caveat about Fuller was his deep commitment to study. During his study, he was reluctant to be disturbed by casual visitors. He would block the doorframe with his presence and dismiss them as quickly as possible. He often pointed to a plaque on his wall that read: "He who steals my purse, steals money, but he who steals my time, steals my life!")[4]

It seems that William Carey was greatly influenced by Fuller's fervor, and the Baptist Missionary Movement was launched. In my opinion, for anyone to suggest that Fuller or William Carey's *Enquiry* were not part of the awakenings shows that person to be more committed to dates than results. While some would dismiss this movement as a lingering result of the awakening, other accounts of "outpourings" or "infusions" of God's presence were noted at the turn of the century beyond the missionary movement. For example, excerpts from exchanged letters of a Colonel Robert Patterson to Dr. King of September 25, 1801, said:

> On the 1st of May, at a meeting at Fleming Creek, KY, about sixty persons were "struck down" publicly confessing sins, praying for pardon, recommending Jesus to sinners, etc. . . . On the next Sabbath over 100 persons were "struck down" in the same manner. A great Solemn appeared all day. There was rejoicing, cries of distress among sinners, praying, singing. About 4,000 persons attended, twelve wagons brought a number of people from great distance with provisions to last. The Lord's Supper was to be held at Point Pleasant, on Stony Creek. The flame spread more and more. About 40 wagons, four carriages, in all about 8,000 persons. There were 350 confessions of faith in Christ, 250 struck down. There was opposition by some who appeared to be real Christians, by normal professors, and by Deists. . . .[5]

---

[4] James Leo Garrett, *Baptist Theology: A Four Century Study* (Macon, GA: Mercer University Press, 2009), 153–212.

[5] H. Shelton Smith, Robert T. Handy, and Lefferts A. Loetscher, *American Christianity: An Historical Interpretation with Representative Documents* (New York: Charles Scribner's Sons, 1960), 566–70.

What shall we say then? While I don't expect everyone to jump on the proverbial bandwagon with me on this, let me conclude on Myth #1 that whether classified as two awakenings or one Great Awakening with two stages, or one long awakening that waned in some areas as it ignited in others, it must be concluded that the "anointing" that began with the Wesleys, Edwards, and Whitefield was the same inspiration that touched Fuller and Carey, and ignited fires of revival at the turn of 1800 that continued through the 1830s.

Myth # 2 "Removing Barriers of Offense to Unbelievers Will Lead to Larger Church Membership"

It may or may not surprise the reader that the strategy for removing barriers of offense to nonbelievers was not birthed in the "seeker sensitive" movement of the 1990s. Whether it was the General Assembly of General Baptists of the 1700s and their embracing of "Unitarianism" to appeal to those bound to the world's influences, or the "Old Light Hyper-Calvinist" who believed you were so secure in your election that habitual sin prompted no need for rebuke (similar to the gnostics' attempt to influence the early church), we church leaders have always been tempted to acquire a crowd through human persuasion rather than conversion.[6]

But a close look at messages such as Edwards' "Sinners in the Hands of an Angry God," in which he described the sinner as "a loathsome spider suspended by a slender thread over a pit of seething brimstone," or Fuller's work, "The Atonement of Christ," in which he said we should "hold up the blessings of His salvation for acceptance, even to the chief of sinners," or when he chided pastors by saying, "I conceive there is scarcely a minister amongst us whose preaching has not been more or less influenced by the lethargic systems of the age," it seems that during the time of awakening, whether in the cities of New England or the prairies of the West, the preaching of the

---

[6] Murray, *Revival and Revivalism*, 113–42.

"narrow road leading to life in Christ" did more to increase church membership than a road made easy by powerless preaching.[7]

> Whatever else we may say, during the awakenings, standards of membership increased, but church membership grew as well! Referencing an event in the 1990s about a large Evangelical church in Texas that set up a wrestling ring in the sanctuary so the ministerial staff (having been trained by someone from WWF) would throw each other around the ring to the delight of the crowd, my friend, in his book titled *Common Sense Church Growth*, said: "Those from the world who are searching and looking for something not found in the world . . . they've tried the world's way and are looking for something 'separate' from the world." After all, Jesus Himself did not lower the standards of the Law in His Sermon on the Mount. (He opened up a five-gallon can of worms, and there wasn't a Pharisee within earshot that wouldn't have given his last denarius to see Jesus strung up by sundown.) Jesus said, "You have heard that it was said to our ancestors, Do not murder, and whoever murders will be subject to judgment. But I tell you, everyone who is angry with his brother will be subject to judgment. And whoever says to his brother, 'Fool!' will be subject to the Sanhedrin. But whoever says, 'You moron!' will be subject to hellfire." (Matt 5:21–22)

That doesn't sound as if He is "lowering" the standards. You may have heard it said, "When Jesus is in the house, people will come to the house." I believe that in each of the awakenings, people had a sense that God was there, and they didn't want to miss it, even camping out for days at a time, lest they miss an outpouring of God's presence.[8]

---

[7] Terry L. Matthews, Wake Forest University, Religion 166: Religious Life in the United States. Lectures: "The Great Awakening," 1995.

[8] Howard Batson, *Common Sense Church Growth* (Macon, GA: Smith & Helwys, 1999), 37–42.

Myth # 3 "The Awakenings Were the Result of a "Push-Back" from Calvinism"

Those who know me, know that I have never been accused of even slightly being a defender of Calvinism. As a matter of fact, there were a few times when I was afraid that if I went to the "Founders' web site," there would be a "most wanted" posting for me: "Dead or alive!" I must confess, with the number of conversions that took place as a result of each of the awakenings, I assumed this was because of a "push-back" against Calvinism.

But in a close examination of the awakening years from 1730–1830, you will find that the context of the initial awakenings occurred among those who were not "hyper-Calvinists," but were strongly Calvinist preachers. It seems that "true Calvinists" were the ones who were successful in beating back the "hyper-Calvinism" of those such as Tobias Crisp and the Old Lights. I personally believe, although you may disagree, that men such as Alvery Jackson and Abraham Booth, both Particular Baptist and Calvinist, were the ones who sought to stamp out the non-missional "hyper-Calvinism" with works such as *The Reign of Grace*, which were preludes to this great renewal.[9]

If Jonathan Edwards could influence the missionary movement of William Carey, and George Whitefield (a die-hard Calvinist) could partner with the Arminian Wesleys, then surely we can find mutual ground that allows us to move forward as Southern Baptists for the sake of reaching the lost for Jesus Christ.

Now the Awakening of 1850–1900 was marked more by what has been labeled "a practical Arminianism" led by men such as Finney, Beecher, and Ashbury. But it can be argued that their focus was more experience based rather than the doctrinal-based earlier awakening. This might account for some of the more unfavorable offshoots of the later awakening such as the Mormons and other less doctrinally sound movements.

---

[9] Murray, *Revival and Revivalism*, 113–42

If there was a "push-back" that helped spur the First Great Awakening, it started with the sermons of Solomon Stoddard in 1679 as he embraced heavily the great gulf between the sovereignty and holiness of God and the depravity of man. This "push-back" of Stoddard was in response to Isaac Newton's *Principle Mathematics*, which attempted to close the gap in the ability of man to discover the formula of the universe and control his own destiny. Lest someone assume that Stoddard and others were rejecting academics, I would offer that there did not seem to be a denial of the science of Newton's thought, except his suggestion that man could control the science and thereby control his destiny.[10]

Myth # 4 "Prayer Meetings Were the Catalyst for the Awakenings"

Again, I approach this with some caution, hoping you will hear what I say, and not what I didn't say. I do agree with Charles Finney who said, "Revival has not come every time people prayed, but it has never come when people did not pray." I also know the great story of Jeremiah Lanphier and the Fulton Street Church (Sept. 23, 1857), when he opened the church to pray at noon, and was soon joined by 20, then 40, 100, and then 1000s. But, as was the case of the Haystack Prayer Meeting of 1806, led by students from Williams College (which inspired a burden for missions among young people), prayer meetings became the context for the awakening, but not the catalyst. Whether we are referencing the experience of the prophet in Isaiah chapter six, or Lanphier's prayer meeting in 1857, the catalyst for awakening seemed to be a realization of God's holiness in contrast with man's sinfulness.[11]

It cannot be denied that when people caught a fresh vision of God's holiness and sovereignty, prayer became a natural response and

---

[10] Matthews, Lectures at Wake Forest University.

[11] Roy Fish, Southwestern Baptist Theological Seminary, *Evangelism: The Awakenings* (class notes, 1986).

thereby the context for God's refreshing. We should not conclude that the "prayer emphasis" was limited to the Awakening of 1850–1900, because it was reported that in the First Awakening, Isaac Backus and Stephen Gano prayed with an expectancy for God's response. Gano once led a prayer meeting for rain in the midst of a great drought, and young people left the meeting saying: "We must hasten home, for after a prayer like that, the rain shall overtake us." Within an hour, rain came pouring down![12]

I should also say, and I am guilty of this charge, that with prayer meetings today having more resemblance to religious "gossip sessions" than true heartfelt desire for God's visitation, prayer might not even be the context for revival, much less the catalyst.

Results of the Awakenings

1. Whether Edwards, Whitefield, the Wesleys, Baackus, Stearns, or William Carey of the First Awakening; or Finney, Ashbury, or Moody of the Awakening of 1850–1900, *the awakenings led to a new and more fervent commitment to evangelism and missions.* Interestingly enough, in the awakenings, the burden for foreign missions first grew out of a burden for reaching neighbors and family. (The society mission movement and the Triennial Convention, formed on the tide of the First Awakening and formation of the Southern Baptist Convention in 1845, met for the forming of mission sending agencies, and became the SBC as the Second Awakening was birthed.) The Second Awakening obviously spurred the growth of the SBC as well as its mission focus.[13]

2. *The awakenings led Baptists to cooperate with other Evangelicals.* This may have been more evident in the First Awakening than the Awakening of 1850–1900. It wasn't that Southern Baptists didn't

---

[12] Murray, *Revival and Revivalism*, 304.
[13] Ibid, 123–25.

want to cooperate; the denomination was growing at such a pace that they didn't feel the need to partner with anyone.[14]

I might say relative to the First Awakenings: Baptists were at first hesitant to embrace the awakening that was ignited among the New Lights. But with help from men such as Richard Furman, Baptist of all Baptists (who had a Presbyterian deliver his funeral message), that cooperation grew. The British also put a contract on his life because he was such a patriot. It should be noted that Princeton graduate James Manning was the founder of Brown University, the premier Baptist school of the day. It seemed that the greater causes of Colonial America had a way of uniting like minds of Baptists and other Evangelical types of the day. Some suggest that the First Great Awakening unified as much as 80 percent of Americans in a common understanding of the Christian faith and life.[15]

3. *The awakenings led to a greater need and desire for education for all.* Great schools grown from the fruits of revival included Princeton, Brown, Furman, and others.[16]

4. *The awakenings led to anti-slavery views, and a greater sense of responsibility for slaves and Indians.* Whitefield was one of the first white ministers to preach to the slaves. A correspondent in Richmond County wrote: "When I go among Mr. Davies people, religion seems to flourish. It is like the suburbs of heaven. Gentlemen praying their morning and evening prayers and their slaves devoutly joining them."[17]

5. *The awakenings waned, not because of persecution from secular society, but from religious establishment of the day.* Some things never change (see Acts 4 and Peter and John). I might add that as popular as Jonathan Edwards was, as the awakening waned, he caught young people in his church looking at an "obstetrics book" containing female anatomy (studying in a less than educational manner), and

---

[14] Garrett, *Baptist Theology*, 153–212.
[15] Matthews, Lectures at Wake Forest University.
[16] Ibid.
[17] Murray, *Revival and Revivalism*, 13.

he reprimanded them from the pulpit. Parents thought he had over-reacted, and a movement banished him from his pulpit. He moved to Stockbridge and died working with the Indians.[18]

Conclusion

Whatever else we may say about our desire or need for awakening, it seems clear to me that God has visited His presence among His people in this unusual way as a result of the "Isaiah 6 factor." Isaiah enters the temple as the "best of the bunch" in religious terms, but quickly has a "woe is me" moment when he beholds the holiness of God. It boils down to what I call "relative holiness" and "absolute holiness." As we look around and compare our sins with the sins of others, we conclude that, relatively speaking, we are as good as anyone. But awakenings seem to occur, not by looking around for relative holiness, but looking up for absolute holiness. It is my desire that the next cry we hear from Baptists will be "woe is me, for we have seen the King, the Lord of Hosts!" May we once again become a body of living water because what flows to us also flows through us.

---

[18] Matthews, Lectures at Wake Forest University.

Chapter 8

Recovering the Gospel for the Twenty-first Century

HARRY L. POE, CHARLES COLSON PROFESSOR OF FAITH
AND CULTURE, UNION UNIVERSITY

At the end of the Cultural Revolution in China, in 1972, after Mao Tse-tung had massacred millions of Chinese and destroyed much of the country's infrastructure, Richard Nixon made diplomatic overtures to that nation. As a result of those overtures, China opened its doors to trade with the United States and others in the West. By the late 1970s, the Chinese government allowed religious groups from the West to visit China on goodwill missions. I was a seminary student when the president of my seminary went to China with a group of Christian leaders from other countries to discover what remained of the church there after many years of Communism. He reported in chapel on his return that no signs of Christianity in China could be found. The gospel faith had been eliminated.

Shortly after this trip, the Chinese government announced a change in policy related to organized religion. Any Christians

remaining in China would be permitted to worship openly at designated locations beginning on a specified date. On that date, over
a million Chinese appeared at the designated locations to worship
God in the name of Jesus Christ. Since that day some 30 years ago,
as many as 100 million Chinese have come to faith in Jesus Christ.
Why?

Christian faith brings no discernable advantage in China, eco-
nomically, socially, or politically. On the contrary, Christians remain
in a disadvantaged position, although the persecution is somewhat
less severe than it was during the Cultural Revolution. What is so
powerful about the Christian message that it would draw so many
followers in a culture that is hostile to it? One might also wonder
who spread the message when the Communist regime had been so
effective in removing Western missionaries. Catholics and Protestants
had established missions in Western spheres of influence in China
in the nineteenth century, but these missions never achieved much
more than nominal success. They managed only to leave the gospel
with a tiny group of people after the Communist Revolution of 1948.

We might even wonder whether the removal of Western missionaries made the spread of the gospel possible. Protestants had taken
a 500-year-old tradition and Catholics had taken a 1,500-year-old
tradition to a land that had a 5,000-year-old cultural tradition. The
original missionaries barely dealt with the deep spiritual issues that
the Chinese culture raised. They merely imported the theological
questions and answers of medieval and Reformation Europe, confusing the theological tradition with the faith once delivered to the
saints (Jude 3).

The essential Christian faith embodied in the gospel never
changes, but the questions that people and cultures ask change with
each generation and each age. Jesus is the answer, but Christians do
not always attend to the question so that they can explain how this
is true. It is much easier to rely on the answers that previous generations gave to their questions, and functionally behave as though it is
wrong to have other questions.

The twentieth century was the great pragmatic age for Protestant Christianity in America. The pragmatic programs of the denominations, linked to the pragmatic church politics, witnessed the development of strong and powerful denominational institutions by mid-century. By the end of the century, however, the Protestant denominations had collapsed in on themselves. No area of church life witnessed this pragmatism more than evangelism. Pastors and churches looked for programs that would work. Denominations and parachurch groups developed evangelism programs designed to produce converts. Without taking time and space to critique the history of evangelism in the twentieth century, one example should illustrate the problem. American Protestants managed to reduce the gospel to a simple presentation, a "plan of salvation" that was easily recited and easily understood. If this presentation addressed a person's spiritual issues, then they very well may have come to faith. As America began to lose its cultural consensus in the mid-twentieth century, however, people within the culture began to ask questions that went beyond the standard answers.

Witness training programs were almost unknown until the second half of the twentieth century. To a certain extent, evangelism programs represent a sign of failure. They suggest that Christians and churches no longer talk about their faith in Christ as a normal part of everyday life. In the late nineteenth century, little booklets designed to convey the gospel appeared throughout the English-speaking world. A variety of missions organizations, churches, denominations, and individuals produced these tracts, which were filled with compelling stories. There was huge variety in these tracts. They may not have represented the high point of English prose, but they applied the gospel to the experiences of life in a helpful and compelling way. In the mid-twentieth century all of that changed.

The "gospel presentation" was standardized in the mid-twentieth century with one basic approach that appeared in a variety of mass-produced tracts. It was developed, adapted, modified, and popularized by several prominent leaders from the Reformed wing of Protestant

Christianity. It had a four-point, dialectic argument that alternated between God and people, people and God. John Stott presented the format in his book *Basic Christianity* in 1958. Stott divided his book into four parts with several chapters assigned to each part:[1]

Christ's Person
    The claims of Christ
    The character of Christ
    The resurrection of Christ

Man's Need
    The fact and nature of sin
    The consequences of sin

Christ's Work
    The death of Christ
    The salvation of Christ

Man's Response
    Counting the cost
    Reaching a decision
    Being a Christian

Bill Bright used this basic outline in 1965 for his *Four Spiritual Laws* tract that became the centerpiece of the evangelistic efforts of Campus Crusade for Christ.[2] The outline remains the same, but Bright adopted the metaphor of law to carry the storyline:

Law One: God loves you and offers a wonderful plan for your life.
    God's love (John 3:16)
    God's plan (John 10:10)

---

[1] John R. W. Stott, *Basic Christianity* (London: Inter-Varsity Press, 1958).
[2] Bill Bright, *Four Spiritual Laws* (San Bernardino, CA: Campus Crusade, 1965).

Law Two: Man is sinful and separated from God. Thus he cannot know and experience God's love and plan for his life.
> Man is sinful (Rom 3:23)
> Man is separated (Rom 6:23)

Law Three: Jesus Christ is God's only provision for man's sin. Through Him you can know and experience God's love and plan for your life.
> He died in our place (Rom 5:8)
> He rose from the dead (1 Cor 15:3–6)
> He is the only way to God (John 14:6)

Law Four: We must individually receive Jesus Christ as Savior and Lord; then we can know and experience God's love and plan for our lives.
> We must receive Christ (John 1:12)
> We receive Christ through faith (Eph 2:8–9)
> When we receive Christ, we experience a new birth (John 3:1–8)
> We receive Christ by personal invitation (Rev 3:20)

Campus Crusade has distributed millions upon millions of the *Four Spiritual Laws*, which have been instrumental in the conversion of large numbers of people, particularly on college campuses.

In the early 1960s, James Kennedy developed an evangelism training program for the Coral Ridge Presbyterian Church in Florida. He called his program Evangelism Explosion.[3] This program involves the memorization of a gospel presentation. Churches from many denominations adopted this training method in the late twentieth century as a way to encourage members to share their faith. It employs a modified version of Stott's outline:

---

[3] D. James Kennedy, *Evangelism Explosion*, rev. ed. (Wheaton, IL: Tyndale House, 1977), 16.

Grace
>Heaven is a free gift
>It is not earned or deserved

Man
>Is a sinner
>Cannot save himself

God
>Is merciful—therefore doesn't want to punish sin
>Is just—therefore must punish sin

Christ
>Who He is—the infinite God-man
>What He did—he paid for our sins and purchased a place in heaven for us which He offers as a gift

Faith
>What it is *not*—mere intellectual assent nor temporal faith
>What it *is*—"trusting in Jesus Christ alone for our salvation"

So many Southern Baptist churches began using the Evangelism Explosion plan that the Home Mission Board of the Southern Baptist Convention developed its own version of Kennedy's plan that it marketed as Continuous Witness Training. This approach employed a memorized "model presentation" like Kennedy's plan, and it collapsed the separate points on God and Christ from Kennedy's plan back to a single point as Stott had arranged it. The Southern Baptists later published the model presentation as a tract called the *Eternal Life* booklet:[4]

---

[4] *Eternal Life*, Personal Evangelism Section, Home Mission Board, SBC, Atlanta, n.d.

God's Purpose (is that we have eternal life)
    We receive eternal life as a free gift (Rom 6:23b)
    We can live a full and meaningful life right now (John 10:10)
    We will spend eternity with Jesus in heaven (John 14:3)

Our Need (is to understand our problem)
    We are all sinners by nature and by choice (Rom 3:23)
    We cannot save ourselves (Eph 2:9)
    We deserve death and hell (Rom 6:23a)

God's Provision (is Jesus Christ)
    Jesus is God and became man (John 1:1, 14)
    Jesus died for us on the cross (1 Pet 3:18)
    Jesus was resurrected from the dead (Rom 4:25)

Our Response (is to receive Jesus)
    We must repent of our sin (Acts 3:19)
    We must place our faith in Jesus (Eph 2:8)
    We must totally surrender to Jesus as Lord (Rom 10:9–10)

Although the different versions of this presentation of the gospel have their own distinctive flavors, they rely on Stott's basic outline.

Besides relying on Stott's outline, American gospel presentations in the late twentieth century also relied on the Roman Road and the Bridge Illustration. The Roman Road involves the recitation of four passages from Romans:

For all have sinned and fall short of the glory of God. (Rom 3:23 HCSB)

For the wages of sin is death, but the gift of God is eternal life in Jesus Christ our Lord. (Rom 6:23 HCSB)

> But God proves His own love for us in that while we were still sinners Christ died for us. (Rom 5:8 HCSB)

> If you confess with your mouth, "Jesus is Lord," and believe in your heart that God raised Him from the dead, you will be saved. With the heart one believes, resulting in righteousness, and with the mouth one confesses, resulting in salvation. Now the Scripture says, No one who believes on Him will be put to shame, for there is no distinction between Jew and Greek, since the same Lord of all is rich to all who call on Him. For everyone who calls on the name of the Lord will be saved. (Rom 10:9–13 HCSB)

Like Stott's outline, this selection of verses from Romans deals with the death and resurrection of Jesus and how they relate to the punishment and forgiveness of sin. They do this very well. We should recall, however, that Paul was addressing a specific issue in the opening of his letter to the Romans. Romans deals with the problem of sin for people who know about God and His moral laws (the Jews) and people who do not know God or the Bible (the Gentiles). In other words, Romans provides the answer to the specific problem of how God deals with guilt. But what might the Galatian Road or the Ephesian Road or the Philippian Road look like?

The Bridge Illustration pictures a great chasm between the sinner and God. The problem posed is how to get from earth to heaven without falling into the chasm of hell and eternal punishment.

All these approaches to presenting the gospel depend on the person hearing the presentation caring about sin and feeling guilty for wrongdoing. If the person's issue is the same issue that beset Martin Luther 500 years ago, then this way of presenting the gospel goes straight to the heart of the matter.

What happens if people no longer believe in sin? What happens if people think that sin is just a matter of breaking the rules, and they do not believe in the rules? What happens when a culture begins to collapse and the values of the culture erode? What happens when relativism replaces a sense of right and wrong? What happens is that the old way of presenting the gospel ceases to communicate with the changing culture and its questions.

This situation creates no particular problem unless Christians have confused a way of presenting the gospel with the gospel itself. This would correspond to confusing a sermon with the Bible. A sermon provides a format in which to discuss one aspect of the Bible. A sermon about stewardship may be perfectly true, but it does not deal with every spiritual issue that needs to be addressed from the pulpit in the course of a year. To repeat the same sermon every Sunday would seem strange, but we do that when we think that the gospel addresses only one spiritual issue. A gospel presentation provides a format in which to discuss one aspect of the gospel. The gospel answers the deep spiritual questions of every culture, but it focuses on a particular issue. A presentation that "works" in 1960 America may not communicate to Generation X, because the new generation deals with different issues from the Baby Boomers and the Greatest Generation. A presentation that "works" in America may not communicate well in Kenya or China. The presentation of the gospel should always address the ultimate questions that people or cultures ask.

Remembering the Gospel

Witnessing tracts, witness training plans, and evangelism aids for the Christian represent a sign of failure. They provide a tool for the person who does not know what to say. Perhaps it is not too much to suggest that a person becomes a Christian by believing the gospel of Jesus Christ. Since every person who is a Christian has believed the gospel, why would a Christian not know what to say? Not too many years ago, critics might complain of the general ignorance of basic theology and doctrine among Christians in America. One might reasonably voice concern now about the general ignorance of the gospel itself among Christians in America. The gospel has not traveled quickly in China during the last quarter century through the use of

witnessing tracts, witness training plans, and other stock presentations of the gospel. Chinese Christians simply know the gospel.

One of the biggest problems for American Christianity came in
the mid-twentieth century when evangelism efforts "simplified" the
gospel by reducing it to two points: (1) Jesus died for our sins and
(2) He rose from the dead. The biblical reference to support this revi-
sionist reductionism comes from 1 Cor 15:1–4 in which Paul stated:

> Now brothers, I want to clarify for you the gospel I proclaimed
> to you; you received it and have taken your stand on it. You
> are also saved by it, if you hold to the message I proclaimed to
> you—unless you believed to no purpose. For I passed on to you
> as most important what I also received: that Christ died for our
> sins according to the Scriptures, that He was buried, that He was
> raised on the third day according to the Scriptures. . . .

On the surface, Paul seems to say that the gospel involves only the
death of Christ for sins and His resurrection from the dead. Unfortunately, this kind of surface reading of the Bible is typical of American
Christianity over the last half century. Oddly enough, it leaves out a
point that Paul believed was so critical that he repeats it: the gospel
is not a new religion that Jesus invented but it is the fulfillment of all
that God had been planning since before creation itself. The fulfillment of Scripture is a vital aspect of the gospel.

The first time I remember anyone teaching me about the gospel
occurred on a youth retreat when I was in high school. The leader used
this text from 1 Corinthians to teach us that the gospel is only about the
death and resurrection of Jesus. The leader went on to make the point
that we should never add anything to the gospel. That summer of 1967
we were warned that anyone who teaches otherwise is not biblical and
should not be trusted. I now know that the leader picked out only one
passage in which Paul mentioned the gospel. In fact, Paul constantly
referred to the gospel in all his letters. For a biblical understanding of
the gospel, we need to go beyond one passage of Scripture and read all
that Paul, the other apostles, and even Jesus taught about the gospel.

Paul's Gospel

To understand Paul's meaning, we should recall that Paul did not write any evangelistic works. He addressed all his writings to Christians who already believed the gospel. He did not write to make converts, but to teach disciples who already believed. Each church had a different set of issues. Groups within churches had different issues. Whether the issues involved worship, doctrine, leadership, ethics, stewardship, spiritual gifts, marriage, or anything else, Paul always rooted his teaching in the gospel. The gospel is not only the message of how to be *saved*, it is also the message of how to *be* saved. It is the message of both evangelism and discipleship. All Christian doctrine and practice have their basis in the gospel. Practices and beliefs of Christians that are not rooted in the gospel are not Christian. They may be cultural or personal, but all Christian belief and practice comes as an implication of the gospel.

Because Paul based his teaching on the gospel, he only needed to remind his readers about the point of the gospel that formed the basis of his teaching. In 1 Cor 15, Paul is answering a question raised by the Corinthians (1 Cor 7:1). As in other cases, when he turned to a new question, he began his answer by saying "now" (1 Cor 8:1; 12:1,31b; 16:1). Chapter 15 is not about the gospel; it is about the resurrection. Paul mentions only enough of the gospel to remind the Corinthians that the resurrection has always been a part of the gospel. In that Greek city where the concept of the physical body was viewed as evil, the idea of resurrection was regarded as opposed to the best of Greek philosophical thought. Paul expounds the doctrine of resurrection because it is an essential aspect of the gospel.

Should we risk violating the warning of the youth retreat leader and add anything to the gospel? What does Paul say? He began his Letter to the Romans with a summary statement of the gospel that goes far beyond what he said in 1 Cor 15. He described the gospel of God as

> . . . (that) which He promised long ago through His prophets in the Holy Scriptures— concerning His Son, Jesus Christ our Lord, who was a descendant of David according to the flesh and was established as the powerful Son of God by the resurrection from the dead according to the Spirit of holiness. (Rom 1:2–4)

Note that Paul does not mention that Christ died for our sins. That omission does not mean that the death was an optional feature of his gospel. On the contrary, the death becomes a major matter of discussion in the Letter to the Romans. At the beginning, however, he merely states those matters of the gospel that are assumed but would not be discussed in depth. By the end of his letter, he will have added to his list. He emphasizes that the gospel includes the fulfillment of the prophecies, the full humanity and deity of Christ, the resurrection, and another critical aspect of who Christ is that is embodied in his title: Jesus Christ is our Lord.

The disciples spoke of Jesus in a new way after the resurrection. They had assumed he was the human Messiah or Christ descended from King David. After the resurrection, however, they understood that He was also the divine Son of Man of Daniel's prophecy who shares the glory, power, sovereignty, and worship of God. After the resurrection, Jesus is Lord. By the first century, the Jews had stopped calling God by the name He had revealed to them: Yahweh. Instead of calling Him by name, the Jews had begun to refer to Him as the "Lord." When the English Bible spells the word with all capital letters, it does not do so out of respect. It does so out of tradition. Whenever the Jews found the name "Yahweh" in the text of Scripture, they spoke the word "Adonai," which we translate as "Lord." The capital letters signify that the word in the text is Yahweh. Whenever the apostles refer to the Lord Jesus, they speak of His present activity exalted to the right hand of the Father where He has a name that is above every name. The exalted Lord rules all of creation. All other powers must bow before Him.

After affirming the aspects of the gospel that would not form the central argument of the letter, Paul immediately began to deal with the problem on the minds of the Roman Christians. It was a problem that disturbed many Christians in the first century, and it concerned the relationship between Jews and Gentiles. It concerned whether God was fair in not making the law known to the Gentiles the way He had done to the Jews. People today still ask the same question when they say, "What about the natives on an island who never heard?" Paul deals with their questions by expounding four other aspects of the gospel: God as Creator, the return of Christ to judge the world, the death of Christ for our sins, and the gift of the Holy Spirit.

The last judgment is rooted in the reason that God has the right to judge the world: God created the world. After reminding the Romans that the gospel "is God's power the salvation to everyone who believes . . . " (Rom 1:16), Paul roots the judgment in creation:

> For God's wrath is revealed from heaven against all godlessness and unrighteousness of people who by their unrighteousness suppress the truth, since what can be known about God is evident among them, because God has shown it to them. From the creation of the world His invisible attributes, that is, His eternal power and divine nature, have been clearly seen, being understood through what He has made. As a result, people are without excuse. (Rom 1:18–20 HCSB)

After exploring the phenomenon of world religions and human depravity, Paul explained that the law never saved anyone. In fact, some Gentiles did the works of the law without ever having heard of the law. With respect to salvation, however, there was no advantage to the Jews because everyone faced the judgment that would take place "on the day when God will judge men's secrets through Jesus Christ, as my gospel declares" (Rom 2:16 NIV). Thus, the gospel is a message of salvation that begins before the beginning of the world and lasts beyond the ending, stretching from everlasting in one direction to everlasting in the other direction, from creation to new creation.

Paul concluded his introductory section to Romans with an explanation of how God dealt with the universal problem of sin through the death of Jesus:

> God presented Him as a propitiation through faith in His blood,
> to demonstrate His righteousness, because in His restraint God
> passed over the sins previously committed. He presented Him
> to demonstrate His righteousness at the present time, so that He
> would be righteous and declare righteous the one who has faith
> in Jesus. (Rom 3:25–26 HCSB)

He then explained how salvation affects people. It does not come as a legal decree but as the coming of God into a person who believes. Salvation is the gift of the Holy Spirit of God, for "God has poured out his love into our hearts by the Holy Spirit, whom he has given us" (Rom 5:5 NIV).

We can see that Paul's gospel includes eight basic points:

1. God is a Creator.
2. The Scriptures have been fulfilled by Jesus.
3. Jesus is both fully human and fully divine.
4. Jesus died for our sins.
5. Jesus rose from the dead.
6. Jesus is exalted to the Father.
7. The Father and Son dwell in each believer through the Holy Spirit.
8. Jesus will return to judge the world and institute the new creation.

An examination of Paul's other letters along with the other apostolic literature will reveal that these basic affirmations of faith formed the common message of all the apostles.

The Gospel of Jesus Christ

Some people talk about Paul and his teachings as though he made it all up. In fact, a group of modern scholars do take the position that Paul invented Christianity. Where did Paul get his gospel? Was it unique to him? He took a hard line on this point in the first book he wrote:

> Now I want you to know, brothers, that the gospel preached by me is not based on a human point of view. For I did not receive it from a human source and I was not taught it, but it came by a revelation from Jesus Christ. (Gal 1:11–12 HCSB)

Do we find anything approaching Paul's version of the gospel in the Gospel accounts of Jesus? We do. Of course, people who like a surface reading of the Bible will be left trying to fit the first-century round peg into their modern square hole.

The easiest part to match up comes after the resurrection. Luke provides us with the account of Jesus meeting two disciples on the Emmaus Road on the afternoon of the resurrection. They do not recognize Him in His glorified form. Perhaps only Peter, James, and John who had seen Him transfigured recognized Him at first (Matt 17:1–9). When the disciples expressed their incomprehension of the stories circulating about the empty tomb, Jesus remarked,

> "How unwise and slow you are to believe in your hearts all that the prophets have spoken! Didn't the Messiah have to suffer these things and enter into His glory?" Then beginning with Moses and all the Prophets, He interpreted for them the things concerning Himself in all the Scriptures. (Luke 24:25–27 HCSB)

Jesus next appeared to the disciples gathered in Jerusalem and expounded to them the core of the gospel message:

> Then He told them, "These are My words that I spoke to you while I was still with you—that everything written about Me in the Law of Moses, the Prophets, and the Psalms must be fulfilled." Then He opened their minds to understand the

> Scriptures. He also said to them, "This is what is written: The
> Messiah would suffer and rise from the dead the third day,
> and repentance for forgiveness of sins would be proclaimed in
> His name to all the nations, beginning at Jerusalem. You are
> witnesses of these things. And look, I am sending you what
> My Father promised. As for you, stay in the city until you are
> empowered from on high." (Luke 24:44–49, HCSB)

In His resurrection, Jesus began to remind the disciples of what He had told them for three years, and it included: (1) the fulfillment of Scripture, (2) the death related to forgiveness, (3) the resurrection, and (4) the gift of the Holy Spirit. He also made a statement about (5) His full humanity and full deity, but He did not use those words as Americans use them today. Instead, He spoke of Himself as the Christ and He referred to His Father. Looking back through 2,000 years of Christian faith, we often mistakenly think that "Christ" means Son of God. But it does not. It is the Greek word for Messiah, a Jewish word that means "anointed one." The anointed one is the heir to the throne who has been anointed as king. In the prophecies, the Christ or the Messiah was the human descendant of King David whom God had sworn would establish an everlasting throne. Thus, the Christ is a fully human descendant of King David. When Jesus speaks of God as His Father, however, He makes Himself equal to God. In the terminology of the first century, Jesus has said that His message includes the announcement that Jesus is both God and Christ, divine and human. So, we add the fifth element.

Jesus, however, was never one for lists when He could tell a story or riddle instead. Instead of saying, "I will rise from the dead" when the skeptics asked for a sign, He said that He would only give them "the sign of Jonah." Here was an enigmatic way to say that just as Jonah was in the belly of the fish for three days before being spit out, so Jesus would be in the belly of death for three days before rising. He would also cryptically remark of His resurrection, "Destroy this temple and I will raise it up again in three days." Of His deity,

He quoted the familiar messianic prophecy about the descendent of King David who would sit on David's throne,

> The LORD declared to my Lord: "Sit at My right hand until I make Your enemies Your footstool." (Ps 110:1 HCSB)

and then asked His critics,

> "David calls Him 'Lord'; how then can the Messiah be his Son?" (Luke 20:44 HCSB)

Jesus was not so cryptic, however, when facing the Sanhedrin court. While the high priest tried to paint Him as a claimant to the throne of David and, thus, an enemy of Rome worthy of execution for sedition, Jesus admitted that He was not only the Messiah, but also the divine Son of Man (6) who would judge the world at the end of time (Matt 26:64). So, we find the sixth element of Paul's gospel, the second coming of Christ and the last judgment.

By His actions as well as His words, Jesus declared the gospel. In the Gospels, the preaching of the gospel of the kingdom of God also involved demonstrations of the power of God. Matthew mentioned it (Matt 4:23–25). Nicodemus mentioned it (John 3:2). Jesus mentioned it in His first recorded sermon in Luke's Gospel (Luke 4:18–19; cf. Isa. 61:1–2). Jesus mentioned it again when John the Baptist sent messengers to Jesus from prison seeking reassurance that Jesus was the promised one (Matt 11:4–6). By His demonstrations of power over the forces of nature, disease, death, the demonic, and physical infirmity, Jesus identified Himself (7) with the God of Creation. So, we find the seventh element of Paul's gospel, the God of Creation.

Finally, Jesus explained to His disciples that when He completed His mission on earth, He would return to His Father (John 14:2,7,20; 16:5–7,13–15,28; 17:1–5). Throughout His ministry He had consistently referred to Himself as the Son of Man from Daniel's prophecy of the mysterious figure who shared God's authority, glory, sovereign power, and worship, and who would come on the clouds of heaven to judge the world on the last day (Dan 7:13–14; Matt 26:64; 28:18). At the Last Supper, He explained that He would return to the Father, but that the Father and Son would make their home in the hearts of every believer (John 14:23). Jesus taught that following His death and resurrection, (8) He would be exalted to His proper place with His Father (John 20:17). So, we find the last element of Paul's gospel, the exaltation of Christ, in the teachings of Jesus.

Paul and the other disciples did not invent a gospel that was different from the gospel Jesus taught. They did, however, explain the teachings of their Jewish Master in a way that Gentiles could understand. The Gentiles did not have the background to understand the way Jesus spoke to the Jewish community of first-century Palestine; therefore, the apostles translated the gospel into the Hellenistic culture of the Roman Empire. The Gentiles knew nothing of the Jewish law of Moses, the ancient Israelite King David and the prophecies about his descendant, or the visions of Daniel about the divine judgment of the world by one "like a Son of Man." The apostles did not change the message about Jesus, but they put it into terms that could be understood by people from another culture. They explained how Jesus answered not only the deepest questions of Jewish culture, but also the deepest questions of Gentile culture.

The Symbols of the Gospel

Even though we find all of the gospel, as Paul and the other apostles told it, in the teachings of Jesus, some might wonder why Jesus did not leave for His followers a clear, systematic presentation of the gospel that could cross all cultural barriers. In fact, He did.

Many people regard the cross as the primary symbol of Christianity, but it really is not. It is a widely held, popular sign of the Christian faith because of its association with the death of Jesus and the place of His death in the theology of the medieval Roman church. But it remains a static sign or image. Jesus left His followers two symbols to convey who He is. These two symbols embody the gospel, but they are not static, lifeless objects, like a cross. They are dynamic events or dramas that exist only when Christians reenact them. They are baptism and the Lord's Supper.

The church has had many important ceremonies over the last 2,000 years that hold greater or lesser importance for different Christian groups, but all Christians (except those small sects that "spiritualize" ceremonies) have given importance above all other ceremonies and worship practices to baptism and the Lord's Supper. These two symbols given by Jesus proclaim the gospel faith.

When Jesus instituted the Lord's Supper, He said that it represents:

1. His death. As the Passover meal, however, the Lord's Supper conveys a sacrificial death that delivers others from death, as the Angel of Death passed over the homes that bore the blood of the lamb.

2. Fulfillment, not only of the prophecies, but also the Law.

3. Establishment of the long-promised new covenant. The new covenant was not written on stone (Jer 31:31–34), but involved the coming of the Holy Spirit within the hearts of the people of God.

4. Fulfillment of the kingdom of God. Paul explained to the Gentiles that the fulfillment of the kingdom of God meant the return of Christ (1 Cor 11:26).

5. The full humanity of Jesus who bled and died.

Baptism represents:

1. Jesus' resurrection from the dead. Baptism completes the mystery of how the sacrificial death of Jesus affects people. As the Lord's Supper symbolizes the sacrifice that begins the new covenant of the Holy Spirit, the water of baptism symbolizes the Holy Spirit who swallows and envelops the believers. By the power and presence of the Holy Spirit, a person is baptized or inserted "into" Christ.

2. The joining of a person by the Holy Spirit to Christ who now lives and reigns as the Lord of Glory, the exalted Christ who lives to bring us to God. Christ commanded His disciples to baptize everyone

"into" the Father, Son, and Holy Spirit, because all power in heaven and earth had been given to Him (Matt 28:18–19).

The foundational belief of the gospel does not appear explicitly in the Lord's Supper or baptism. These symbols do not expressly teach that God created the physical world. At one time in their history, the people of Israel had wavered in their belief in the one God who created the heavens and the earth. The belief in the one God is the first of the Ten Commandments and the basis for all the others. It was the Creator God who freed Israel from Egyptian bondage and instituted the Passover. The Psalms and the Prophets continuously return to the theme that God created the world and all living things. The judgment on Israel, according to the prophets, came because Israel failed to recognize Yahweh as the only God, the Creator, who had expectations of how people would relate to Him as well as to one another. After the fall of Jerusalem to the Babylonians in 586 BC, the people of Israel never again flirted with other gods or other concepts of deity. By the time of Jesus, the cardinal tenet of faith permeated the belief system of the Jews. It did not require expression, because of its absolute, pervasive acceptance. The very tangible experience of physical bread, wine, and water affirm creation and the significance of the physical realm as a pointer to spiritual reality. But what about people who do not believe that the material world came from the creative activity of a single supreme being?

The Gospel Connecting with Culture

When Peter preached the gospel on Pentecost just 10 days after Jesus Christ ascended to heaven, He began by announcing that the prophecies had been fulfilled. In the shadow of the temple, on one of the high holy days of Israel, with pilgrims gathered from all over the Roman and Persian empires, Peter could assume his audience already believed in the God who created the heavens and the earth. It was this God who spoke by the prophets, who brought the plagues upon Egypt and parted the Red Sea, who commanded the armies of

Babylon only to destroy those armies later with his servants the Persians. Peter did not need to explain what kind of God exists.

Paul found a different situation, however, when he and Barnabas embarked on their first missionary journey through southern Galatia in present-day Turkey. After healing a crippled man in Lystra, Paul and Barnabas received a grand reception from the local crowd who concluded that Barnabas must be the god Zeus and Paul must be Hermes, the messenger of Zeus. The local priest of Zeus brought bulls and ceremonial wreaths to offer as sacrifices to Paul and Barnabas before they realized what the Lystrans were saying. When they finally understood the situation, Paul and Barnabas tore their clothes, probably in horror that they were about to be objects of the violation of the First Commandment, and cried out,

> Men! Why are you doing these things? We are men also, with the same nature as you, and we are proclaiming good news to you, that you should turn from these worthless things to the living God, who made the heaven, the earth, the sea, and everything in them. In past generations He allowed all the nations to go their own way, although He did not leave Himself without a witness, since He did good: giving you rain from heaven and fruitful seasons, and satisfying your hearts with food and happiness. (Acts 14:15–17 HCSB)

Whatever else they may have said, Luke only reported their fervent effort to proclaim what kind of God exists, for on this issue all else depends.

When the apostles encountered a culture that had no concept of a Creator God, they apparently began the gospel story here. They settled the matter of presuppositions at the outset to avoid any confusion over what they meant when they spoke of "God." Paul found himself in the same situation when he visited Athens. In Athens he had the complicating issues not only of a view of multiple gods, but also a philosophical tradition that offered alternative explanations for the nature of reality. He encountered the philosophy of the Stoics and Epicureans as well as the polytheism of traditional Greek culture.

In presenting the gospel to the Athenians, Paul made use of the religious sensibilities of the pagans and the intellectual tradition of the philosophers. He referred to the altar to an unknown god and to the poets:

> Then Paul stood in the middle of the Areopagus and said: "Men of Athens! I see that you are extremely religious in every respect. For as I was passing through and observing the objects of your worship, I even found an altar on which was inscribed:
>
> ### TO AN UNKNOWN GOD.
>
> Therefore, what you worship in ignorance, this I proclaim to you. The God who made the world and everything in it—He is Lord of heaven and earth and does not live in shrines made by hands. Neither is He served by human hands, as though He needed anything, since He Himself gives everyone life and breath and all things. From one man He has made every nation of men to live over the whole earth and has determined their appointed times and the boundaries of where they live so that they might seek God, and perhaps they might reach out and find Him, though He is not far from each one of us. For in Him we live and move and exist, as even some of your own poets have said, 'For we are also His offspring.' Being God's offspring then, we shouldn't think that the divine nature is like gold or silver or stone, an image fashioned by human art and imagination.
>
> "Therefore, having overlooked the times of ignorance, God now commands all people everywhere to repent, because **He has set a day on which He is going to judge the world** in righteousness by the Man He has appointed. He has provided proof of this to everyone by **raising Him from the dead**." (Acts 17:22–31 HCSB, emphasis mine)

Paul began by introducing the concept of a Creator God who has the right to establish justice by virtue of His creation of all people and things. He then went straight to the idea of the last judgment. Without a Creator, sin does not exist. Without a Creator, people have no need of a savior. Paul had to explain what kind of God exists before the idea of Jesus dying for our sins would make any sense. As it happens, Paul did not even mention the death of Jesus to the Athenians. Instead, he focused attention on the resurrection of Jesus, another idea that would have seemed at odds with the Greek understanding of the world in which material things are considered evil and the goal of life is to escape the body, not to have the body resurrected to everlasting life!

Conclusion

So why has the gospel traveled so quickly in China during the last 25 years? For one thing, Chinese Christians do not regard presenting the gospel as a logical syllogism as is so often the case in the United States. For the Chinese, the gospel involves presenting a person: Jesus. Second, the Chinese begin by explaining what kind of God exists. In a land with a culture that stretches back 5,000 years, a complicated worldview dominates the concept of the physical universe and its relationship to the spiritual world. For several thousand years, the king or emperor served as the intermediary between the people and the gods. The gods and spirits of nature, villages, and families populate the religious beliefs of the Chinese. Interlaced with traditional Chinese religion, however, come strands of philosophical approaches to the spiritual and physical such as Taoism and Confucianism. To these must be added the Chinese version of Buddhism that denies the reality of the physical world as Westerners understand it. For the faithful Buddhist of China, the material world is an illusion. Against this complex religious tradition, which allows a person to accept or participate in the full variety of systems, the Communist government tried for years to enforce the view that only the material world exists and that the spiritual world is foolish superstition. By introducing people to the knowledge of the Creator God, Chinese Christians bring clarity to a confusing situation. Belief in one God who made the universe makes sense, and the rest of the gospel follows naturally from it.

Ten years ago, I explained the ideas in this article to a former president of the Southern Baptist Convention and a group of other pastors. He said, "Give me a model and show me three places where it has worked." He smiled graciously and walked away.

This chapter does not propose a new model or gimmick for boosting church enrollment. Rather, it attempts to help American Christians recover something that American corporate religion has lost. The Chinese have not invented something new. They have discovered something very old.

Chapter 9

Emergent or Emerging?
Questions for Southern Baptists and
American Evangelicals

MARK DEVINE, ASSOCIATE PROFESSOR OF
DIVINITY, BEESON DIVINITY SCHOOL

My interest in the Emerging Church phenomenon was neither planned nor expected. I backed into it. My concern was the specter of death looming over a historical Baptist church I found myself pastoring in midtown Kansas City, Missouri. It was founded in 1840, five years before a group of ministers would gather in Augusta, Georgia, to launch the denomination these Missouri Baptists would soon join. I found at First Calvary Baptist Church an urban congregation halfway into its third decade of decline. We gathered to worship in a magnificent sanctuary adorned with stained glass bearing the names of Wornall and Ward, names also attached to two of Kansas City's famed boulevards. A balcony stretches into an impressive gallery on both sides of the pulpit. An arched ceiling terminates in an ornate alcove framed by carved wood and beveled glass acting as prisms that throw off narrow but brilliant rainbow light here and there. In the church's heyday two services were required to accommodate the more than one thousand Baptists who made their way to First Calvary on a typical Lord's Day.

I was mesmerized by this worship space, not because of its beauty alone but because of its beauty set as it was in a strategic location for the advance of the gospel and the fact that it was a Southern Baptist church. I am incurably Southern Baptist—a malady from which fewer and fewer folks suffer. Indeed, fewer and fewer folks are incurably Baptist, Methodist, Presbyterian, or anything else where religious affiliation is concerned. Across the denominational spectrum, folks are just not sitting all the way down in their pews. The fastest-growing segment of Christian identity in North America is nondenominational. But I remain permanently and hopelessly afflicted with congenital denominational loyalty. I remember as a child flipping through my Baptism Bible, confused that Lottie Moon's name did not appear in the concordance at all! What kind of Bible was this anyway? Even if I changed denominational affiliation, I think I would still be Southern Baptist somehow. Is this what it is like to be Jewish? I wonder. When I learned that John A. Broadus had preached the dedicatory sermon for an earlier sanctuary of First Calvary, my denominationally protective instincts toward this Baptist congregation only increased.

The spectacle of this once-vibrant congregation dying before our very eyes cut me to the quick, spiritually speaking. The impending demise of First Calvary threatened the loss of gospel witness in the historical Westport section of Kansas City, just as this midtown section of the true gateway to the West was witnessing an influx of residents. Westport was then an urban landscape in transition, energized by a vibrant entertainment district and a magnet for singles and young couples attracted to the ethnically and socially diverse environment this neighborhood provided. A stroll down Westport Road promised encounters not only with a pierced and tattooed populace, but also with bankers, business people, musicians and artists of most every stripe, and even the occasional new mother proudly pushing her child along in a stroller. New residential construction alongside established neighborhoods held out the possibility of ripe and fascinating fields for gospel advance amid perhaps the most resistant of settings for such advance in the twenty-first century, not only in North America but around the globe—the great cities.

Over the course of seven years I poured myself into the pursuit of a new future for First Calvary Baptist Church. In 2008 fewer than 70 active members were losing the battle to maintain the magnificent but rapidly deteriorating facilities. We voted to merge with an Emerging Southern Baptist church in St. Louis, a church that embraced the Baptist Faith and Message 2000 without apology. This St. Louis congregation deployed a replanter to First Calvary. As this chapter goes to press, more than 800 worshipers now gather in two services each Lord's Day at the replanted First Calvary, newly renamed Redeemer Fellowship. The balcony and gallery and baptistery are needed again to accommodate worshipers and new converts at the Baptist church in Westport. Where the shadow of impending death once hovered over a declining flock and a deteriorating and gravely threatened facility, now the most pressing problems at the corner of 39th Street and Baltimore Avenue are those precipitated by rapid growth right smack in midtown Kansas City.

Defining the Emerging Church

I want to survey a few of the benefits I believe the Emerging Church can bring to Southern Baptists, but first a brief word about the Emerging Church itself and the stream within the movement to which I shall be referring in this chapter. I have found it appropriate and helpful to divide the movement into two major streams: one doctrine-friendly stream and another stream, which I identify as Emergent, composed of two sub-streams—one doctrine averse and the other doctrine wary. It is the doctrine-friendly stream that especially interests me as I consider the future of the Southern Baptist denomination. The doctrine-averse Emerging Churches subscribe to no formal doctrinal stance whatsoever. Significant influencers among this group are becoming less and less interested in protectiveness even for the adjective "Christian" to describe who they are and where they are headed. The doctrine-wary communities of faith are those Emerging Churches that may have launched themselves without doctrine but have now taken on usually the Apostles' Creed or Nicene Creed or both. While the transition from a doctrine-averse posture to mere wariness for doctrine marks a welcome development, a potentially deadly blind spot remains, the failure to fully recognize the irreducibly doctrinal character of Christianity.

Be that as it may, my main interest in the movement centers around the doctrine-friendly stream of Emerging. These communities of faith embrace fully orbed confessions of faith that situate them squarely within orthodox and Evangelical Christianity. They affirm historical Christian thinking on the doctrine of the Trinity and the person of Jesus Christ as articulated in the Apostles' Creed and Nicene-Constantinopolitan Creed of the early church. They affirm both the formal and material theological bases of the Protestant Reformation, namely insistence on salvation by grace alone, through faith alone, in Jesus Christ alone, on the basis of the testimony of Holy Scripture alone. Unlike most of the doctrine-averse and doctrine-wary contingent of the Emerging Church, they do not shy away from objective understandings of the atonement accomplished by Jesus Christ through His incarnation and death on the cross. The left wing of the Emerging Church, in ways and for reasons reminiscent of Protestant liberalism, tends to reduce the work of Jesus Christ to variations of moral influence and other exemplarist construals of the meaning of Christ's life and death. But the doctrine-friendly contingent tends to embrace robust affirmation of vicarious substitutionary atonement. Also, while the left wing of the Emerging Church, as happened among many Protestant liberals, has developed a bad conscience for proselytizing and speaks of belonging before believing within the church, the doctrine-friendly stream encourages and practices conversion-seeking evangelism and covenant-shaped membership within the church.

So what do these theologically orthodox and Evangelical Emerging communities bring to the table? How might Southern Baptists benefit from their efforts, their vision, and even from them?

Church Planting-Fixated

The entire Emerging Church phenomenon is characterized by an impressive zeal for church planting. Dissatisfied for a variety of reasons with the models of church that nurtured them or those they have otherwise encountered, Emerging Church leaders plant churches. Perhaps the most misinformed comments I encounter about the Emerging Church are those that apply a quick and dirty analysis that ends by reducing and dismissing the phenomenon as the convulsions of typical youth rebellion against Grandma and Grandpa's religion. Admittedly, Emerging Church leaders do tend to be quite young. The first wave involved mostly young men in their 20s and early 30s, and young people do act like young people. That much is true. But the first wave of these church planters has aged 10 to 15 years since then. The "typical youthful rebellion" interpretation is quickly losing its saliency.

And let's ask ourselves this question: When young men dissatisfied with the models of church that nurtured them strike out on their own and plant churches, how typical is that? Church planting is not child's play; neither is church replanting of the type that took place at First Calvary in Kansas City. It's not play at all. It is an impressive way to rebel, I think. And many of these church-planters are Southern Baptist. Some would like to stay Southern Baptist. Others, I believe, could be attracted to the SBC.

Citified Church Planting

The Emerging Church phenomenon is not only a church-planting movement, but one in which many church planters are attracted to urban settings. For many, the more citified the context, the more they salivate at the prospect of seeing the gospel advance. I live in Alabama, not a state boasting a great megalopolis for sure. But if you want to find Emerging Churches here, go to downtown Birmingham or downtown Huntsville and you will find these young men laboring away in challenging ministry settings. As North America and indeed the world become more urban, missiologists can tell us much about how forbidding urban terrain proves to be from Birmingham to Boston to Bangkok, where I once served on a church-planting team. Yet here, right under our noses, we find not a few ecclesiologically baptistic and theologically Evangelical church planters pouring their lives out to reach the lost with a zeal and willingness to sacrifice comparable to the great missionaries we Baptists have long revered. Some of these communities of faith have been very successful, some spectacularly so.

Ought not such a spectacle of missionary effort expended in some of the most difficult settings imaginable animate the Baptist mind and tug at Baptist heartstrings? It does mine. At a time when so many Baptist churches are seemingly stuck in a downward spiral—at a loss as to the path forward and in something of an embattled mode and in retreat from the strange, changing, and increasingly post-Christian culture around them—what a bright and shining light to see young church planters who believe in the inerrancy and full authority of the Bible so immersed in such a marvelous work in the cities of America. There is a vibrant and robust missionary zeal at work within some of our young people. Where strong and deep theological affinity prevails, let us be slow to view with a jaundiced eye those who have embraced such work. Let us allow shared theology to do its proper work and make way for patience and time for communication and understanding of these young church planters.

Missional

These Emerging Church planters attempt to build what they call missional churches. I want to highlight two ways in which they employ this term. First, missional churches are contrasted with attractional ones. An attractional church focuses disproportionate energy into what takes place within the walls of its buildings: worship services, religious education, clubs, recreation, and other programs. All of these are advertised and promoted and are meant to attract both unchurched believers and unbelievers to the church's facilities, where enjoyment of the programmatic offerings keep them there. Once someone crosses the threshold of that church facility, most of the work of church growth is done.

Emerging Churches may recognize the appropriateness of attractional methods for some, but they are also convinced that growing proportions of the unbelieving population will not be reached by such an approach. Increasingly, unbelievers must be reached outside the church building. They must be reached where they live, work, study, and play. That brings us to a second meaning the word "missional" carries for the Emerging Church. All Christian believers are equally and always on mission. Every believer bears the burden and enjoys the responsibilities of missionary service, and every follower of Jesus Christ should be equipped for such missionary service here at home. Tuscaloosa must be approached with full seriousness as a mission field as surely and profoundly as one might approach Turkey or Tajikistan or Timbuktu.

Culture-Conscious

The missional posture of the movement brings us to what might prove to be the most welcome and most enduring contribution of the Emerging Church to North American Christianity. It is the conviction that, increasingly, North America is made up of multiple subcultures. No longer can Christian believers and would-be evangelists expect to encounter unbelievers with whom they share a deep and wide and rich cultural heritage across great swaths of geography, not even in the South. Even in the heart of Dixie you can drive across town or even walk across the street and find yourself plunged into a subculture where familiar speech and custom and, most importantly, shared meanings are difficult to come by. The cultural diversification in North America matters for those who would see the gospel advanced and Bible-believing Evangelical churches planted, for the same reason culture has always mattered when a missionary is, let us say, dropped from rural or suburban Kansas City into urban Thailand as I once was, because culture profoundly affects the conveyance of meaning and the gospel is a message with a meaning that must be conveyed in order to be believed.

The cultural distances we are traversing as we make our way in and around the lower 48 states does not always feel as significant, and certainly not as jarring, as one experiences between, say, Jackson, Tennessee, and Jakarta, Indonesia, but the Emerging Church is here to tell us that these lesser cultural distances are real and that nonchalance with respect to them will inhibit communication of the gospel. Yes, millions of Americans can still understand the gospel communicated in ways largely unchanged from the language and techniques that prevailed and proved effective in the 1950s in, say, Knoxville, Tennessee; but, warns the Emerging Church, fewer and fewer of those we wish to reach can understand them.

Therefore, the Emerging Church insists, culture should be studied with great care and with missiological questions in mind in much the same way as it has been studied by the great mission-sending agencies for decades, perhaps best symbolized and illustrated by the recognition that efforts to put tops on bare-breasted natives in Asia and Africa inhibited the advance of the gospel by erecting unnecessary stumbling blocks to faith. We study culture not to discover the gospel but to discover the best ways of communicating that gospel within a cultural context.

Ironically, what these missional Emerging Church planters are striving to approximate, whether they realize it or not, is perhaps the most spectacular church-planting movement North America has seen, namely the rise of the Southern Baptist Convention between 1845 and whenever we stopped growing. Part of what accounts for the exponential growth of Southern Baptists is the fact that pretty much optimal cultural conditions prevailed across an enormous geographical expanse, which allowed an ease of communication, a natural or—to use a favorite Emerging Church word—"organic" conveyance of meaning. The difference is that Southern Baptists grew up out of that soil. But now that soil has changed and become a different kind of mission field.

Direct Conversion-Seeking Evangelism Delayed?

Many left-wing Emerging Church leaders suffer from a bad conscience when it comes to proselytizing. But the doctrine-friendly stream of Emerging, the right wing if you will, believes strongly in conversion-seeking evangelism. Nevertheless, some do practice a kind of patience in evangelism that may make some Southern Baptists a little nervous. Such patience may suggest an unseemly lack of urgency where heaven and hell hang in the balance. Nevertheless, many Emerging Church leaders welcome a delay in direct, conversion-seeking evangelism.

Why do they do this? Once again, culture matters here. Conveyance of meaning matters. Many wise Southern Baptists these days are expressing the need to recover zeal for the historical Baptist insistence on a regenerate church membership. Are not many of us convinced that we have, because of a variety of causes, unwittingly and unintentionally perhaps, helped many unconverted persons to think themselves born again? Neither the baptized unconverted nor the local congregations they inhabit are helped where such scenarios play out. In fact, both are harmed—by our praiseworthy but overanxious and imprudent evangelistic zeal. Emerging Churches are convinced that, where evangelism must be done in a context increasingly post-Christian and subculture-shaped as prevails in North America, taking time to gain more confidence that the gospel has truly been communicated and truly believed before filling up the baptismal pool is warranted. Perhaps the place where Evangelicals have been most willing to accept deliberate delay in direct conversion-seeking evangelism is in the adoption on the international mission field of the methods of New Tribes Mission. New Tribes spends months teaching foundational biblical truths to tribal peoples in order to establish a minimal knowledge base without which New Tribes believes such groups, because of profound cultural and worldview differences, simply cannot comprehend the gospel. Yet New Tribes has frequently, at the end of months of teaching and sharing their lives with tribal peoples, seen stunning response to the gospel. For Emerging Churches as for New Tribes, evangelism demands a greater or at least a different kind of investment where significant cultural distance must be traversed in order for the gospel message to be faithfully conveyed, and potentially embraced.

Delay of direct conversion-seeking evangelism, and especially delay of baptism and formal incorporation to the local body of believers, are meant to honor the seriousness of the commitment expected within these doctrine-loving and discipline-practicing congregations. Such caution and conscientiousness would seem to share much with early Baptists who pressed the claims of Christ promiscuously but also guarded the baptismal pool with a bit more vigilance than Baptists of the last six decades or so have been inclined to do. To quote Tertullian, that brilliant and sarcastic sometimes orthodox and sometimes heretical North African teacher of the third century, "If we understood better the true character of Baptism, we might fear its reception more than its delay."

Community

Now I want to spend some time exploring one of the most consistently and fervently expressed pursuits of Emerging Church pastors—the quest for community in the context of church. This yearning for community is variously expressed as the search for authentic relationships, authentic community, and organic, embodied Christianity. They want communities characterized by transparency, mutual

openness, forgiveness, and love—places where brokenness is welcome, where shattered lives find genuine healing within an authentic
Christian siblinghood. They want churches in which, in the deepest sense of the word, members belong to one another, and together
to their Savior and Lord. They want a church that is worthy of the
theme song of the television series *Cheers*:

> Making your way in the world today takes everything
>   you've got.
> Taking a break from all your worries, sure would help a lot.
> Wouldn't you like to get away?
> Sometimes you want to go
> Where everybody knows your name,
> and they're always glad you came.
> You wanna be where you can see,
> our troubles are all the same
> You wanna be where everybody knows your name.[1]

One of the most prominent interests of the Emerging Churches
surely dovetails with one of the most eroded dimensions of church
life and indeed of human life in our time. The significance of the
human longing evoked by mention of the word "community" is evidenced perhaps most concretely by the massive effort investors are
making these days in the construction of mixed-use developments.
Attempts to approximate some of the conditions that once characterized small-town America or even safe urban neighborhoods that
accommodated and facilitated frequent and intimate human interaction abound today across the fruited plain.

Emerging Church leaders want to see a deeper and higher quality
of relationship and depth of community within their congregations
and are convinced that, while such a vision accords with the body

---

[1] See http://www.lyricsondemand.com/tvthemes/cheerslyrics.html.

life described in, for example, I Corinthians 12 and elsewhere in the Bible, it is eluding more and more followers of Jesus in our time. Was not more of this quality and depth of community enjoyed by a much higher percentage of Southern Baptists between 1845 and 1975 than today? Urbanization and suburbanization together with drastically increased mobility and proliferation of community-undermining technologies have rendered the cultural soil on which churches must be planted much less hospitable to the building and nurturing of intimate and durable or—to use an Emerging Church word—"authentic" Christian fellowship.

Job changes that uproot people, but perhaps just as significantly the increasing distances people drive to church, together with distances between places where people worship, work, play, and study, are all obstacles to development of authentic relationships recognizable as anything like the body life desirable for every believer in Jesus Christ. The economic and sociological factors identified by David Wells 16 years ago as profound and insidious enemies of Evangelical theology continue to undermine the best efforts of many churches to recover authentically covenant-shaped, relationally deep, and disciplined communities of faith.[2]

Relationship-inhibiting gadgets and portals and patterns of living foster conditions in which people generally, but including Christian believers, settle into compartmentalized lives, physically isolated and almost cornered into more privatized practice of spirituality. Unless and until more Christian believers participate in communities of faith in which mutual encouragement, love, and accountability become dominant dimensions of their lives, the conditions for robust Christian living will continue to elude us. Is not some minimum amount of time spent with one another, some frequency of contact on a weekly basis, required for the formation and nurturing of something worthy of being called a Christian community? Emerging Church leaders think so.

---

[2] David Wells, *No Place for Truth: Whatever Happened to Evangelical Theology?* (Grand Rapids: Eerdmans, 1994).

Where such minimum contact is not achieved, the means of theological shaping necessary to the people of God is undercut. God's chosen arena for blessing, sanctifying, disciplining, and deploying his children for the enjoyment and advancement of the gospel, namely the church, is simply not being inhabited by believers in sufficient measure to achieve community. Where believers are deprived of the time and means required to develop commitment to one another, how can they be led to an appreciation of and commitment to their own local church, much less to a denomination?

What can be done? The obstacles to the formation and nurturing of genuine Christian community are enormous. They have worked their way into the warp and woof of our lives and, I fear, our psyches. But the stakes also are enormous. We can and must fight back. Mark Dever and Paul Alexander encourage believers who move to pick out a church first, then find a house or apartment. Where possible, try to worship in proximity to where you live and work.[3]

Some Emerging leaders are establishing house churches or small-group Bible studies in homes, and focus on the immediate neighborhood, not only as a strategy for penetrating those neighborhoods with the gospel, but also as an attempt to foster Christian community worthy of the name. Other congregations, when they grow, are deciding to launch new church starts to discourage long commutes. One urban congregation started a church in the suburbs to prevent the suburbanization of its urban venue. These are strategic decisions driven by concern for community shaped by the theological conviction that the gospel is, by divine design, community-creating and community-nourished and that steps must be taken to develop and protect conditions favorable to that community.

The Emerging Church is not calling for a new asceticism. They love their laptops and iPods, and do not consider such contraptions intrinsically evil, but they also believe that the Devil always makes

---

[3] Find this and much helpful advice on the building of Christian community in Mark Dever and Paul Alexander, *The Deliberate Church: Building Your Ministry on the Gospel* (Wheaton, IL: Crossway, 2005).

good use of whatever is available—that goes for both our mobility and these new technologies.

Much excellent reflection has been given in answer to the question, What ought to characterize Southern Baptist churches in the twenty-first century? They ought to be biblical, theologically orthodox and Evangelical, rooted in the Baptist past, evangelistic, missional, etc. Yes, yes, and yes! But in what context do we envision the accomplishment of such goals? I would suggest that the extent to which settings where authentic community is achieved with high quality and depth will prove a fairly accurate harbinger of how effective such efforts prove to be over time. Where theologically and relationally shallow communities develop, however large they may become, enduring gains will likely prove elusive.

For Southern Baptist churches, one indispensable key to accomplishment of most of what needs to happen seems strikingly clear—it is the ability of pastors to stay put in churches for the long haul. This is not happening in many of our churches, but where it does happen, where pastors stay and gain the trust of their congregations, they can pretty much have their way with them, for good or ill. They can work for authentic community, for a renewed denominational loyalty, or for a thousand other things and do so successfully, but only if they stay put.

Commitment

The Emerging Church emphasis on community runs up against a formidable obstacle that I believe characterizes my own generation, the younger Baby Boomers, and subsequent generations of younger adults. I refer to a pernicious refusal, almost an inability, to commit to much of anything. One explanation for the hankering after community is that fewer and fewer of those we want to reach have much if any experience of community or commitment. Many have never known commitment from others, perhaps even from their parents. They lack models. The notion of a man and woman keeping marriage vows till death parts them some five to seven decades after they say "I do" may strike many as a fantastic pipe dream, not something that takes place in the real world. Larger proportions of those we are trying to reach grew up in broken homes in which the biological father was absent and perhaps no father figure was present at all. I have known my whole life that there are at least a handful of people who would give their lives for me without thinking. But many we seek to reach are confident and correct that not a tear would be shed if they dropped dead tomorrow. This growing broken and love-deprived population has no plans to commit to anyone or anything, least of all to a church and even less to a denomination. They may, in certain ways, welcome the Christian-consumer, winner-take-all landscape in which our urban and suburban sprawl churches are set, but in profound ways they do not sit all the way down in their pews.

Great irony arises here—which the Emerging Church, with its quest for community, seems particularly conditioned to detect—the same folks yearning for genuine community characterized by authentic relationships exhibit palpable wariness for and even inability for one of the indispensable building blocks of that true community: commitment.

The same powerlessness to make and keep commitments that results in serial marriage, or the refusal to enter the bonds of marriage at all, displays itself in church hopping and in the refusal to join a church. This same fierce protectiveness for the right to (and even expectation that one eventually will) opt out of any relationship also helps to account for the fastest-growing self-identification among believers in America—namely, as nondenominational.

I have noticed that when a pastor leaves a congregation, those who joined that church during his tenure are more likely than others to consider leaving after the pastor's departure. The church just does not feel as much like home anymore. In an attempt to combat this tendency, before I left one church I had pastored, I met several times with the families that had joined during my tenure. I asked them to tell me what they wanted in a church. They said they wanted a place where they felt at home, where they belonged, where they could count on others in times of need. They sought not merely a place of worship but a church family and a true church home. I asked them, "Well, do you think that the Parkers, the Wilsons, and the Smiths have that?" "Oh yes, of course," they responded, almost in unison. These were the long-tenured families of the congregation. I asked them how they thought these families had achieved what they themselves wanted? I told them that each of these families, typically after the departure of the pastor under whom they had joined, had themselves considered leaving. One thing is for sure, these families had to stay put to gain what these other families wanted. "If you leave," I warned, "you will have to start over. Your stated desires cannot be satisfied without commitment and time." I am convinced that "staying put" is an essential ingredient of true community and an important means for achieving much not only of what we need and want but also of what God, according to His revealed purposes, means for us to enjoy. The relationship of commitment, longevity, and genuine community that prevails within local churches also prevails where denominational identity is concerned.

One of my students, a former Southern Baptist, pastors a nondenominational, doctrine-friendly Emerging Church in an urban setting. I asked him why he left the denomination. His answer was fairly easy to anticipate. He said it seemed as though the denomination was stuck in a lot of fighting and politics, and that younger pastors like him have no voice in what goes on. The denomination seemed to him to be more of a distraction than anything else. I asked him how things were going now that he was out there engaged in ministry, free from the denomination. He said it was fine but he did feel a bit isolated, a bit disconnected. That bothered him because one of the reasons Emerging Church leaders give for leaving denominational ties behind is that they think of themselves as fellow believers with many Christians around the globe and stretching back through history. They are repulsed by the kind of denominational pride that reflexively touts its superiority and distances itself from other believers. Yet breaking from the denomination did not seem to provide the more widely connected Christianity they sought.

The bottom line for this pastor was that church ought to feel like family, and the denomination did not.

Within a month of this conversation, mission-sending agencies of various types descended on Beeson Divinity School where I teach, and I found myself seated at a table with this young pastor and a young woman around my son's age whom neither of us had met before. I soon discovered that she lived in Richmond and worked for the International Mission Board (IMB) of the Southern Baptist Convention. I had served with the IMB in Bangkok. Next thing you know we discover mutual friends and acquaintances. The young woman had been to Bangkok, for heaven's sake! After she left I asked the young pastor, "Did you see what just happened?" Although I had never met this woman before, because of the denominational tie, my time with her quickly took on the atmosphere of a meeting between distant family members. Both of us left the conversation knowing that we were very much connected to one another and serving together in a very large Christian family with a long history, and that we face the future together as spiritual siblings. Without the denominational connection this could not have happened.

A middle-aged Thai Christian man addressing college students on the subject of dating and marriage said this: "The most important predictor of a long healthy marriage is the ability of the husband and wife to 'put up with stuff'." No doubt about it, staying put these days in a marriage, a local church, or a denomination is not easy. You have to put up with stuff. But in return, they put up with your stuff, too, and the next thing you know, something like authentic community, spiritual siblinghood, the family of God, starts to take root and grow.

Southern Baptists:
Understanding the Past in Order to Explore the Future

Chapter 10

Reflections on 400 Years
of the Baptist Movement:
Who We Are, What We Believe

JAMES A. PATTERSON, UNIVERSITY PROFESSOR AND
ASSOCIATE DEAN, SCHOOL OF THEOLOGY AND MISSIONS,
UNION UNIVERSITY

The immense scope and thorny intricacies of the Baptist heritage
constitute daunting challenges for any who would attempt to provide
a worthy synopsis of it in an essay of modest length. Furthermore,
a widespread historical amnesia in the Evangelical community as a
whole can render the crafting of a credible denominational narrative
a thankless project.[1] Even when contemporary believers cultivate a

---

[1] For an insightful discussion of this common ill, see Dean C. Curry, "Evangelical
Amnesia," *First Things*, no. 176 (October 2007): 15–17. For some useful antidotes to
specifically Baptist amnesia, see these representative surveys of the Baptist past: Bill
J. Leonard, *Baptist Ways: A History* (Valley Forge, PA: Judson Press, 2003); H. Leon
McBeth, *The Baptist Heritage: Four Centuries of Baptist Witness* (Nashville: Broadman
Press, 1987); Tom Nettles, *The Baptists: Key People Involved in Forging a Baptist Iden-
tity*, 3 vols. (Fearn, Rosshire, UK: Christian Focus/Mentor, 2005–7; and C. Douglas

commendable interest in the legacy of their forebears, they sometimes project current agendas backwards in such a way as to distort the past. Indeed, what *First Things* editor Joseph Bottum has cautioned about employing memory for autobiographical purposes applies equally well to our denominational recollections: "Memory may be our best tool for self-understanding, but only when we remember how weak a tool it really is: prone to warping under the narrative drive of story-telling, vulnerable to self-interest, susceptible to outside influence."[2]

In the context of utilizing our historical memories to help ascertain Baptist identity, our manifest diversity points to additional hurdles for the conscientious historian. Wake Forest Dean and scholar Bill Leonard advises against an overly simplistic account of our denominational roots: "Baptists should not succumb to the fallacy of origins, that noble but naïve belief that there exists a pristine, systematic, and unified source of Baptist identity in the beginning that need only be discovered and installed. In fact, there are multiple Baptist traditions—theological, regional, and institutional—from which churches may choose."[3] Memories must be not only sharp and reliable but also wide-ranging, to be of service in describing and clarifying our denominational identity.

The primary thesis of this chapter is that history—in particular, Baptist history—is messy. The Baptist heritage is composed of competing stories that cannot be easily disentangled. The multifaceted character of our past, moreover, suggests some notable implications for the conduct of the Baptist historical enterprise.

First, Baptist history is not reducible to a bald, integrating theme such as "freedom" or "experience." For instance, Charles Deweese, former executive director of the Baptist History and Heritage Society,

---

Weaver, *In Search of the New Testament Church: The Baptist Story* (Macon, GA: Mercer University Press, 2008).

[2] Joseph Bottum, "The Judgment of Memory," *First Things*, no. 181 (March 2008): 30.

[3] Bill J. Leonard, "Whose Story, Which Story? Memory and Identity among Baptists in the South," in *History and the Christian Historian*, ed. Ronald A. Wells (Grand Rapids: Eerdmans, 1998), 135.

summed up the essential Baptist soul and genius in this shortsighted manner: "Baptists' primary gift to civilization and to Christianity has been, is, and must remain the legacy of liberty."[4] Even an approach that broadens this constricted perspective by focusing on Baptist "distinctives," principles, or as Walter Shurden once put it, "convictional genes," may not always do justice to the rich complexity of the Baptist past.[5] This kind of historiography may misleadingly imply that the principles and practices in place today have at all times and places been intrinsic features of Baptist life and thought.

Second, for 400 years Baptist history has been significantly interwoven with the narratives of other groups, movements, and denominations that have also witnessed to the gospel. Baptists essentially have been and still are Evangelical Protestants; hence, the wider stories in church history cannot be ignored when Baptists address who they are and what they believe. While Baptists historically have been marked by ideas and practices that set them apart from other Christians, they also share some considerable common ground that has significant consequences both for how we interpret our own history and how we relate at present to those outside the Baptist fold.

Third, our untidy Baptist past should function as a hedge against excessive pride and triumphalism when we commemorate our history. The high moments and notable developments of the past 400 years almost always had a downside. Our past is messy because—like us—our Baptist forebears were fallen creatures who sinned, stumbled, and otherwise fell short of God's glory and His desires for them.

---

[4] Charles W. Deweese, *Freedom: The Key to Baptist Genius* (Brentwood, TN: Baptist History and Heritage Society, 2006), 23. For an analogous emphasis on experience in the same booklet series, see William E. Hull, *The Meaning of the Baptist Experience* (Nashville: Baptist History and Heritage Society, 2007). James Dunn, onetime head of the Baptist Joint Committee for Religious Liberty, hailed "soul competency" as the greatest Baptist contribution to the Christian world. See "Dunn's Address," *American Baptists in Mission* 195 (January/February 1996): 15.

[5] See Walter B. Shurden, *Turning Points in Baptist History* (Brentwood, TN: Baptist History and Heritage Society and the William H. Whitsitt Baptist Heritage Society, 2001); see also William H. Brackney, *A Capsule History of Baptist Principles* (Atlanta: Baptist History and Heritage Society, 2009).

A fitting salute to the Baptist heritage should not require that we suspend our critical faculties or disregard the awkward or embarrassing features of the Baptist movement since 1609. An outlook of sober realism about our history may actually facilitate constructive relationships with non-Baptist Evangelicals.

Backgrounds to Baptist History

One of the risks in surveying the centuries before the rise of the Baptist movement is that it might stir the imaginative juices of those who hold to a successionist view of Baptist origins; they would reject a 400-year limit on our history and extend the historical path to almost two millennia.[6] At the same time, it is vital to see that the Baptist tradition that emerged in the early seventeenth century was not radically discontinuous with previous developments in church history. Early Baptists, in fact, set forth ideas, doctrines, and practices that were not always original or unique; in some cases, they had deep historical roots. For instance, most Baptists have embraced the trinitarian and Christological beliefs that were elucidated respectively at the Council of Nicaea (325) and the Council of Chalcedon (451). As theologian James Leo Garrett recaps it, "For Baptists the affirmations of the deity of Christ, the complete humanity of Christ, the one person of Christ, and the two natures of Christ imply some indebtedness to these early councils, whether or not that indebtedness is formally acknowledged."[7] Although successionists especially do not invoke the

---

[6] See G. H. Orchard, *A Concise History of Foreign Baptists* (London: George Wightman, 1838), for a classic statement of successionist theory. Landmark patriarch J. R. Graves arranged for the publication of an American edition, for which he wrote an introductory essay. See Orchard, *A Concise History of Baptists from the Time of Christ Their Founder to the Eighteenth Century* (Nashville: Graves & Marks, 1855). Successionism later was popularized in J. M. Carroll's booklet, *The Trail of Blood* (Lexington, KY: American Baptist Publishing Company, 1931). I have critiqued Graves's position in "James Robinson Graves: History in the Service of Ecclesiology," *Baptist History & Heritage* 44 (Winter 2009): 72–83.

[7] James Leo Garrett, *Baptist Theology: A Four-Century Study* (Macon, GA: Mercer University Press, 2009), 3.

early church councils as supporting evidence for Baptist perpetuity, the creeds that stemmed from them clearly shaped the historical orthodoxy that later influenced the majority of Baptist confessional statements.

A few years ago, Steven Harmon, a theology professor at Beeson Divinity School, measured the importance of this patristic tradition for Baptist vision and identity. Based on their seventeenth-century confessions, he even argues that the earliest Baptists demonstrated a "surprisingly catholic ecclesial outlook," one that modern Baptists need to retrieve and apply to their worship and theology.[8] While Landmarkers would surely impugn the entire notion of a "Baptist catholicity" and moderate/liberal Baptists with an uncompromising "freedom" agenda would reject his call to re-envision the nature and function of the ancient creeds, Harmon nonetheless poses some intriguing theses and proposals regarding the connection of an ancient ecumenical tradition to Baptist life and thought.

Since successionist historical portraits typically keep their distance from the early councils and instead accentuate the martyrdom of those who stood against the Roman Catholic Church through the ages, it is not remarkable that their "trail of blood" includes allegedly baptistic groups such as the Montanists, Donatists, Paulicians, Petrobrusians, Albigensians, Waldensians, Lollards, and Hussites. It is true, of course, that seventeenth-century Baptists both in England and British North America frequently assumed a stance of nonconformity over against entrenched religious establishments; in that sense, some parallels can be drawn between their experiences of persecution and those of late-medieval dissenters such as Peter Waldo (d. early 1200s), John Wycliffe (c. 1330–84), and John Hus (c. 1372–1415). At the same time, it would be an illegitimate stretch to presume that pre-Reformation radicals and Reformers necessarily shared the same theological or ecclesiastical agendas as the first generation of Baptists.

---

[8] Steven R. Harmon, *Towards Baptist Catholicity: Essays on Tradition and the Baptist Vision*, Studies in Baptist History and Thought 27 (Bletchley, Milton Keynes, UK: Paternoster, 2006), esp. 71–87.

Despite holding some common convictions and similar enemies with Baptists, medieval sectarians can be categorized at best as "forerunners" of the Baptist movement.[9]

The Protestant Reformation of the sixteenth century provided a more direct backdrop for the rise of the Baptists. Even though successionism's historically suspect claim that Baptists are not Protestants basically trivializes the Magisterial Reformation, the efforts of Reformers such as Martin Luther (1483–1546), Ulrich Zwingli (1484–1531), and John Calvin (1509–64) laid an indispensable foundation upon which the nascent Baptist movement was able to build less than a century later. In essence, the Protestant Reformers—with Luther leading the way—recovered the meaning and breadth of the biblical evangel. Over against a late-medieval system of works righteousness that practically conveyed a salvation based on human merit, the Wittenberg pastor and professor openly proclaimed justification by the imputed grace of God. The believer could not earn God's favor but instead was declared by the Father to be righteous through faith in the finished work of His Son Jesus Christ on the cross (Rom 1:17). To this fresh appropriation of the NT gospel, Luther adjoined a fresh renewal of the priesthood of all believers based on passages such as 1 Pet 2:9 (NIV)—"You are a chosen people, a royal priesthood, a holy nation, a people belonging to God, that you may declare the praises of him who called you out of darkness into his wonderful light." This theme had profound implications for ecclesiastical life in the sixteenth century as it helped to undermine the oppressive Catholic sacerdotalism and sacramentalism of the late Middle Ages. Luther and his Magisterial colleagues buttressed their profound theological principles with an unswerving commitment to the full authority and sufficiency of the Bible—hence their espousal of *sola scriptura*, or perhaps more precisely *suprema scriptura*. For the

---

[9] This term is borrowed from Heiko A. Oberman and used a bit differently from his *Forerunners of the Reformation: The Shape of Late Medieval Thought* (New York: Holt, Rinehart and Winston, 1966).

Reformers, Scripture took priority over tradition, papal decrees, or any other human authority.[10]

Although Landmarkers have distanced themselves from the Lutheran and Reformed traditions in some respects, most Baptists have integrated salvation by grace through faith, the priesthood of all believers, and *suprema scriptura* into their doctrinal formulations. Their commitment to the gospel flows from those basic affirmations. On the other hand, they have rejected certain teachings of the Magisterial Reformers, including infant baptism, a close alliance of church and state, and specific ecclesiological concepts relating to the sacraments and the nature of the church. On these issues, Baptists have exhibited closer kinship to the "Radical" or Anabaptist Reformation as characterized by groups such as the Swiss Brethren, Mennonites, and Hutterites.[11] Anabaptist and Baptist movements have undeniably exhibited some fundamental continuities, especially on matters such as believer's baptism and regenerate church membership. In addition, as persecuted minorities, both Baptists and Anabaptists voiced strenuous opposition to state churches and promoted religious liberty. As a general rule, however, Baptists have not accepted Anabaptist positions on pacifism, oath taking, and soul sleep. Perhaps most seriously, sixteenth-century Anabaptist soteriology—with its synergistic tendencies—has been conspicuous by its absence in Baptist systematic theologies.[12] Because the Baptist tradition drew on the resources of

---

[10] On the theological significance of the Protestant Reformers, see Timothy George, *Theology of the Reformers* (Nashville: Broadman Press, 1988). For a handy overview of the Reformation, see Stephen J. Nichols, *The Reformation: How a Monk and a Mallet Changed the World* (Wheaton, IL: Crossway, 2007). On the relevance of John Calvin for Baptists, see Timothy George, "What Baptists Can Learn from Calvin: The Genevan Reformer's Words Are Still Worth Hearing Today," http://www.christianitytoday.com/ch/thepastinthepresent/historymatters/whatbaptistscanlearnfrom-calvin.html (accessed August 31, 2009).

[11] A classic work on this tradition is William R. Estep, *The Anabaptist Story*, 3rd ed. (Grand Rapids: Eerdmans, 1996). See also George Hunston Williams, *The Radical Reformation*, 3d ed. (Kirksville, MO: Truman State University Press, 2000).

[12] For a helpful summary of Anabaptist-Baptist discontinuities, see James Edward McGoldrick, *Baptist Successionism: A Crucial Question in Baptist History*, ATLA Monograph Series 32 (Metuchen, NJ: Scarecrow Press, 1994), 86–122.

both the Magisterial and Anabaptist reformations, its emergence in the seventeenth century can—in part—be understood as a synthesis of the earlier reform movements.

The later development of the English Reformation likely affords the most immediate context for the initial rise of the Baptist movement. After all, the earliest Baptists identified themselves as English Protestants. These Baptists, nevertheless, selectively borrowed from the English Reformers. They principally admired the Puritans, those Protestants who felt that the Church of England had not been sufficiently reformed, and so they continued to press for further changes in worship, doctrine, polity, and lifestyles. The Puritan brand deeply impressed itself on the figures in early Baptist history, especially as it was mediated through the more radical Puritans who ultimately separated themselves from the established church. It was the English Separatists, then, who passed the notions of a gathered church and congregational autonomy on to the first Baptists. These same Separatists suffered imprisonment and even death under Elizabeth I and James I because of their exodus from the parish churches of the Anglican communion. In reality, early Baptist history cannot be fully explained without reference to this late-Reformation, Puritan-Separatist setting in England.[13]

The Seventeenth-Century Origins of the Baptist Movement

John Smyth (c. 1570–1612) is the primary reason that Baptists celebrated their 400th anniversary in 2009. This cleric was raised in

---

McGoldrick shows that some Anabaptists even deviated at times from historical Christian orthodoxy.

[13] On the broader sixteenth-century picture, see Michael E. Williams Sr., "The Context of Baptist Beginnings: 1517–1609," in *Turning Points in Baptist History: A Festschrift in Honor of Harry Leon McBeth*, ed. Michael E. Williams Sr. and Walter B. Shurden (Macon, GA: Mercer University Press, 2008), 3–12. For an important monograph on a Separatist who did not become a Baptist but had connections to some who did, see Timothy George, *John Robinson and the English Separatist Tradition* (Macon, GA: Mercer University Press, 1982).

the Church of England and later studied at Christ's College, Cambridge, which at the time was known for both Puritan and Separatist influences. One of his tutors was Francis Johnson, who eventually embraced Separatism and pastored a small congregation of English exiles in the Netherlands. Smyth revealed his own Puritan leanings in the early 1600s and, by about 1606, associated with a Separatist body in Gainsborough, England. Like his Cambridge mentor, Smyth soon emigrated to Holland, where he led the Gainsborough group in Amsterdam. By 1608 he publicly advocated a thoroughgoing congregationalism while he simultaneously dismissed the Church of England as a false church. He likewise readily pointed out differences between his small church and other scattered English Separatist congregations in Holland.[14]

On his road to taking positions that would identify him—at least tentatively—as a Baptist, Smyth initially unfolded a strict congregationalist ecclesiology that emphasized the independence of each local assembly. As he worked through the implications of regenerate church membership, he apparently sensed a discrepancy between that feature of congregational polity and the practice of baptizing infants. Furthermore, his contacts with Anabaptists in Amsterdam likely reinforced what he saw as intrinsic in his ecclesiology. At any rate, Smyth transitioned to believer's baptism in 1609 when he first baptized himself (se-baptism) and then others in his tiny congregation, probably by pouring. The church was soon reconstituted on the basis of believer's baptism and—from all appearances—was the first "Baptist" congregation to emerge out of English Separatism. Smyth forcefully attacked the practice of infant baptism in his 1609 publication, *The Character of the Beast*.

---

[14] For an overview of Smyth and his church, see James R. Coggins, *John Smyth's Congregation: English Separatism, Mennonite Influence, and the Elect Nation*, Studies in Anabaptist and Mennonite History 32 (Scottdale, PA: Herald Press, 1991). For a good theological analysis, see Jason K. Lee, *The Theology of John Smyth: Puritan, Separatist, Baptist, Mennonite* (Macon, GA: Mercer University Press, 2003).

Smyth, however, promptly muddied the waters by raising questions about his self-baptism and then entering into discussions with the Waterlander Mennonites in Amsterdam with the aim of merging his church with their movement. His 1610 confessional statement, moreover, revealed that he had shifted from the Calvinism of his Puritan background to the Arminian perspective of the Dutch Anabaptists. While the Smyth group was not officially accepted by the Waterlanders before his death in 1612, it surely seemed that Smyth intended to be identified as an Anabaptist. This did not set well with one of his colleagues, Thomas Helwys (c. 1550–1616), an English country gentlemen who decided to separate from Smyth and take about a dozen former members of Smyth's church back to England. Helwys's diminutive assembly, which gathered outside the walls of London in 1612, thus represented the first tangible planting of the General Baptist movement in the British Isles.[15]

While Smyth's impact on the General Baptist tradition remains somewhat murky, Helwys eventually stood as its chief initiator in England. On the theological front, Helwys had already distanced himself from both Smyth and the Mennonites before taking his followers back to the homeland, in part by his muted Arminianism on matters such as sin and free will. On the other hand, he agreed with Smyth on the necessity of religious liberty, which he vigorously affirmed in his 1612 treatise, *A Short Declaration of the Mystery of Iniquity*. He chided his British sovereign, James I, with the oft-quoted query, "is it not most equal that men should choose their religion themselves, seeing that they only must stand themselves before the judgement seat of God to answer for themselves[?]"[16] This forthright sentiment abruptly landed Helwys in Newgate Prison, London, where he died sometime before 1616.

---

[15] On the Smyth-Helwys division, see James E. Tull, *Shapers of Baptist Thought* (Valley Forge, PA: Judson Press, 1972), 24–29.

[16] Thomas Helwys, *A Short Declaration of the Mystery of Iniquity*, ed. Richard Groves (Macon, GA: Mercer University Press, 1998), 37. For Helwys's 1611 *Declaration of Faith*, see William L. Lumpkin, *Baptist Confessions of Faith* (Valley Forge, PA: Judson Press), 116–23. Cf. Smyth's *Short Confession*, ibid., 102–13.

Because Smyth and Helwys divided over relatively minor issues, it should not be shocking that even deeper ruptures plagued English Baptists for much of the seventeenth century. A disparate group of Separatists associated with the JLJ Church—named after Henry Jacob, John Lathrop, and Henry Jessey, the first three pastors—in London adopted believer's baptism in the 1630s and thus provided groundwork for the Particular Baptist tradition. These Baptists advocated Calvinistic doctrine (e.g., limited atonement), freedom of conscience, and, by 1641, immersion as the biblically correct mode of baptism. In addition to their theological differences with General Baptists, the Particulars also showed a more favorable posture toward congregational hymn singing in their worship services, as reflected in the innovative hymnbooks—*Spiritual Melody* (1691) and *Spiritual Songs* (1700)—of London pastor Benjamin Keach (1640–1704). Then, as General and Particular Baptist polities matured, the latter more commonly shied away from centralized associations that might threaten the autonomy of local congregations. Hence, competing models of thought and practice were in play even at this primitive stage of Baptist history.[17]

Baptist pioneers in seventeenth-century England charted a groundbreaking path for future generations in three important respects. First, both General and Particular Baptists carefully expressed their doctrinal convictions in confessional statements that they designed to establish the parameters of acceptable belief and practice. The Particular Baptists' First London Confession of 1644, with its strong Christological focus and Evangelical Calvinism, was also the first Baptist

---

[17] For an argument that early Baptist history was more complicated than the General/Particular split, see Stephen Wright, *The Early English Baptists, 1603–49* (Woodbridge, Suffolk, UK: Boydell & Brewer, 2006). Wright's book covers a period that is too early to include the Seventh Day Baptists, a Sabbatarian movement that dates back to the Cromwell period (1650s) in England and 1671 in Colonial Rhode Island. See Don A. Sanford, *A Choosing People: The History of Seventh Day Baptists* (Nashville: Broadman Press, 1992). On Keach's contributions to Baptist hymnody, see J. Barry Vaughn, "Benjamin Keach," in *Baptist Theologians*, ed. Timothy George and David S. Dockery (Nashville: Broadman Press, 1990), 63–65.

document of this type to set forth immersion as the proper form of baptism. Although only seven London congregations initially signed on, it arguably became the most influential of all Baptist confessions. The Orthodox Creed of 1678, which shared with the First London a keen interest in Christology, sought to steer General Baptists of the Midlands away from theological error and to unite them with other orthodox English Protestants. The statement incorporated complete texts of the Apostles' Creed, the Nicene Creed, and the Athanasian Creed, thus identifying itself with the patristic trinitarian and Christological traditions.[18] While some Baptists in modern times—particularly those who are fearful that individual conscience and soul competency might be compromised—seem apprehensive about confessional documents, it is clear that from the seventeenth century on, Baptists used them as essential boundary markers. Baptist identity involved fairly specific doctrinal content, and the earliest Baptists did not hesitate to articulate what it entailed.

Second, Baptists in the seventeenth century demonstrated consistency with their Puritan heritage by emphasizing the value of vital Christian experience. Perhaps no Baptist writer of the era illustrated this better than John Bunyan (1628–88), who penned the spiritual classic *The Pilgrim's Progress* (1678) while a prisoner in Bedford jail because he conducted illegal religious services outside the state church. His practice of open membership, which allowed those who had not been immersed as believers to join his church, suggested that he saw himself more as a Nonconformist than as a Baptist. In fact, his ecclesiology brought him into open conflict with some Particular Baptists in London. At the same time, his allegory of the Christian life has resonated with several generations of Baptists, especially his vivid portrait of Christian before the cross, where the burden of sin fell from his back and tumbled into "the mouth of the sepulchre, where it fell in, and I saw it no more." As a result of this life-transforming event, Christian burst forth in triumphant song:

---

[18] See Lumpkin, *Baptist Confessions*, 153–71, 297–334.

Thus far did I come laden with my sin;
Nor could aught ease the grief that I was in;
Till I came hither: what a place is this!
Must here be the beginning of my bliss?
Must here the burden fall from off my back?
Must here the strings that bound it to me crack?
Blest cross! blest sepulchre! blest rather be
The Man that was there put to shame for me![19]

Although Bunyan was a Baptist more by the spirit than by the letter, his cross-centered approach—anchored as it was in Christ's substitutionary atonement—has resounded perpetually in Baptist preaching ever since, most notably in the nineteenth-century London pulpit of Charles Spurgeon, who reportedly read *The Pilgrim's Progress* more than 100 times.[20] Few Baptists have contributed to the characteristic themes of warm piety and gospel proclamation as John Bunyan.

Third, Bunyan's own experience as a prisoner highlighted the reality that early English Baptists advanced their cause in a context of persecution, which was mostly inflicted by the Church of England. Although they enjoyed some respite during the Civil War (1640s) and Cromwell's Commonwealth (1650s), their legal status remained precarious until Parliament passed the Act of Toleration in 1689. Imprisonment of Baptist preachers was not uncommon, particularly during the Restoration of the monarchy and Anglican Church beginning in 1660, when law codes placed numerous obstacles in the pathways of Nonconformist groups including the Baptists. Eventual toleration fell well short of full religious liberty; on a very uneven playing field, the state church continued to hold many advantages over dissenting movements. The historical Baptist insistence on a free

---

[19] John Bunyan, *The Pilgrim's Progress* (New York: Lancer Books, 1968), 55–56. On Bunyan as a Baptist theologian, see Harry L. Poe, "John Bunyan," in *Baptist Theologians*, 26–48.

[20] Eric W. Hayden, "Did You Know? A Collection of True and Unusual Facts about Charles Haddon Spurgeon," *Christian History* 10, no. 1, issue 29 (1991): 2.

church in a free state, which had significant long-term implications in both England and America, was undeniably forged in such unfavorable political and legal circumstances.[21]

The broader struggles of seventeenth-century English Nonconformists against the established church indirectly factored into the coincident birth of the Baptist movement in British North America. The iconoclastic Separatist, Roger Williams (c. 1603–83) fled religious persecution in England under Charles I in late 1630, only to find that the Puritan colony of Massachusetts Bay in the New World was just as overbearing and theocratic as the government of the homeland. A Calvinist who shared many theological ideas with the Puritans, Williams openly rejected the emerging state church system in Massachusetts and declared that civil government had no inherent right to enforce Christian belief or worship within its borders. He also repudiated the notion that the church needed to rely on carnal weapons in serving the kingdom of the sovereign God.

By 1635 Williams faced the threat of deportation to England and chose to move south in 1636 to establish a settlement that he called Providence, in what became known as Rhode Island. In sharp contrast with Puritan Massachusetts, he offered full religious freedom to those who came to his new colony. His spirited espousal of the separation of church and state ultimately prevailed in America, particularly after the country adopted the Bill of Rights in 1791 and Massachusetts disestablished the last remaining state church in 1833.[22]

Among religious refugees who came to Providence was a small group that met in Williams's home and, by 1638, concluded that believer's baptism was the NT norm. Ezekiel Holliman, who had been a member of a Puritan church in Salem, Massachusetts, baptized

---

[21] See William R. Estep, *Revolution within the Revolution: The First Amendment in Historical Context, 1612–1789* (Grand Rapids: Eerdmans, 1990), 49–71.

[22] J. Bradley Creed, "Baptist Freedom and the Turn toward Separation of Church and State: 1833," in *Turning Points in Baptist History*, 153–66. For a useful, readable overview of Williams's life and contributions, see Edwin S. Gaustad, *Liberty of Conscience: Roger Williams in America*, Library of Religious Biography (Grand Rapids: Eerdmans, 1991).

Williams, who in turn baptized about 10 others. The likely baptismal mode, as in Amsterdam three decades earlier, was pouring. The First Baptist Church of Providence has had a continuing history to the present, although Williams officially disaffiliated from the congregation after a few months and became a fussy and even eccentric "Seeker" after the true church and divinely sanctioned ordinances. Williams nonetheless blazed a trail for Baptists in America by providing a safe haven where in due course the Baptist witness could flourish, and by expounding an influential model of church-state relations.

John Clarke (1609–76), another disillusioned Puritan, left a more direct and enduring legacy to the Baptists of early America. After departing Massachusetts during the Antinomian Controversy, this émigré Englishman helped to found Newport, Rhode Island, in 1638. Perhaps as early as 1640 he participated in the launching of a church there that within a few years showed a genuinely Baptist identity. A Particular Baptist, Clarke stood against both General and Sabbatarian Baptists in Newport, which led to early rifts in the Colonial Baptist movement that closely approximated the divisions in England. In addition, he boldly championed the cause of religious freedom, even daring to conduct unauthorized worship in Lynn, Massachusetts, for which he was promptly arrested. Finally, he exemplified a budding Baptist propensity in America for cultural engagement by balancing his pulpit responsibilities in Newport with political duties as a representative in Rhode Island's General Assembly and as the colony's deputy governor.[23]

By the end of the seventeenth century, more than 300 Baptist congregations could be found scattered throughout various regions of England, with an additional 15 or so in New England, Pennsylvania, New Jersey, and South Carolina.[24] While the movement was

---

[23] See Sydney V. James, *John Clarke and His Legacies: Religion and Law in Colonial Rhode Island, 1638–1750*, ed. Theodore Dwight Bozeman (University Park: Pennsylvania State University Press, 1999).

[24] For information on the number of churches, see Clinton Wolf, "Theological Renewal, Prayer Fueled 18th-Century Renewal, Speaker Says," *Baptist Press*, October

neither large nor especially threatening to older denominational traditions, it had gained a conspicuous identity through its accents on believer's baptism by immersion, regenerate church membership, congregational polity, and religious freedom. Its promising inception, however, was a bit clouded by marked disagreements in matters of both doctrine and practice. Part of the messiness of Baptist history became readily evident in the competing versions of what it meant to be a Baptist that appeared almost from the movement's inaugural in 1609. This untidy character would only intensify in the following century.

The Eighteenth Century: Growth and Further Differentiation

Baptists did not exactly barrel into the eighteenth century with any recognizable momentum that might have stemmed from their earlier successes. In England, for example, they failed to benefit significantly from their enhanced legal status that came with the 1689 Act of Toleration. Instead of exploiting this legislation, both General and Particular Baptists actually declined in the number of churches and members until the mid-eighteenth century. Evangelistic vision dimmed for many reasons, including a preoccupation with constructing churches. Furthermore, General Baptists fell into Christological disputes that revealed Arian and even Unitarian heresies among some of their preachers. Particular Baptists, on the other hand, sometimes succumbed to hyper-Calvinist and antinomian extremes that resulted in peculiar theories, as well as abstract preaching devoid of applications or invitations. The venerable John Gill (1697–1771), who preached for half a century at a Particular Baptist church in the Southwark section of London, has been categorized by some Baptist historians as a hyper-Calvinist obstacle to renewal and growth;

7, 1997, http://www.bpnews.org/bpnews.asp?id=3938 (accessed October 22, 2009); and Robert G. Torbet, *A History of the Baptists*, rev. ed. (Valley Forge, PA: Judson Press, 1963), 207–14.

Timothy George, however, interprets Gill in a more charitable light.[25] All the same, the General and Particular Baptist traditions in England both displayed flaws that pointed to the need for revival, renewal, and reformation.

Meanwhile, Baptists in the North American Colonies dodged most of the theological aberrations of their British cousins yet remained relatively small in number before the mid-eighteenth century. Along with their English counterparts, they profited substantially from the transatlantic revivals that swept through Great Britain and America beginning in the 1730s. Although the contexts and some of the results were different, the awakenings shared common threads that linked them in meaningful ways. For example, non-Baptist preachers on both sides of the Atlantic exercised considerable impact on Baptist evangelists both in terms of priorities and methods. Anglicans John Wesley (1703–91) and George Whitefield (1714–70), both of whom adopted "field preaching" as a strategy for reaching people in England who would not darken the door of a parish church, influenced British and American Protestants well beyond their own communion toward a burden for the lost and a willingness to innovate in order to reach them.

Before long, waves touched off by the English revivalists produced transformations in Baptist circles. Dan Taylor (1738–1816), who as a youth walked miles to hear Wesley and Whitefield hold forth the gospel, became the pastor in 1762 of an independent church in Yorkshire, England, where he introduced customs that he had learned from Wesley such as organizing small-group "experience meetings" to assist his members' spiritual growth. In spite of his admiration for Wesley, within a year Taylor concluded that there was no biblical support for infant baptism. After discovering that his Arminian doctrines disqualified him from affiliating with the Particular Baptists,

---

[25] Timothy George, "John Gill," in *Theologians of the Baptist Tradition*, ed. Timothy George and David S. Dockery (Nashville: Broadman & Holman, 2001), 11–33. For historian Michael Haykin's take on English Baptist decline in the early eighteenth century, see Wolf, "Theological Renewal, Prayer."

he received believer's baptism from the General Baptists and quickly remade his congregation into a General Baptist church. His overall reaction to the conventional General Baptists, however, was largely negative; he noticed, for instance, their persistent Christological laxity, even commenting that "they degraded Jesus Christ and He degraded them."[26] What he had gleaned from the fervor of revival seemed discordant with the dullness and heterodoxy that he perceived among the already established General Baptists.

Finding a closer kinship among some baptistic independents in Leicestershire, Taylor collaborated with them and a remnant of more orthodox General Baptists to organize a New Connection movement in 1770. While not cut off completely from the old-line General Baptists, this new body mapped a strikingly discrete course that promoted hymn singing, education, and journalism; the New Connection thus shaped a fresh denominational identity for General Baptists in England. Since many of the traditional General Baptists veered toward Unitarianism and rationalism, Taylor and the New Connection effectively rescued the General Baptist line from a virtual demise; New Connection Baptists preserved their distinctiveness until their full merger in 1891 with the Baptist Union, which had a majority Particular Baptist constituency.[27] The English Awakening, although not begun by Baptists, clearly had weighty consequences for General Baptist life and thought in the eighteenth century.

Particular Baptists likewise drew inspiration from the revivals, although, for theological reasons, they responded more favorably to Whitefield than to Wesley. In addition, their theological rejuvenation in the late eighteenth century was likely sparked more by American

---

[26] Dan Taylor, quoted in W. E. Bloomfield, *The Baptists of Yorkshire* (London: Kingsgate Press, 1912), 105.

[27] On the New Connection and revivalism, see Bill J. Leonard, "Baptist Revivals and the Turn toward Baptist Evangelism: 1755/1770," in *Turning Points in Baptist History*, 97–99. On the eventual marriage of General and Particular Baptists in Great Britain, see Jerry Faught, "Baptists and the Bible and the Turn toward Theological Controversy: The Downgrade Controversy, 1887," in *Turning Points in Baptist History*, 249–50.

Congregationalist Jonathan Edwards (1703–58) than by any other source. This New England pastor and theologian, who defended the First Great Awakening in America without endorsing its more unusual manifestations, fundamentally roused Particular Baptists in England from their hyper-Calvinism by his synthesis of Reformed theology and a winsome, public proclamation of the gospel message. Edwards's writings powerfully affected Andrew Fuller (1754–1815), the Particular Baptist preacher in Soham and Kettering, England, who challenged the pervasive ultra-Calvinist "theology of glory" with a more biblical and Evangelical "theology of the cross," which focused on what was clearly revealed in Scripture rather than on fruitless speculation about the timing or exact nature of God's eternal decrees. Fuller's *The Gospel Worthy of All Acceptation* (1785) offered Particular Baptists an Evangelical Calvinism that reiterated many of the doctrinal and practical insights that had earlier been expressed by Whitefield and Edwards. His stress on the universal offer of the gospel strengthened the evangelistic resolve of Particular Baptists and allowed them to respond better to the revivalistic currents of the day.[28]

Fuller's theological reformation also contributed to the emergence of a new missionary spirit among British Particular Baptists near the end of the eighteenth century. He helped to mentor William Carey (1761–1834), a shoemaker and Baptist convert from the Church of England who, by 1789, labored with Fuller and other Particular Baptist pastors to stir their people to support overseas efforts for reaching those who had never heard the gospel. After making several appeals to Particular Baptist audiences, Carey and Fuller facilitated the establishment of the Baptist Missionary Society in 1792, with the Kettering cleric serving as its first secretary. Carey, along with his reluctant spouse, sailed to India in 1793 to minister with Dr. John Thomas as the BMS's pioneer missionaries. Labeled by

---

[28] See Tull, *Shapers of Baptist Thought*, 79–100; Phil Roberts, "Andrew Fuller," in *Theologians of the Baptist Tradition*, 34–51.

many as "the father of modern missions," Carey spent over 40 years in the subcontinent as a church planter, educator, businessman, and Bible translator. The impact of his correspondence and courageous example on the birth of an international missionary endeavor among Baptists in America—and more generally in the Christian world—is, of course, legendary.[29]

Revivalism in the American Colonies left its own unique imprint on the Baptist tradition in the New World. Just as the Wesleyan revival aided the emergence of the New Connection in Great Britain, the First Great Awakening in New England brought forth a new type of Baptist that lacked a predecessor in the mother country. In the midst of heated controversies in the Northern Colonies over the nature and efficacy of the revivals—including the role of itinerant preachers—the Congregationalists divided into pro- and anti-revival parties. Separate or New Light Congregationalists both promoted the awakening and challenged the spiritual integrity of the churches that were closely connected to governmental authority in colonies such as Connecticut, Massachusetts, and New Hampshire. The Separates, as a logical response to revivals that emphasized the new birth, attempted to rejuvenate the practice of regenerate church membership; in turn, some of them started to question the practice of infant baptism, which they could not harmonize either with Scripture or their dissident ecclesiology.[30]

Beginning in the 1740s, many Separate Congregationalists became Separate Baptists, thus launching a new and distinctly American variety of the Baptist tradition. In contrast with the already recognized Regular Baptists, the Separates tended to be less educated, more rural, more apprehensive of doctrinal statements such as the

---

[29] See Timothy George, *Faithful Witness: The Life and Mission of William Carey* (Birmingham, AL: New Hope Press, 1991).

[30] The classic treatment of the divisions within New England Congregationalism during the First Great Awakening is C. C. Goen, *Revivalism and Separatism in New England, 1740–1800: Strict Congregationalists and Separate Baptists in the Great Awakening* (New Haven: Yale University Press, 1962).

Philadelphia Confession (1742), more suspicious of strong associations, and more likely to endorse the loud and emotional preaching
that characterized some of the itinerants who stirred discord in New
England. Unlike the General Baptists who emigrated from England,
Separates rejected Arminian theology and showed more affinity for
the Calvinism of the Regulars (and their own Congregationalist heritage). Most important, Separates vigorously contended for the full
independence of each local congregation. As a minority movement
that faced discrimination and even overt persecution, Separate Baptists treasured freedom and localism.[31]

Not coincidently, the most renowned champions of religious
liberty in late eighteenth-century New England were rooted in the
Separate Baptist movement. Isaac Backus (1724–1806), for instance,
was converted in the Great Awakening and identified for a number
of years with Strict Congregationalism. After embracing believer's
baptism, he sought to lead a "mixed" congregation in Middleborough,
Massachusetts, but later saw the need to organize a Separate Baptist
church in that locale. Through his peripatetic preaching, writings,
associational activities, and relentless lobbying for religious freedom,
he stood as the most dominant personality among Separate Baptists
in the northeast. He is rightfully credited with helping to undermine
the Congregational state church in Massachusetts, even though it
was not officially disestablished until 1833. He also bequeathed to
Baptists in America a conspicuously local church ecclesiology that
influenced later movements such as Landmarkism.[32]

Another product of both the revival and Separate Baptist traditions was the more unconventional preacher and activist John Leland
(1754–1841). A native New Englander, he preached in Virginia from

---

[31] Ibid., 288–95; and LeRoy Benjamin Hogue, "A Study of the Antecedents
of Landmarkism" (ThD diss., Southwestern Baptist Theological Seminary, 1966),
114–23.

[32] On Backus, see Stanley J. Grenz, *Isaac Backus—Puritan and Baptist: His Place
in History, His Thought, and Their Implications for Modern Baptist Theology* (Macon,
GA: Mercer University Press, 1983); and William G. McLoughlin, *Isaac Backus and
the American Pietistic Tradition* (Boston: Little, Brown, 1967).

around 1777 until 1791, a period marked by local awakenings under his leadership. After urging his friend James Madison to add a Bill of Rights to the proposed U.S. Constitution, Leland returned to Massachusetts to pastor and itinerate for many more years. A staunch opponent of the state churches in both Virginia and Massachusetts, he also affirmed the Separate Baptist ecclesiology which emphasized the autonomy of each congregation. Leland's lively rhetoric, moreover, incorporated localism, individualism, and the republican spirit of post-Revolutionary America.[33] Both he and Backus nudged Baptists in America toward intentional engagement with the public square, especially regarding religious liberty and church-state relationships.

A final important area of eighteenth-century Baptist endeavor in both England and America was Christian higher education. In the British Isles, the impetus for Particular Baptist ministerial and theological training predated the age of revivals. As early as 1679, a will that was drawn up in Bristol provided funds for those called to the Baptist ministry. Some mentoring occurred early in the eighteenth century, and classes commenced in 1734 with the opening of the Bristol Baptist Academy, which became Bristol Baptist College. Evidence suggests that some of the original students contributed to the awakenings in England and Wales.[34]

In America, the gospel preachers of the First Great Awakening apparently saw the formation of denominational colleges that would train the next generation of clergy as one way to preserve the fruits of revival. Along with their Anglican, Congregationalist, and Presbyterian counterparts, Baptist preachers unfolded a vision for ministerial education and thus chartered the College of Rhode Island in 1764.

---

[33] For one of the better historical and ideological assessments of Leland, see John Bradley Creed, "John Leland, American Prophet of Individualism" (PhD diss., Southwestern Baptist Theological Seminary, 1986).

[34] See Roger Hayden, "The Contribution of Benjamin Foskett," in *Pilgrim Pathways: Essays in Honour of B. R. White*, ed. William H. Brackney and Paul S. Fiddes, with John H. Y. Briggs (Macon, GA: Mercer University Press, 1999), 189–206. For the broader account of the school in Bristol, see Norman S. Moon, *Education for Ministry: Bristol Baptist College 1679–1979* (Bristol: Bristol Baptist College, 1979).

Originally located in Warren, it was moved to Providence in 1770 and became Brown University in 1805, named after an early alumnus who provided a gift of $5,000. The Philadelphia Baptist Association, the largest and most dynamic Baptist organization in the American Colonies, assisted in the formation and early development of this school. James Manning (1738–91), a leader in the association, served as the college's first president. New England was ably represented by the prominent Separate Baptist, Isaac Backus, who was a longterm trustee. Perhaps the most significant president in the nineteenth century was Francis Wayland (1796–1865), a Baptist pastor-theologian who led Brown for 25 years. Although the university dissolved its relationship with the Northern Baptist Educational Board in the early twentieth century and became an elite Ivy League institution with a secular ethos, its earlier development suggested a model for Baptist colleges and universities in the United States, some of which have managed to retain a distinctively Christian identity.[35]

The Baptist movement in both Great Britain and America found itself at the end of the eighteenth century in a more mature and stable condition than had been the case a hundred years earlier. Not surprisingly, it continued to display conspicuous fissures related to doctrinal, practical, and cultural differences. At the same time, "Baptist" as a denominational moniker implied some level of coherence because of a basic consensus on virtually the same core of principles that had marked the tradition at the end of the seventeenth century. In

---

[35] On the founding and early history of Brown, see Reuben Aldridge Guild, *The Early History of Brown University Including the Life, Times and Correspondence of President Manning 1756–1791* (Providence: Snow and Farnham, 1896). For the bigger picture of Baptist higher education in America, see William H. Brackney, "Baptists Turn toward Education: 1764," in *Turning Points in Baptist History*, 128–40. On Wayland and Baptist colleges in the nineteenth century, see David B. Potts, "Baptist Colleges in the Development of American Society, 1812–1861" (PhD diss., Harvard University, 1967). For an evangelical Baptist perspective on contemporary Christian higher education by the president of a school—Union University—that has held on to its Baptist roots and Christian character, see David S. Dockery, *Renewing Minds: Serving Church and Society through Christian Higher Education* (Nashville: B&H Academic, 2008).

addition, most Baptists on both sides of the Atlantic imbibed deeply from the streams of spiritual awakening that ran through English and American Protestantism. Nourished and invigorated by the revivals, Baptists stood poised for their greatest advances thus far. Once again, however, they could not avoid what seemed to be the almost inevitable cycle of conflict and schism that had been part of their legacy for some time.

The Nineteenth Century: Storms of Controversy in the Midst of Expansion

Taking their cues from William Carey and other British Baptist missionaries in India, Baptists in America took some initially tentative steps toward organizing for mission ventures in the early nineteenth century. In the context of the Second Great Awakening, which spawned numerous benevolent and missionary societies to meet the religious and humanitarian needs of the time, New England Baptists in particular showed a propensity for this model; in part, they believed that several decentralized societies in the denomination could prevent the rise of an ecclesiastical structure that might threaten the autonomy of local churches. Agencies such as the Massachusetts Baptist Missionary Society, founded in 1802 with close ties to the Warren Baptist Association, focused primarily on home missions yet also alerted supporters to the Baptist work in India through a magazine that frequently published the letters of British Baptist missionaries who labored there. The Baptist societies thus established the foundation for a more ambitious missionary enterprise that would surface beginning in 1814.

The appointment of Baptist foreign missionaries, however, did not really ensue by design. New England Congregationalists, mostly as the result of a fervent prayer meeting in 1806 on the campus of Williams College in Massachusetts, set up the American Board of Commissioners for Foreign Missions in 1810. By 1812, the ABCFM sent to India five young men, some with their wives. Among this group were Adoniram Judson (1788–1850) and his wife, Ann, and Luther Rice (1783–1836). Both men had sensed a missionary call as students at Andover Theological Seminary, where they were influenced by Samuel Mills, one of the participants in the Haystack Prayer Meeting at Williams. After arriving at their destination on separate ships, the Judsons and Rice became convinced—largely through study of the Greek NT that the Judsons had undertaken en route—that the immersion of believers was the only truly biblical mode of baptism. Soon all three were baptized by British Baptist missionaries in India, and conscientiously resigned their ABCFM appointments.[36]

Suddenly Baptists in America found themselves blessed with three missionaries in India; these courageous pioneers, however, lacked both funding and an effective support mechanism on the home front. At the suggestion of William Carey's son Felix, the Judsons made plans to redirect their mission efforts to Rangoon, Burma. Adoniram Judson spent the rest of his career—except for one furlough in 1845—in that challenging field, enduring chronic physical troubles, imprisonment, and the deaths of his first two wives. Like William Carey, he generated a compelling missionary biography, especially as a Bible translator, church planter, and role model for fellow Baptists at home.[37]

In 1813 Luther Rice returned to Boston to raise support for the Judsons and himself, since he expected to return to foreign missionary service. Although he never resumed his overseas ministry, the

---

[36] On Judson and the broader context of these developments, see Joan J. Brumberg, *Mission For Life: The Story of the Family of Adoniram Judson, the Dramatic Events of the First American Foreign Mission, and the Course of Evangelical Religion in the Nineteenth Century* (New York: Free Press, 1980). My first scholarly article covered some of the early dynamics of Baptist missionary advance. See James A. Patterson, "Motives in the Development of Foreign Missions among American Baptists," *Foundations* 19 (October-December 1976): 298–319.

[37] William H. Brackney, "The Legacy of Adoniram Judson," *International Bulletin of Missionary Research* 22 (July 1998): 122–27. The classic biography is Courtney Anderson, *To the Golden Shore: The Life of Adoniram Judson* (Boston: Little, Brown, 1956).

indefatigable Rice traveled throughout the eastern United States for several years promoting Baptist missionary, educational, and journalistic endeavors. Moreover, he was a major catalyst for an 1814 meeting in Philadelphia that created the General Missionary Convention of the Baptist Denomination in the United States for Foreign Missions.[38]

The use of "denomination" in the longer title for the Triennial Convention could be viewed as a misnomer; at the time, this new mission agency represented the first authentic attempt by Baptists in America to initiate something beyond the associational level. For 30 years the Triennial Convention, managed in day-to-day operations by the Baptist Board of Foreign Missions for the United States, connected Baptists North and South in a cooperative undertaking that not only directed an expanding foreign missions program, but also— for a shorter period (1817–26)—sponsored initiatives in home missions and education. While this broader agenda caused the Triennial Convention to function for a season as an extended association, it ultimately opted for the societal model of the British Baptists when it restricted its scope to international work; this move blocked the development of a centralized denominational umbrella, much to the chagrin of some Baptist leaders in the South.[39]

While the Baptist movement in America experienced growth and some measure of unity in the first half of the nineteenth century, the new missionary enterprise spawned debate and division that threatened to undercut the successes and cooperative spirit that had been attained. On the American frontier, particularly in the Ohio and

---

[38] The secondary literature on Rice is slim. For a brief overview of his contributions, see Michael Foust, "Prof: Today's Missionaries Owe Much to Baptist Pioneer Luther Rice's Work," *Baptist Press*, November 27, 2000, http://www.bpnews.org/BPnews.asp?ID=6927 (accessed November 5, 2009).

[39] On the early history of the Triennial Convention (and its relationship to earlier developments in India and Burma), see Carol Crawford Holcomb, "Baptist Missions and the Turn toward National Denominational Organizations: The Baptist Missionary Society and the Triennial Convention: 1792/1812," in *Turning Points in Baptist History*, 114–27.

lower Mississippi River valleys, an "anti-mission" bloc emerged with an antagonistic attitude toward mission societies, Sunday schools, and an educated or paid clergy. For some, anti-mission sentiment grew out of a hyper-Calvinist theology that opposed any organized human effort in reaching the lost. Others argued that mission organizations were designed by humans without biblical support. Still others suspected that untrustworthy Baptists in the eastern U.S. controlled agencies such as the Triennial Convention in a hierarchical manner that would weaken the autonomy of local congregations. The movement's diversity was reflected in groups such as Daniel Parker's Two-Seed-in-the-Spirit Predestinarian Baptists, the many varieties of Primitive Baptists, and the more nebulous "Hardshell" Baptists.[40] Although anti-mission Baptists were relatively few in number, they pointed to a recurring problem in Baptist life similar to what British Baptists confronted in the late eighteenth century. Being Baptist has not always meant being missions-minded.

Alexander Campbell (1788–1866), a former Presbyterian who had migrated with his family from Scotland to America to join his father, Thomas, brought an added dimension to anti-missionism. As an Arminian, he did not share the antipathy of the hyper-Calvinists toward missions and evangelism; instead, it was his intense desire to duplicate the primitive church of the first century that fired his opposition to Bible and mission societies. As a strict biblicist, he found no explicit support in the NT for such institutions. Furthermore, his hermeneutic led him to oppose musical instruments in worship and to tilt toward baptismal regeneration, even while agreeing with Baptists on believer's baptism by immersion and local church autonomy. Campbell's Brush Run church was officially part of the Redstone Baptist Association in western Pennsylvania for over a decade, but the Restorationist preacher and polemicist caused much consternation among frontier Baptists when they discovered that his "Reformed"

---

[40] For a thorough discussion of the anti-mission forces, see Byron Cecil Lambert, "The Rise of the Anti-Mission Baptists: Sources and Leaders, 1800–1840 (A Study in Religious Individualism)" (PhD diss., University of Chicago, 1957).

agenda diverged in substantive ways from traditional Baptist positions. In 1832 he joined with revivalist Barton Stone (1772–1844) to organize the Disciples/Christian movement, and took several formerly Baptist congregations with him.[41]

A more significant division relating to missions occurred in 1845 when Baptists in the South concluded that they could no longer collaborate effectively with the Triennial Convention or the American Baptist Home Missions Society, which they perceived to be dominated by Northern, antislavery Baptists. While Baptist leaders in the South such as Richard Furman (1755–1825)—pastor of First Baptist in Charleston, South Carolina, and first president of the Triennial Convention—had pointed to the alleged benefits of slavery, Northern Baptists who desired viable missionary agencies helped to uphold a policy of neutrality on the peculiar institution. By 1844, however, that strategy was in collapse as Baptist state conventions in the South received responses from the ABHMS and the Triennial Convention's Board of Managers that revealed an unwillingness to continue appointing slaveholders as either home or foreign missionaries. The prospects appeared to be slim for holding together the fragile missionary consensus of the previous 30 years.

Indeed, at a called gathering in Augusta, Georgia, in 1845, delegates from Baptist churches and societies across the South voted to establish the Southern Baptist Convention along the lines of the associational model. Hence, a Foreign Mission Board and a Board of Domestic Missions were presently organized under the umbrella of the SBC and not as independent societies. Most mission-minded Baptists in the South quickly transferred their allegiances from the Triennial Convention—soon to be renamed the American Baptist Missionary Union—and from the ABHMS to the new entities. While

---

[41] Recent scholarship on Campbell includes Richard J. Cherok, *Debating for God: Alexander Campbell's Challenge to Skepticism in Antebellum America* (Abilene, TX: ACU Press, 2008); and Peter Allan Verkruyse, *Prophet, Pastor, and Patriarch: The Rhetorical Leadership of Alexander Campbell* (Tuscaloosa: University of Alabama Press, 2005).

Baptists in the South had for some time preferred a convention structure for doing missions and also squabbled with the ABHMS over the geographic distribution of funds and missionaries, irreconcilable positions on slavery among Baptists North and South figured prominently in the steps that were taken in 1845. Moreover, as Ouachita Baptist Professor Terry Carter has remarked, this context of controversy over a significant moral and political question left an enduring mark on the SBC: "Slavery laid the groundwork for attitudes and actions that would plague the Southern Baptist Convention for more than a century and a half."[42] When the SBC celebrated its 150th anniversary in 1995, it formally repented of the racism and apologetic for slavery that constituted such a problematic moral and cultural heritage.[43]

Despite the fact that the founding of the SBC occurred in less than ideal circumstances and with mixed motives, this new body promptly commenced a robust missionary program that would characterize the denomination down to the present. In the early history of the FMB, for example, China emerged as its earliest and most important field of service. Among the many missionaries who served there, Charlotte Diggs Moon (1840–1912) stirred the passions of Southern Baptists on the home front with her intrepid spirit of sacrifice, commitment to reaching the millions in the Far East with the gospel, and great affection for the Chinese people. Today, of course, what is now called the International Mission Board benefits from the annual Christmas offering named after Lottie Moon. As the SBC has become the largest Protestant denomination in the United States with 16 million adherents, the IMB is one of the largest Evangelical Protestant

---

[42] Terry Carter, "Baptists and Racism and the Turn toward Segregation: 1845," in *Turning Points in Baptist History*, 167. For an insightful discussion of the components of the early SBC, see Walter B. Shurden, "The Southern Baptist Synthesis: Is It Cracking?" *Baptist History and Heritage* 16 (April 1981): 2–11. Shurden delineates the Charleston, Sandy Creek, Tennessee (Landmark), and Georgia traditions. Cf. H. Leon McBeth, "The Texas Tradition: A Study in Baptist Regionalism (Parts I and II)," *Baptist History and Heritage* 26 (January 1991): 37–57.

[43] For coverage of the 1995 apology in Atlanta, see Timothy C. Morgan, "Racist No More? Black Leaders Ask," *Christianity Today* (August 14, 1995): 53.

mission agencies in the world, with more than 5,000 missionaries in more than 180 countries.[44]

Even as the SBC was in its infancy as a denomination, additional conflict within the ranks held implications for mission structures. James Robinson Graves (1820–93), a Yankee transplant from Vermont, used the *Tennessee Baptist*, a widely circulated denominational paper in the mid-South, to promote an ecclesiological agenda that became known as Landmarkism. For journalist-preacher Graves, bona fide Baptists affirmed that the only valid NT meaning of *ekklesia* was the local, visible assembly of believers. He denied the concept of a church universal. He connected this ecclesiology to a successionist view of Baptist history, maintaining that Baptists had existed in an unbroken chain of true churches since the first century. Furthermore, the Landmark patriarch vigorously attacked practices such as open communion, the acceptance of immersion done by non-Baptist ministers, and the friendly exchange of pulpits between Baptist and non-Baptist preachers. Finally, Graves brusquely expressed skepticism about any denominational mission organizations beyond the level of the local church, fearing that such entities might infringe on the prerogatives and overall freedom of autonomous congregations.

At the Richmond meeting of the SBC in 1859, Graves—for all practical purposes—attempted to dismantle the Foreign Mission Board, which for him epitomized the dangers of consolidation and centralization in missions. The FMB showed some inclination to channel funds for individual churches or groups of churches that wanted to appoint their own missionaries, but the overall pattern for missions that had been in place since 1845 remained intact. The SBC survived later controversies related to Landmarkism; pockets of the

---

[44] On Lottie Moon, see Catherine B. Allen, "Charlotte (Lottie) Moon, 1840–1912: Demonstrating 'No Greater Love'," in *Mission Legacies: Biographical Studies of Leaders of the Modern Missionary Movement*, ed. Gerald H. Anderson, et al. (Maryknoll, NY: Orbis Books, 1994), 205–15. Statistics are from various links found at http://imb.org (accessed November 10, 2009).

movement persisted in some areas of denominational life, as well as in Landmark groups that broke away such as the American Baptist Association and the Baptist Missionary Association of America.[45] The historical Baptist penchant for conflict had manifestly flared up, even in a relatively homogeneous denomination that was at the time primarily regional in nature.

Meanwhile, British Baptists experienced a major dispute late in the nineteenth century. The immediate setting was the Baptist Union, which was organized in 1813 by Particular Baptists and expanded through the century with the admission of General Baptists. By the late 1880s, the Baptist Union betrayed tendencies toward doctrinal drift as some pastors and other leaders apparently embraced aspects of Darwinism, higher criticism of the Bible, and universalism. Charles Haddon Spurgeon (1834–92), arguably the greatest pulpiteer in Baptist history, feared that the union had "downgraded" biblical orthodoxy, so he used his *Sword and Trowel* in 1887 to sound the alarm concerning liberal inroads in the Baptist fellowship. The London Metropolitan Tabernacle pastor called on the union to adopt a more specific confessional statement to replace its more generalized Declaration of Faith. The union responded negatively to Spurgeon's request and he withdrew from it, leading to a highly critical union resolution against him in 1888.[46] The Downgrade Controversy anticipated similar theological and political struggles among Baptists in America, including a Northern Baptist conflict in the 1920s and the SBC "Controversy" that erupted in 1979. A common thread in these denominational clashes turned out to be the authority and inspiration

---

[45] I am working on a book about Graves, tentatively titled *Staking the Boundaries: James Robinson Graves and Baptist Identity in the Nineteenth-Century South*. See my preliminary work in James A. Patterson, "The J. R. Graves Synthesis: American Individualism and Landmarkist Ecclesiology," *Tennessee Baptist History* 7 (Fall 2005): 9–18; and id, "James Robinson Graves: History in the Service of Ecclesiology," 72–83.

[46] See Mark Hopkins, "The Down-Grade Controversy: What Caused Spurgeon to Start the Most Bitter Fight of His Life?" *Christian History* 10, no. 1, issue 29 (1991): 31–32; and Faught, "Baptists and the Bible and the Turn toward Theological Controversy," 249–60.

of Scripture; the Baptist Union's reluctance to take a strong stand on this doctrinal matter may well have contributed to its marked decline in the twentieth century, which in some ways paralleled a less-pronounced slide in the Northern Baptist Convention/American Baptist Churches, USA.

After a century of ecclesiastical discord, albeit with clear progress in many venues, Baptists might have paused in 1890 or 1900 and asked probing questions about their identity. The diversity that had contributed to the overall messiness of Baptist history almost from the beginning broadened considerably in the nineteenth century. The Baptist missionary enterprise itself, which required some basic level of agreement to be successful, also brought more richness and complexity to the denominational portrait. The Baptist movement, which had flourished mainly in Great Britain and America, now had become global. Churches planted in Europe, Asia, Africa, and Latin America would not look or function the same as those in the lands that sent out cross-cultural missionaries. Even on the home front, the basic theological harmony on the meaning of the gospel, which made the great missions surge of the nineteenth century possible, would not survive for long in a swiftly changing world.

Trends since the Late Nineteenth Century

By the end of the nineteenth century, a growing theological diversity represented a palpable and disquieting trend in the Baptist movement. Historical orthodoxy still commanded a sizable following among Baptists, particularly in America. Among Southern Baptists, who faced less immediate threats from overtly liberal theology than did their Northern colleagues, James P. Boyce (1827–88) exemplified both a Reformed impulse in doctrine and a vision for effective ministerial training that was fleshed out in the early history of The Southern Baptist Theological Seminary, which he helped to found in 1859 and continued to guide until his death. The Princeton Seminary graduate's chief written contribution to Baptist thought, *Abstract of*

Systematic Theology, was published in 1887.[47] Although Southern Seminary shifted theologically leftward in the next century, current President Albert Mohler sparked something of a Boyce renaissance at the school beginning in 1993.

The twentieth century likewise saw the emergence of a later generation of Baptist thinkers who essentially echoed Boyce's classical and rational approach to theology, albeit with more subdued Calvinistic tones. In particular, Carl F. H. Henry (1913–2003) earned a justifiable reputation as one of the premier Evangelical Protestant theologians of the post-World War II era. Although he plainly influenced fellow Baptists, he exercised a much wider impact in American religious life as a seminary professor, *Christianity Today* editor, and interpreter and defender of what was dubbed the "new Evangelicalism." His voluminous writings include his magnum opus, the multivolume *God, Revelation and Authority*.[48]

In the post-Boyce period at Southern Seminary, fourth President Edgar Young Mullins (1860–1928) stood as an important mediating theologian who marked some distance between himself and his predecessor. Mullins conveyed a basically orthodox doctrinal perspective; he served, for instance, as the primary author of the SBC's first Baptist Faith and Message statement (1925). At the same time, his *Axioms of the Christian Religion* (1908) and *Freedom and Authority in Religion* (1913) bestowed on Christian experience and the doctrine of soul competency a much greater centrality than Boyce would have ascribed to them.[49] In the long run, Mullins not only helped to shape

---

[47] James P. Boyce, *Abstract of Systematic Theology* (Philadelphia: American Baptist Publication Society, 1887). On his life and thought, see Timothy George, "James Petrigu Boyce," in *Theologians of the Baptist Tradition*, 73–89; and Gregory A. Wills, *Southern Baptist Theological Seminary, 1859–2009* (New York: Oxford University Press, 2009), esp. 3–188.

[48] Carl F. H. Henry, *God, Revelation and Authority*, 6 vols. (Waco, TX: Word Books, 1976–83. A reprint edition in paperback has been published: Wheaton, IL: Crossway, 1999. For an overview of the Henry legacy, see R. Albert Mohler Jr., "Carl F. H. Henry," in *Theologians of the Baptist Tradition*, 279–96.

[49] Edgar Young Mullins, *The Axioms of Religion* (Philadelphia: American Baptist Publication Society, 1908); and ibid., *Freedom and Authority in Religion* (Philadelphia:

the SBC's twentieth-century confessional tradition, but also opened the door for the incursion of neoorthodox thinking in state convention-sponsored Baptist colleges and SBC seminaries.[50]

The late nineteenth century also witnessed the rise of the social gospel movement in American Protestantism. Perhaps the most acknowledged leader of the movement was Walter Rauschenbusch (1861–1918), a Baptist who taught church history for two decades at Rochester Theological Seminary. His prior experience at Second German Baptist Church in New York City brought him in direct contact with social problems caused by rapid urban and industrial growth. Although he did not repudiate the Evangelical piety of his youth, the budding social gospel promoter enthusiastically utilized social and economic themes to articulate his understanding of the kingdom of God. The most mature expression of his thought can be found in *A Theology for the Social Gospel* (1917), which originated as the Taylor Lectures at Yale Divinity School.[51] Many Baptists remain ambivalent about the Rauschenbusch legacy; his predilections for pacifism, socialism, and some elements of theological liberalism have all been contested.

The impact of Rauschenbusch's social gospel became vividly evident in the life and ministry of Martin Luther King Jr. (1929–68), the African-American civil rights activist of the 1950s and 1960s. What is sometimes missing from the accounts of King's accomplishments is that he pastored Dexter Avenue Baptist Church in Montgomery,

---

Griffith & Rowland Press, 1913). See also Fisher Humphreys, "Edgar Young Mullins," in *Theologians of the Baptist Tradition*, 181–201.

[50] See Tim Ellsworth, "Mullins' Legacy Tied to Both Sides of SBC Controversy, Mohler Recounts," *Baptist Press*, April 5, 2000, http://www.bpnews.org/bpnews.asp?id=5579 (accessed November 12, 2009). Mohler attributes the "autonomous individualism" in the SBC to Mullins.

[51] Walter Rauschenbusch, *A Theology for the Social Gospel* (New York: Macmillan, 1917). One of the better biographies is Paul M. Minus, *Walter Rauschenbusch: American Reformer* (New York: Macmillan, 1988). I have discussed his relationship to foreign missions in James Alan Patterson, "The Kingdom and the Great Commission: Social Gospel Impulses and American Protestant Missionary Leaders, 1890–1920," *Fides et Historia* 25 (Winter/Spring 1993): 51–52, 57–60.

Alabama, and Ebenezer Baptist Church in Atlanta during the time he became an international figure through his campaigns for civil rights and peace. His studies at Crozer Theological Seminary, a Northern Baptist institution in Chester, Pennsylvania—now part of the Colgate Rochester Divinity School complex—drew him to Rauschenbusch's optimistic vision for social change; then again, this line of thought was tempered by his exposure to Reinhold Niebuhr's more realistic assessment of the social order.[52] Nonetheless, this Progressive National Baptist preacher shared Rauschenbusch's passion for social justice and infused his civil rights speeches—which he delivered in an obviously sermonic style—with copious biblical allusions. King also tapped a longstanding Baptist tradition of public engagement, even if more pietistic Baptists remained uncomfortable with the time he spent away from his pulpit. Baptist political activists such as Jerry Falwell (1933–2007) borrowed a page or two from King's *modus operandi*, even though their theologies were widely divergent.

Another twentieth-century Baptist preacher who digested Rauschenbusch's writings as a seminary student was Harry Emerson Fosdick (1878–1969). Ultimately, however, the pastor of Riverside Church in New York City was probably more indebted to the liberalism of Northern Baptist theologian William Newton Clarke (1841–1912), who mentored Fosdick at Colgate University. Because his congregation was aligned with what are now called the American Baptist Churches and the United Church of Christ, it is not surprising that his influence extended well beyond Baptist circles. Through his attacks on fundamentalists, his strategically located pulpit, his radio ministry, and his books, he might have been one of the best known Protestant liberals of his day; he appeared on covers of *Time* magazine in 1925 and 1930. He also contributed to Baptist hymnody with

---

[52] See David J. Garrow, *Bearing the Cross: Martin Luther King, Jr., and the Southern Christian Leadership Conference* (1986; repr., New York: Vintage Books, 1988), 42–43.

the stirring lyrics, "God of Grace and God of Glory."[53] His popularity in the middle of the twentieth century underlined just how big the Baptist tent had become theologically, particularly in the Northern Baptist Convention/American Baptist Churches.

In the context of a doctrinal pluralism that marked some denominational bodies, many grassroots-level Baptists continued to uphold the venerable Baptist revival tradition. Many local Baptist churches, particularly in the SBC, regularly held revival services and meetings. Full-time Baptist evangelists often filled pulpits during these special events. On a larger scale, Baptists around the world ardently supported the ministries of itinerant preachers, of whom the most legendary was William Franklin Graham (1918–). Although raised as a Presbyterian, young Billy became a Baptist as a college student in Florida and thereafter held membership in Baptist congregations; most recently he has been affiliated with First Baptist in Dallas, and now First Baptist in Spartanburg, South Carolina. Probably no other Baptist preacher in history has been heard live by more people than Graham. Since his Los Angeles crusade in 1949, this energetic evangelist has built a large evangelistic organization, written many popular books, utilized mass media, befriended U.S. presidents, and preached around the world. Now in his 90s, Billy Graham, while openly identifying himself as a Baptist, has epitomized the modern Evangelical movement perhaps better than any other individual.[54]

Another important trend in Baptist life since 1900 has been an expanding institutional base that has helped to consolidate and strengthen the Baptist cause. Two examples help to illustrate this development. On the international scene, several Baptist groups

---

[53] *The Baptist Hymnal* (Nashville: Convention Press, 1991), 395. For a biography of Fosdick, see Robert Moats Miller, *Harry Emerson Fosdick: Preacher, Pastor, Prophet* (New York: Oxford University Press, 1985). For a survey of the growth of liberalism among Northern Baptists, see Gregory A. Thornbury, "The Legacy of Natural Theology in the Northern Baptist Theological Tradition, 1827–1918" (PhD diss., Southern Baptist Theological Seminary, 2001).

[54] One of the better biographical studies is William C. Martin, *A Prophet with Honor: The Billy Graham Story* (New York: W. Morrow & Company, 1991).

launched the Baptist World Alliance in London in 1905. Currently based in Falls Church, Virginia, the BWA has been committed to both religious liberty and congregational autonomy since its founding. It also has conducted congresses roughly every five years, promoted Baptist distinctives, distributed news items about Baptist life, supported humanitarian relief efforts, and sponsored evangelistic missions. A truly global entity, the BWA represents 216 Baptist unions and conventions that encompass 37 million baptized believers and an overall Baptist community of over 100 million, although its membership does not include all Baptists. The Southern Baptist Convention, for example, departed from the organization in 2004, expressing concerns about the presence of theological liberalism in some BWA bodies, as well as the alliance's acceptance of the Cooperative Baptist Fellowship into its ranks the previous year.[55] While certainly one of the most visible and diverse expressions of the worldwide Baptist movement, it remains to be seen whether the BWA can attain a sufficient doctrinal unity or consensus to be a comprehensive agency.

A second illustration of Baptist institutional life is the SBC's Cooperative Program, which officially began at the 1925 annual meeting in Memphis. A post-World War I financial campaign in the denomination fell about $17 million short of its $75 million goal, leaving several institutions and agencies with significant debt. The messengers hence approved a new program that allowed the SBC to be a genuine convention in both its structure and funding mechanism; any remnants of a societal approach to raising money were essentially eliminated. For 85 years the Cooperative Program (CP) has reinforced denominational loyalty and unity in a remarkable way; furthermore, it has provided an efficient channel for monies from the

---

[55] See the BWA website at http://www.bwanet.org (accessed November 16, 2009); and Richard V. Pierard, ed., *Baptists Together in Christ, 1905–2005: A Hundred-Year History of the Baptist World Alliance* (Birmingham, AL: Samford University Press, 2005). Pierard also has penned a helpful article about the global impact on Baptist historiography. See "The Globalization of Baptist History," *American Baptist Quarterly* 19 (June 2000): 164–76.

churches to be distributed to the state Baptist conventions and the various entities of the SBC. The 2008-2009 CP allocated more than $205 million, with about 95 percent divided among the SBC seminaries (22 percent), the North American Mission Board (almost 23 percent), and the International Mission Board (50 percent).[56] While the CP system has endured challenges from the right and the left—particularly since 1979—it effectively carries out its work and functions as a testimonial to what Baptist collaboration can accomplish that local churches or associations could never do by themselves.

One downside of effective institutional life is that it can lead to an undue accent on pragmatic considerations. Western Christian churches on the whole have suffered from a marked strain of pragmatism that has dimmed their vision for kingdom work and weakened their social, cultural, and spiritual impact. In Baptist life, for instance, it appears that a mid-twentieth-century preoccupation with denominational programs in the SBC reaped a bloated bureaucracy, and an inability or unwillingness to confront theological deviations in colleges and seminaries.[57] There are no guarantees even now that a more conservative SBC will dodge the damaging effects of overly pragmatic agendas. Seeker-friendly paradigms, budgetary pressures, and utilitarian rationales all have the potential to compromise an authentically biblical witness.

Concluding Thoughts

First, even though their past is messy, Baptists have managed to maintain a clear and distinct denominational identity for 400 years. They have shown more consistency on some principles such as baptism by immersion, but somewhat less on others. Believer's baptism,

---

[56] See the CP website at http://cpmissions.net (accessed November 16, 2009); and Chad Brand and David Hankins, *One Sacred Effort: The Cooperative Program of Southern Baptists* (Nashville: Broadman & Holman, 2005).

[57] "Inerrancy Controversy Roots Deeper Than Past 12 Years, Dockery Says," *Baptist & Reflector* (February 6, 1991): 5.

regenerate church membership, and congregational polity all have been upheld in theory but compromised in practice.

Second, in the past century or so, liberalism, pragmatism, and cultural conformity have undermined doctrinal integrity in many contexts. The conservative resurgence in the SBC, which was launched in 1979, constitutes a qualified exception to this trend. The efforts of leaders such as Paige Patterson (1942–), Paul Pressler (1930–), and Adrian Rogers (1931–2005) helped to bring about major institutional and theological changes in the SBC, including a new Baptist Faith and Message statement in 2000 that aptly reflected what had occurred in the previous two decades. In spite of this seismic denominational shift, it remains to be seen how all the implications will play out in the next several years. Hazards to be navigated include wrangling over secondary and tertiary doctrinal and practical matters, which is already evident in SBC life. Perhaps a more serious danger is the lurking historical amnesia referred to at the beginning of this essay; Dean Curry has observed that this malady easily leads to a loss of interest in theology, which in turn engenders indifference toward denominational distinctions. The results would be tragic for a meaningful Baptist identity in the twenty-first century.[58]

Finally, the apostle Paul's words in 2 Cor 4.7 (HCSB) suggest an application to the study of Baptist history: "Now we have this treasure in clay jars, so that this extraordinary power may be from God and not from us." In light of the messiness of the Baptist past, these words point to the need for humility in celebrating our heritage, as well as

---

[58] Curry, "Evangelical Amnesia," 16. The literature on the SBC conflict since 1979 is vast. For two very different perspectives, see David T. Morgan, *The New Crusades, the New Holy Land: Conflict in the Southern Baptist Convention, 1969–1991* (Tuscaloosa: University of Alabama Press, 1996); and Jerry Sutton, *The Baptist Reformation: The Conservative Resurgence in the Southern Baptist Convention* (Nashville: Broadman & Holman, 2000). For a detailed comparison of the 1925, 1963, and 2000 BFM statements, see "Report of the Baptist Faith and Message Study Committee to the Southern Baptist Convention," June 14, 2000, published as a booklet separate from the convention proceedings. On the pressing need for SBC unity, see David S. Dockery, *Southern Baptist Consensus and Renewal: A Biblical, Historical, and Theological Proposal* (Nashville: B & H Academic, 2008).

recognition that ultimately we will be measured by how faithful we have been to God's glorious and eternal gospel. Our denominational distinctives are important, but not so much as ends in themselves, and not nearly as urgent as the gospel message that we proclaim in common with those in the wider body of Christ.

Chapter 11

Southern Baptists and Evangelicals: Passing on the Faith to the Next Generation

NATHAN A. FINN, ASSISTANT PROFESSOR
OF CHURCH HISTORY AND BAPTIST STUDIES,
SOUTHEASTERN BAPTIST THEOLOGICAL SEMINARY

Introduction

This chapter addresses how Southern Baptists and Evangelicals can pass on their faith to the next generation. I have a vested interest in this subject for a couple of reasons. As a seminary professor who teaches courses in Baptist history and American religious history, I am self-consciously attempting to pass on the faith to the next generation of ministers and missionaries. I let my students know up front that I am not a secular historian, that I am not ideologically detached from these subjects, and that although I attempt to be fair and balanced when it comes to recounting the past, I have a definite agenda when it comes to their spiritual and ministerial formation. But as a historian in my early 30s, I also recognize that I am a participant-observer in this next generation, both an interpreter and an actor. As a member of the emerging generation, I am keenly aware of some of the challenges inherent in cultivating a strong sense of both Evangelical convictions and Southern Baptist identity among some of my peers.

Although I am excited to address the relationship between Southern Baptists and American Evangelicals, this topic is not one that lends itself to neat and tidy answers that are universally affirmed. In attempting to get my mind around this dicey subject, I have decided to follow the example of the Baptist historian Walter Shurden, who has been known to "exegete" the titles of his lectures as a roundabout and (dare I say?) *preachy* way to make a point. I have structured this chapter around two key ideas worth considering if we are to pass on a Southern Baptist and Evangelical faith to those who come behind us. First, we need to revisit the scholarly debate surrounding the relationship between Southern Baptists and Evangelicals. Second, we need to consider what it means to pass on the Southern Baptist and/ or Evangelical faith to the next generation by means of catechesis and narrative. Along the way I will offer some general observations, as a participant-observer, about younger Southern Baptists and Evangelicals between the ages of 20 and 40.

Southern Baptists and Evangelicals

As Duane Litfin notes in his chapter, there are a variety of ways to define words such as *Evangelical* and *Evangelicalism*, some of which are more helpful than others. In this chapter, I will focus on how confessed Evangelical scholars and various Southern Baptist scholars have understood these terms. I will also offer my own understanding of these concepts and make some suggestions pertaining to the relationship between Southern Baptists and Evangelicals.

Evangelicals Defining Evangelicalism

Evangelical scholars argue for at least four different understandings of Evangelical identity, though some overlap exists among them. Following historians including David Bebbington and Garth Rosell, some describe Evangelical Christianity using primarily theological categories.[1] Many theologians adopt this approach, especially those with more conservative theological inclinations.[2] This strategy works on some levels because Evangelicals share some common convictions about biblical authority, the basic gospel message, the importance of conversion, and the necessity of missions and evangelism. But the devil is in the details: confessed Evangelicals frequently differ among themselves concerning how best to articulate these core beliefs. There are also a variety of other hotly debated issues that are not addressed in most scholarly catalogs of Evangelical beliefs, but nevertheless remain borderline foundational convictions in at least some segments of Evangelicalism. (Ongoing debates about gender roles and Calvinism versus Arminianism come to mind.). Various polls demonstrate that many professing Evangelicals are confused, or at least indifferent, about basic Christian doctrine, which further muddies this approach.[3]

A second approach, advanced by scholars such as Donald Dayton and Robert Johnston, underscores Evangelical diversity by

---

[1] See David W. Bebbington, *Evangelicalism in Modern Britain: A History from the 1730s to the 1980s* (London: Unwin Hyman, 1989), 3–17; and Garth M. Rosell, *The Surprising Work of God: Harold John Ockenga, Billy Graham, and the Rebirth of Evangelicalism* (Grand Rapids: Baker Academic, 2008), 26. Although Bebbington's work focused on British Evangelicalism, his approach has been widely adopted by historians of North American Evangelicalism.

[2] David Wells is one recent example. See David F. Wells, *No Place for Truth: Whatever Happened to Evangelical Theology?* (Grand Rapids: Eerdmans, 1993).

[3] For example, see "Americans Draw Theological Beliefs from Diverse Points of View," The Barna Group (October 8, 2002), http://www.barna.org/barna-update/article/5-barna-update/82-americans-draw-theological-beliefs-from-diverse-points-of-view (accessed September 25, 2009).

emphasizing activism.[4] While those in this camp do not discount the-ology's importance to Evangelical identity, they nevertheless argue that one knows Evangelicals more by what they do than what they believe. At the popular level, this approach is evident among many politically engaged Evangelicals. Activists as diverse as Jim Wallis and Ron Sider, on the one hand, and Tony Perkins and James Dobson, on the other, tend to treat Evangelicalism as if it were primarily a prophetic cultural (or countercultural) renewal movement. Many journalists, particularly those transfixed on the Religious Right, fre-quently adopt this view and portray Evangelicals, at least those of a politically conservative disposition, as more of a political action com-mittee than a fundamentally religious movement. For example, when *Time* magazine ran a 2007 story on "The 25 Most Influential Evan-gelicals in America," the authors so emphasized activism that at least two of those named were politically conservative Roman Catholics.[5]

Joel Carpenter and George Marsden are notable advocates of a third approach, which focuses on an affinity among Evangelicals.[6] By this reckoning, what Marsden calls "card-carrying" Evangelical-ism includes conservative Protestants who embraced Christianity at a Billy Graham Crusade, subscribe to *Christianity Today*, send their teenagers to Wheaton College, pursue ministerial training at Gordon-Conwell Seminary, and give financial support to World Vision and Campus Crusade for Christ. This understanding seems reasonable

[4] See Donald W. Dayton, *Discovering an Evangelical Heritage* (New York: Harper and Row, 1976); Donald W. Dayton and Robert K. Johnston, *The Variety of American Evangelicalism* (Downers Grove: InterVarsity, 1991); Timothy L. Smith, "The Evan-gelical Kaleidoscope and the Call to Christian Unity," *Christian Scholar's Review* 15, no. 2 (Spring 1986): 125–40.

[5] David Van Biema et al., "The 25 Most Influential Evangelicals in America," *Time* (February 7, 2005), http://www.time.com/time/covers/1101050207/ (accessed September 25, 2009).

[6] See Joel Carpenter, "From Fundamentalism to the New Evangelical Coalition," in *Evangelicalism and Modern America*, ed. George M. Marsden (Grand Rapids: Eerd-mans, 1984): 3–16; and George M. Marsden, *Understanding Fundamentalism and Evangelicalism* (Grand Rapids: Eerdmans, 1991), 4–6. Marsden has referred to Evan-gelicalism as a denomination of sorts. See Marsden, "Introduction: The Evangelical Denomination," in *Evangelicalism and Modern America*, vii–xix.

enough, although at times it so focuses on parachurch ministries to the exclusion of denominational identity that some scholars, most notably Darryl Hart, contend that contemporary Evangelicalism is really a myth perpetuated by journalists, historians, and sociologists.[7] Hart provocatively argues that authentic Evangelicalism is more or less those Protestants who still adhere to their historical confessional documents, an approach that leaves little room for those who identify primarily with parachurch ministries or nondenominational churches.[8]

A final way to understand Evangelical identity is by advocating a common Evangelical piety. Stanley Grenz is the key scholar to make this argument, which for him led to an ambitious project to rethink the nature of Evangelical theology in a postmodern context.[9] Many self-proclaimed "postconservative" Evangelical theologians such as Roger Olson and John Franke identify with Grenz's vision.[10] Key leaders in the left wing of the Emerging Church movement, particularly Brian McLaren, often cite Grenz for inspiration in their attempt to rethink what Evangelicalism should look like in the twenty-first century.[11]

---

[7] The term *parachurch* literally means "alongside the church." For the purposes of this chapter, a parachurch ministry is any religious organization that is independent of local church and/or denominational oversight that devotes its energies and resources to specialized ministry objectives.

[8] D. G. Hart, *Deconstructing Evangelicalism: Conservative Protestantism in the Age of Billy Graham* (Grand Rapids: Baker Academic, 2005).

[9] See Stanley J. Grenz, *Revisioning Evangelical Theology: A Fresh Agenda for the 21st Century* (Downers Grove: InterVarsity, 1993); id, *Renewing the Center: Evangelical Theology in a Post-Theological Era* (Grand Rapids: Baker Academic, 2000); Stanley J. Grenz and John R. Franke, *Beyond Foundationalism: Shaping Theology in a Post-Modern Context* (Louisville: Westminster John Knox, 2001).

[10] See Roger Olson, *Reformed and Always Reforming: The Postconservative Approach to Evangelical Theology*, Acadia Studies in Bible and Theology (Grand Rapids: Baker, 2007); ibid., *How to Be Evangelical without Being Conservative* (Grand Rapids: Zondervan, 2008); John Franke, *The Character of Theology: An Introduction to Its Nature, Task, and Purpose* (Grand Rapids: Baker, 2005). The cover of Franke's book describes it as a "postconservative evangelical approach." For a critique of the postconservative paradigm, see Millard J. Erickson, *The Evangelical Left: Encountering Postconservative Evangelical Theology* (Grand Rapids: Baker, 1997).

[11] See Brian J. McLaren, *A Generous Orthodoxy* (Grand Rapids: Zondervan, 2004), 28–29. For recent critiques of Emergent tendencies, see Gary L. W. Johnson

But the postmodern chic among us do not possess a monopoly on a "piety-centric" understanding of Evangelicalism. Anecdotally, I would suggest that a version of this approach is the default position among many grassroots Evangelicals and Southern Baptists, even those who in theory very firmly adhere to conservative theology. Many readers of this chapter likely know Christians who do not concern themselves with too much doctrine—they just want Jesus. Whatever that means.

One thing all these approaches have in common is that they focus predominantly on white, or at least Western, believers. Yet recent scholarship indicates that the ethnic ethos of American Evangelicalism is changing. Philip Jenkins contends that over the last two or three generations the numeric center of Christian gravity has shifted from North America and Europe to Asia, Africa, and South America.[12] Church historians such as Martin Marty and Robert Bruce Mullins argue that church history should incorporate more non-Western Christian movements and contributions.[13] Mark Noll applies a similar approach in telling the story of American Christianity.[14] In a provocative recent book titled *The Next Evangelicalism: Freeing the Church from Western Cultural Captivity*, Soong-Chan Rah argues that first- and second-generation immigrant congregations from Asia and Africa are the fastest-growing demographic among American

---

and Ronald N. Gleason, *Reforming or Conforming? Post-conservative Evangelicals and the Emerging Church* (Wheaton: Crossway, 2008); William D. Henard and Adam W. Greenway, eds., *Evangelicals Engaging Emergent: A Discussion of the Emergent Church Movement* (Nashville: B&H Academic, 2009). For attempts to constructively appropriate elements of the Emergent Church without abdicating more-traditional approaches, see Mark Liederbach and Alvin L. Reid, *The Convergent Church: Missional Worshipers in an Emerging Culture* (Grand Rapids: Kregel, 2009); Jim Belcher, *Deep Church: A Third Way Beyond Emerging and Traditional* (Downers Grove, IL: IVP, 2009).

[12] See Philip Jenkins, *The Next Christendom: The Coming of Global Christianity* (New York: Oxford University Press, 2002); ibid., *The New Faces of Christianity: Believing the Bible in the Global South* (New York: Oxford University Press, 2008).

[13] See Martin E. Marty, *The Christian World: A Global History* (New York: Modern Library, 2008); Robert Bruce Mullin, *A Short World History of Christianity* (Louisville: Westminster John Knox Press, 2008).

[14] See Mark A. Noll, *The New Shape of World Christianity: How American Experience Reflects Global Faith* (Downers Grove: InterVarsity, 2009).

Evangelicals. He asserts that American Evangelicals must break free from the "white captivity" of the church and embrace a more multi-ethnic, multicultural future.[15] Whenever we think of passing on the faith to the next generation, we must understand that many of them will not identify with some of our Evangelical and Southern Baptist experiences because many of those experiences reflect our predominantly white, North American, and Southern context.

Southern Baptists Defining Evangelicalism

Southern Baptists have periodically debated their relationship to Evangelicalism since at least the 1970s. The same definitional ambiguities that characterize the aforementioned scholars also plague Southern Baptists who have addressed this issue. Reflecting both a denominational insularity and likely equating Evangelicalism with fundamentalism, Foy Valentine famously quipped in a 1976 *Newsweek* article that Evangelicalism is a "Yankee word" that real Southern Baptists eschew.[16] In a 1983 book titled *Are Southern Baptists "Evangelicals"?* Glenn Hinson, Southern Baptist Theological Seminary historian, argued similarly to Valentine, while James Leo Garrett, Southwestern Baptist Theological Seminary theologian, countered that Southern Baptists are Evangelicals, albeit Evangelicals with a strong denominational identity. James Tull, Southeastern Baptist Theological Seminary theologian and moderator for this debate, remained unsure of Southern Baptists' Evangelical credentials.[17] Significantly, these Southern Baptist scholars failed to agree on an understanding of Evangelicalism. The debate continued into the early 1990s, when David S. Dockery, then Southern Baptist Theological

---

[15] Soong-Chan Rah, *The Next Evangelicalism: Freeing the Church from Western Cultural Captivity* (Downers Grove: InterVarsity, 2009), 22.

[16] See Kenneth L. Woodward et al, "Born Again! The Year of the Evangelicals," *Newsweek* 88 (October 25, 1976): 76.

[17] James Leo Garrett Jr., E. Glenn Hinson, and James E. Tull, *Are Southern Baptists "Evangelicals"?* (Macon, GA: Mercer University Press, 1983).

Seminary administrator, edited a collection of essays titled *Southern Baptists and American Evangelicals: The Conversation Continues*. The Dockery volume is noteworthy because it includes contributions from both Southern Baptist scholars and several "Northern" Evangelical scholars. But as with the Hinson-Garrett debate, the contributors did not have a common understanding of Evangelicalism and thus differed in their beliefs concerning how Southern Baptists relate to Evangelicalism.[18]

This discussion endures into the early years of the twenty-first century. In 2005, Steve Lemke, New Orleans Baptist Theological Seminary provost, gave an address at Mid-America Baptist Theological Seminary titled "The Future of Southern Baptists as Evangelicals." Although the bulk of the paper focused on his personal concerns about the future of the convention, Lemke seemed to assume that Southern Baptists are Evangelicals in at least some sense, although he distanced the SBC from progressive trends among some Evangelicals such as egalitarianism and inclusivism.[19] In 2006, Malcolm Yarnell, Southwestern Baptist Theological Seminary theologian, authored a "second decadal reassessment" of the relationship between Southern Baptists and Evangelicals. Yarnell was a bit more cautious than Lemke about lumping Southern Baptists with Evangelicals, although he agreed that Southern Baptists have many common beliefs with Evangelicals. Yarnell argued that Southern Baptists should both maintain a separate existence from Evangelicalism and engage Evangelicalism, all the while safeguarding our unique identity, especially concerning ecclesiological matters.[20]

---

[18] David S. Dockery, ed., *Southern Baptists & American Evangelicals: The Conversation* Continues (Nashville: Broadman and Holman, 1993).

[19] Steve W. Lemke, "The Future of Southern Baptists as Evangelicals." Unpublished paper delivered at the Maintaining Baptist Distinctives Conference, Mid-America Baptist Theological Seminary (April 2005), 2–3, http://www.nobts.edu/Faculty/ItoR/LemkeSW/Personal/SBCfuture.pdf (accessed September 23, 2009).

[20] Malcolm B. Yarnell III, "Are Southern Baptists Evangelicals? A Second Decadal Reassessment," *Ecclesiology* 2, no. 2 (2006): 211–12. Yarnell recently expanded his arguments in an attempt to commend a uniquely "Free Church" theological method.

So *Evangelical* and *Evangelicalism* remain somewhat ambiguous concepts that lend themselves to multiple definitions, among both professing Evangelicals and Southern Baptists. How do we wade through these murky waters? For my part, I prefer to make a distinction between the terms *Evangelical* and *Evangelicalism*. I agree with Bebbington and Rosell that an Evangelical affirms a high view of Scripture, a conversionist piety, the centrality of the cross in human salvation, and a gospel-inspired activism, especially (although not exclusively) evangelism and missions. Any piety that might be common to Evangelicals must flow from these core convictions and priorities. I believe these sentiments also characterize the growing number of American Evangelicals with non-Western backgrounds. But I do want to make what I think is an important clarification. While I certainly believe that there are many individual Roman Catholic (and Eastern Orthodox) Christians who embrace these convictions, the historian in me finds the roots of modern Evangelical Christianity in the various reform movements that rejected Catholicism during the sixteenth and seventeenth centuries. For this reason, I am hesitant to speak of Catholic "Evangelicals," although again I think there are many Catholic believers who are sympathetic to what we might call "Evangelicalish" beliefs.[21] Although I am thankful for the increased dialog and cooperation among some Evangelicals and some Roman Catholics in recent years, the Reformation is not over.

Having shared my understanding of what it means to be an Evangelical, I would suggest that not all Evangelicals are participants in Evangelicalism; the latter is more a movement than a set of beliefs and priorities. On this point I agree with scholars including Marsden who argue for a network of interdenominational parachurch ministries

---

See Malcolm B. Yarnell III, *The Formation of Christian Doctrine* (Nashville: B&H Academic, 2007).

[21] This is perhaps especially true of evangelicals who convert to Roman Catholicism. See Francis Beckwith, *Return to Rome: Confessions of an Evangelical Catholic* (Grand Rapids: Brazos, 2008). For a larger discussion of these matters, see Mark A. Noll and Carolyn Nystrom, *Is the Reformation Over? An Evangelical Assessment of Contemporary Roman Catholicism* (Grand Rapids: Baker Academic, 2005).

that influence and inform the faith of many millions of card-carrying Evangelicals. But there are many Evangelicals content to live out their faith in their local churches or denominations and who remain oblivious to this movement. This would characterize many Southern Baptists, who I think Garrett rightly terms "denominational Evangelicals." Although we Southern Baptists are normally Evangelical in our beliefs, denominational loyalty has historically run deep among us, and our ecclesiology focuses on the centrality of local churches rather than parachurch ministries. Furthermore, I agree with those raising concerns that there are some of at least questionable Evangelical convictions who identify with movement Evangelicalism.[22] So while *Evangelical* and *Evangelicalism* are related concepts, they are by no means coterminous.

Southern Baptists and Evangelicals Revisited

Based on this distinction between the terms *Evangelical* and *Evangelicalism*, I would propose three ways to think about the relationship between Southern Baptists and Evangelicals. The first is *Southern Baptists as Evangelicals*. Most Southern Baptists would have no trouble affirming a list of basic Evangelical convictions about the Bible, conversion, and the cross, although like all Evangelicals we further nuance these categories in ways that clarify our beliefs. The same goes for activism; from its inception the SBC has drawn together autonomous churches for the purpose of gospel endeavors, especially missions and evangelism. We should think of Southern Baptists as Evangelicals in the sense that the vast majority of us embrace basic Evangelical sentiments about doctrine and the Christian life. This is perhaps even more the case in the years since conservatives gained control of the SBC in the 1980s and 1990s, which resulted in at least some Southern Baptists who reject or are hesitant about Evangelical

---

[22] I am thinking particularly of the Open Theist controversy, which preoccupied the Evangelical Theological Society a few years back and caused controversy in several evangelical colleges and universities.

beliefs withdrawing from the denomination and forming new coalitions.[23] Many progressive Baptists remain suspicious of the Evangelical label. Mercer University ethicist David Gushee (himself now a self-described left-of-center Evangelical) noted in a recent op-ed piece in the progressive-friendly *Associated Baptist Press* that he is regularly reminded by some of his colleagues that "*Moderates are not to be understood as evangelicals.*"[24]

Because we should think of Southern Baptists as Evangelicals in some sense, this means that, for better or worse, trends among other Evangelicals often influence Southern Baptists. A few examples will suffice. First, beginning in the mid-1970s, Evangelical missiologists such as Ralph Winter began calling for a re-centering of foreign missions around ethno-linguistic people groups rather than geographic national boundaries.[25] Southern Baptist missiologists adopted this approach, and our missionaries now focus on planting churches among people groups with minimal Christian presence. Second, during the 1970s and 1980s, many Evangelical scholars affiliated with the International Council on Biblical Inerrancy reasserted the importance of inerrancy in light of rejection of that doctrine by some Evangelicals since at least the 1960s. The group published three books and drafted the Chicago Statement on Biblical Inerrancy in 1978.[26] We

---

[23] All of the living contributors to *Southern Baptists & American Evangelicals* who raised serious concerns about identifying Southern Baptists as Evangelicals are now identified with moderate groups such as Cooperative Baptist Fellowship and the Alliance of Baptists.

[24] David Gushee, "Opinion: What is the Future of Moderate Baptists?" Associated Baptist Press (September 29, 2009), http://www.abpnews.com/index. php?option=com_content&task=view&id=4439&Itemid=9 (accessed October 1, 2009). Emphasis in original. Progressive Baptists, particularly in the South, prefer to call themselves *moderates* in an effort to cast themselves as a balanced middle between their perceptions of liberalism and fundamentalism.

[25] Winter's address calling for engaging unreached people groups was given at the Lausanne Missions Congress in 1974. The audio of that address is available online, http://www.uscwm.org/about/rdw.html (accessed September 26, 2009).

[26] The books were Norman L. Geisler, ed., *Inerrancy* (Grand Rapids: Zondervan, 1978); Earl D. Radmacher and Robert D. Preus, eds., *Hermeneutics, Inerrancy, and the Bible* (Grand Rapids: Academie, 1984); and Kenneth S. Kantzer, ed., *Applying the Scriptures* (Grand Rapids: Academie, 1987).

Southern Baptists endured our own controversy over inerrancy during the last two decades of the twentieth century, the roots of which are also found in theological changes during the 1960s.[27] Finally, the so-called "New Calvinism" has become increasingly popular among many, especially younger Evangelicals, a trend that is also very much evident in Southern Baptist life.[28]

Although Southern Baptists are Evangelicals in one sense, there are times that *Southern Baptists must be against Evangelicals*, understood in this usage as those card-carrying Evangelicals who find their primary identity in parachurch Evangelicalism. Southern Baptists are *denominational* Evangelicals, and although loyalty to our convention's programs and initiatives seems to be on the decline, I think most Southern Baptists remain committed to primacy of the local church. This makes sense in light of our history because the Baptist movement is essentially an ecclesiological renewal movement that began among English churches of Evangelical conviction in the early seventeenth century. Our identity as Baptists centers on our understanding of the church, particularly our emphasis on voluntary local congregations of regenerate believers who have undergone believer's baptism by immersion.

Because Southern Baptists are a movement that has historically focused on local churches, we will at times be at odds with the fundamentally parachurch nature of American Evangelicalism. The authors of *The Prospering Parachurch* claim that almost half the money Americans give to religious organizations goes to parachurch ministries rather than to local churches and denominations. This pattern reflects a supposed paradigm shift from what the authors call

---

[27] For the pre-1979 roots of the Conservative Resurgence, see Jerry L. Faught, "The Genesis Controversies: Denominational Compromise and the Resurgence and Expansion of Fundamentalism in the Southern Baptist Convention" (PhD diss., Baylor University, 1995).

[28] Colin Hansen, *Young, Restless, Reformed: A Journalist's Journey with the New Calvinists* (Wheaton: Crossway, 2008), 69–93; and C. Douglas Weaver and Nathan A. Finn, "Youth for Calvin: Reformed Theology and Southern Baptist Collegians," *Baptist History and Heritage* 39 (Spring 2004): 19–41.

a "church-centered" model of God's work to a "kingdom-centered" model.[29] In his recent study, *Faith in the Halls of Power*, sociologist D. Michael Lindsay claims that many of the Evangelical leaders he interviewed more readily identify with parachurch ministries than with local churches and invest the bulk of their financial resources in parachurch organizations. Lindsay argues that "the parachurch sector has become the fulcrum of Evangelical influence in American Society."[30]

As long as Evangelicalism remains a parachurch-driven coalition, Southern Baptists will remain nervous about certain types of cooperation with the broader Evangelical movement. We will continue to resist the trend among many Evangelicals to downplay ecclesiology as a tertiary matter that unnecessarily impedes Evangelical cooperation and so-called "kingdom" advance. While pan-Evangelical confessions understandably often avoid nuanced ecclesiological statements for the sake of wider cooperation, this at times gives the impression that parachurch ministries are "the church" in the same sense as local churches are "the church."[31] It is hoped that Southern Baptists, particularly those engaged in the wider Evangelical movement, will resist this tendency. While we can and should cooperate with other Evangelicals in a variety of worthy endeavors, such cooperation must not come at the expense of an ecclesiological downgrade that would transform us into something other than Baptists. On this point I admittedly share some of Darryl Hart's uneasiness with Evangelicalism and resonate with his fears that the movement has replaced local churches and denominations with a product that is in many ways inferior.

---

[29] Wesley K. Willmer, J. David Schmidt, and Martyn Smith, *The Prospering Parachurch: Enlarging the Boundaries of God's Kingdom* (San Francisco: Jossey-Bass, 1998), xi–xii.

[30] D. Michael Lindsay, *Faith in the Halls of Power: How Evangelicals Joined the American Elite* (New York: Oxford University Press, 2007), 194–95, 201, 204, 207.

[31] Most parachurch confessional statements focus on the church universal and say little if anything about local churches. Those confessions that do focus on local churches tend to be silent or ambiguous about issues such as baptism, the Lord's Supper, church discipline, and specific forms of polity, each of which factors significantly into basic Baptist identity.

While Southern Baptists are Evangelicals who at times must be against Evangelicals, I think we must also continue to be *Southern Baptists among Evangelicals*. Having noted my concerns, I favor continued Southern Baptist engagement with other Evangelicals, even within segments of movement Evangelicalism. I say "continued" because some Southern Baptists have been engaging Evangelicalism since the 1940s. Although the convention never took any formal action in this regard, some Southern Baptists were early participants in the National Association of Evangelicals. Southern Baptists were sometimes speakers at interdenominational evangelism, preaching, and prophecy conferences. Several Southern Baptists were part of the aforementioned International Council on Biblical Inerrancy. Individual Southern Baptists are contributing editors to Evangelical periodicals including *Christianity Today*, sit on the board of interdenominational networks such as The Gospel Coalition, advocate theological positions in organizations such as the Alliance of Confessing Evangelicals and the Council on Biblical Manhood and Womanhood, teach in more broadly Evangelical colleges and seminaries, and most notably participate in the Evangelical Theological Society. In recent years, Southern, Southwestern, and Southeastern seminaries have provided ETS with several of its presidents, and the current editor of the *Journal of the Evangelical Theological Society* teaches NT at Southeastern.

As this ETS participation might indicate, considerable Southern Baptist and Evangelical interchange takes place in some of our denominational colleges and seminaries. Many Southern Baptist seminaries employ at least some professors who hail from non-SBC backgrounds and who previously were closely identified with the broader Evangelical movement. This is perhaps especially true of Southern Seminary, where several noteworthy Evangelical scholars joined the faculty after some moderate faculty members' early retirement in the mid-1990s.[32] Baptist-related universities such as Union University

---

[32] Gregory A. Wills, *Southern Baptist Theological Seminary, 1859–2009* (New York: Oxford University Press, 2009), 541, 544–45.

and especially Baylor University have also recruited faculty members from within the ranks of Evangelicalism. Beeson Divinity School was launched in 1988 as a self-consciously Evangelical divinity school anchored to the self-consciously Baptist Samford University. All these aforementioned institutions have hosted several major conferences that included Evangelical speakers, and most Baptist-related schools periodically host guest lecturers from the broader Evangelical world. In addition, some schools normally associated with Evangelicalism such as Trinity Evangelical Divinity School, Gordon-Conwell Theological Seminary, Dallas Theological Seminary, Wheaton College, Taylor University, and even Reformed Theological Seminary have employed Southern Baptists (or professors with SBC roots) on their faculties in recent years.

Individual Southern Baptists have never been aloof of Evangelicalism. Timothy George notes that "the 1970s and 1980s were marked by increasing fellowship and cooperation between Southern Baptists and evangelicals."[33] Both Timothy George and Barry Hankins have argued that Evangelical authors, especially Carl Henry and Francis Schaeffer, influenced some key leaders of the Conservative Resurgence.[34] Not coincidentally, growing numbers of Southern Baptists have participated in pan-Evangelical endeavors since the convention took a conservative turn. Nevertheless, recent Southern Baptist engagement has generally tended toward the Reformed, Dispensational, and/or Complementarian wings of the Evangelical movement. One could argue that over the last generation some Southern Baptists have become movement insiders within the more theologically conservative camp(s) in the increasingly diverse Evangelical movement.

---

[33] Timothy George, "Toward an Evangelical Future," in *Southern Baptists Observed: Multiple Perspectives on a Changing Denomination*, ed. Nancy Tatom Ammerman (Knoxville: University of Tennessee Press, 1993), 283.

[34] Barry Hankins, *Uneasy in Babylon: Southern Baptist Conservatives and American Culture*, Religion and American Culture (Tuscaloosa: University of Alabama Press, 2001). Although Henry was a member of a Southern Baptist church, he was more closely identified with movement Evangelicalism.

I resonate with Timothy George's call for an "Evangelical future" for Southern Baptists, one characterized by a "holistic orthodoxy" that permeates every layer of our polity and (Lord willing) results in our thinking rightly about God and our living rightly before God.[35] To that end, I agree with Albert Mohler that a healthy future for the SBC "lies in the rediscovery and reclamation of an authentic and distinctive Southern Baptist Evangelicalism—*genuinely Baptist*, and *genuinely Evangelical*."[36] This means we must recognize that we are Evangelicals who must at times swim against some Evangelical currents, nevertheless always seeking to remain in the Evangelical river. Balancing our identities as Southern Baptists, Evangelicals, and Southern Baptist Evangelicals is crucial to passing on our faith to the next generation.

Passing On the Faith

Having identified what I think are some key characteristics of the next generation of Southern Baptists and Evangelicals, the remainder of this chapter suggests what exactly it means to pass on the faith to that generation. Again, I have in mind those between the ages of 20 and 40 who will emerge as key leaders in the next decade, although I readily concede that some of my generational contemporaries already possess influential voices. Of course, if the next generation is to be a generation *of Southern Baptists and Evangelicals*, then we must win them to the faith and disciple them in that faith. They must be an increasingly diverse group in terms of ethnicity and cultural background, which will require creativity by Southern Baptists and Evangelicals. We could camp out here for a long time, but for the sake of brevity I want to focus on discipleship by commending two concepts

---

[35] George, "Toward an Evangelical Future," 295–96.

[36] R. Albert Mohler Jr., "A Call for Baptist Evangelicals & Evangelical Baptists: Communities of Faith and a Common Quest for Identity," in *Southern Baptists and American Evangelicals*, 238.

I think will help us pass on a robust faith to the rising generation: catechesis and narrative.

Catechesis: Passing On Our Convictions

By *catechesis*, I mean that Southern Baptists and Evangelicals must pass on our convictions in our preaching, discipleship programs, life-on-life mentoring, theological education, and parenting. Many of the convictions we must entrust to the next generation are shared by Southern Baptists and other Evangelicals. As mentioned, all Evangelicals (at least in theory) affirm the supreme authority of Christian Scripture, the need for personal conversion, the cross-centered saving work of Jesus Christ, and a commitment to evangelism and missions. But I want to move from *description* to *prescription* by digging a bit deeper on some of these points. For example, in my mind, passing on a mere intellectual commitment to biblical inspiration and authority is insufficient. We must labor to pass on a commitment to the full truthfulness of Scripture and its sufficiency in all matters of faith and practice. The sufficiency part will be especially important as we assess new trends among Southern Baptists and Evangelicals and seek to allow Scripture to shape our doctrines, priorities, and methodologics. But we must also seek to inculcate a *Christian* way of reading *Christian* Scripture, which would include reading the whole Bible as one grand narrative spanning two testaments with one Main Character, the Lord Jesus Christ. I would suggest that we point the next generation not only to the Bible battles of the late twentieth century but to the best of the wider Christian tradition, if we are to pass on a robust doctrine of Scripture. Our Patristic, Medieval, and Reformation forebears have much to teach us about how to read our inerrant Scriptures *Christianly*.[37]

---

[37] I am encouraged by the recent move toward a "theological interpretation of Scripture" that draws on insights from the pre-critical tradition. For an introduction to this school of thought, see Daniel J. Treier, *Introducing Theological Interpretation of Scripture: Recovering a Christian Practice* (Grand Rapids: Baker Academic, 2008).

We must also seek to pass on a robust view of the gospel. There are Southern Baptists and other Evangelicals providing helpful thoughts in this regard.[38] David Dockery catalogs a number of theological truths that one must expound in order to rightly proclaim the gospel, including God's creation of humanity in His image and His sovereign rule over all things; humanity's rejection of God's rule and fall into sin; God's provision for humanity's sin in the perfect life, penal substitutionary death, and victorious resurrection of Jesus Christ; God's salvation of men and women when they repent of their sins and trust in the person and work of Christ; and God's ultimate redemption of the entire created order.[39] In a helpful statement titled "Theological Vision for Ministry," The Gospel Coalition notes that one finds the good news both "along" the Bible as a story of creation, fall, redemption, and restoration, and "across" the Bible as the true understanding of God, sin, Christ, and faith.[40] John Piper, a non-SBC Baptist Evangelical, reminds us that the gospel is theocentric and is ultimately about our reconciliation with our Creator, while parachurch leader Jerry Bridges reminds us that the gospel is not some password to enter the Christian family but is the good news that sustains us in our faith and strengthens us in times of need.[41] Southern Baptists and Evangelicals must also pass on what I call a "gospel instinct," which I believe will help us to be very hesitant about aberrant doctrines that seem to undermine faithful gospel proclamation. Examples would include inclusivism, universalism, annihilationism, and hyper-Calvinism.

Developing such a gospel instinct will also help us avoid the truncated view of conversion that is rampant among many Southern

---

[38] For an excellent recent example, see Harry Poe's chapter in this volume.

[39] David S. Dockery, *Southern Baptist Consensus and Renewal: A Biblical, Historical, and Theological Proposal* (Nashville: B&H Academic, 2008), 70.

[40] "Theological Vision for Ministry," The Gospel Coalition, http://thegospelcoalition.org/about/foundation-documents/vision/ (accessed September 25, 2009).

[41] See John Piper, *God is the Gospel: Meditations on God's Love as the Gift of Himself* (Wheaton: Crossway, 2005); and Jerry Bridges, *The Gospel for Real Life* (Colorado Springs: NavPress, 2002).

Baptists and other Evangelicals. Some Christians tend to equate personal conversion with a *mere* decision. This is particularly the case among some of those inclined toward revivalism or the church-growth movement. Were we to bring Bonhoeffer back from the grave, he would surely say that "cheap grace" has too often become the order of the day among many conservative, evangelistic, Bible-believing Protestants.[42] Authentic conversion must include repentance from sin and faith in Jesus Christ and must never collapse into repeat-after-me, walking an aisle, raising a hand, attending a class, or even baptism. Salvation by sincerity is not the same thing as salvation by grace through faith, and jumping through hoops will never justify anyone. I am encouraged by the trend among many American Evangelicals, including Southern Baptists, to recover a view of conversion that is more than praying a canned "sinner's prayer" or affirming a handful of propositions about Jesus.

We must also pass on a balanced commitment to activism, including cultural engagement, evangelism, and missions. I need to tread carefully here. I for one am thankful for the broadened social conscience that so many of my generational peers have developed. I am glad that so many of them care about social justice issues such as poverty, racism, and sexism. I am glad they are committed to combating social evils such as the AIDS epidemic in Africa, worldwide human sex trafficking, and religious persecution. I am glad they are asking hard questions and attempting to develop thoughtful Christian answers for issues such as nuclear warfare, torture, and the role that humans play in climate change. And I am glad that most of them seem to embrace their forebears' commitment to the sanctity of human life, including unborn human life, and the dignity of traditional heterosexual marriage. I am encouraged by this trend, which also characterizes many American believers who hail from non-Western backgrounds.[43]

---

[42] See Dietrich Bonhoeffer, *The Cost of Discipleship* (New York: Touchstone, 1995), 43–56.

[43] See Rah, *The Next Evangelicalism*, 39–87.

But despite this encouragement, I am fearful that some of my peers, just like some of my parents' peers, are allowing these and other legitimate cultural issues to become greater priorities than evangelism and missions. When I listen to some of my students, I see a greater zeal for social justice than for the salvation of their friends and family. When I read books by some Evangelicals, I see a greater zeal for the culture wars than the Great Commission. And when I attend the Southern Baptist Convention's annual meeting, I sometimes hear louder shouting and endure longer ovations for Religious Right victories than gospel advances reported by our two mission boards. I wonder whether Lottie Moon would receive the same adulation that some Republican politicians have received at recent convention meetings.

Please do not misunderstand me. I am not opposed to cultural engagement; again, I am in favor of Southern Baptists and other Evangelicals engaging culture, and I want to see us thoughtfully bring our faith to bear on even more issues. But I do not want to see the next generation engage culture at the expense of personal evangelism and church planting, in North America and to the uttermost parts of the earth. We must pass on a commitment to both the cultural commission and the Great Commission. We must not become like some of our fundamentalist cousins and focus only on personal morality and saving souls. But neither can we allow our social conscience to devolve into the social gospel. I believe Jesus would have us weep for the lost *and* the hungry, to share the gospel *and* clothe the poor, to speak out against all manners of injustice *and* speak out about our personal testimonies. A well-worn sermon illustration tells of the Communist politician who traveled around Eastern Europe proclaiming that "Communism will put a new coat on every man." Supposedly a Christian in the audience responded, "But only Jesus will put a new man in the coat!" As near as I can tell, the story is apocryphal, but my point is this: we need to convince the next generation of Southern Baptists and Evangelicals that the gospel should give them the desire to do both.

Southern Baptists and Evangelicals need to make sure that the faith we pass on is a distinctively trinitarian faith. I am not convinced that Evangelicals in general have always given appropriate emphasis to the triune nature of our God. The same criticism applies to Baptists, whom Curtis Freeman has provocatively charged with being "Unitarians who have not yet gotten around to denying the Trinity."[44] While Freeman probably overstates the case, Baptists have tended to assume the Trinity rather than offer robust articulations of trinitarian theology. But that has begun to change, at least in part because of an intramural discussion among Baptists and other Evangelicals about the relationship between the Trinity and gender roles. In recent years Evangelical theologians such as Millard Erickson and Robert Letham and Southern Baptist scholars such as Bruce Ware and Andreas Köstenberger have written notable works about the Trinity.[45] Timothy George has edited a collection of essays on the Trinity that includes contributors from several denominations, and recently called on Southern Baptists to retrieve the best of the wider Christian tradition for the sake of our own renewal.[46] Surely all Evangelicals, and Southern Baptists in particular, can heed his advice when it comes to the Trinity, that most foundational of Christian doctrines. As Southern Baptists attempt to pass on a trinitarian faith, we should consider following the example of the General Baptist *Orthodox Creed*

---

[44] Curtis W. Freeman, "God in Three Persons: Baptist Unitarianism and the Trinity," *Perspectives in Religious Studies* 33, no. 3 (Fall 2006): 324.

[45] Millard Erickson, *God in Three Persons: A Contemporary Interpretation of the Trinity* (Grand Rapids: Baker, 2005); id, *Making Sense of the Trinity: Three Crucial Questions* (Baker Academic, 2000); id, *Who's Tampering with the Trinity? An Assessment of the Subordination Debate* (Grand Rapids: Kregel Academic, 2009); Robert Letham, *The Trinity: In Scripture, History, Theology, and Worship* (Phillipsburg, NJ: P&R Publishing, 2005); Bruce A. Ware, *Father, Son, and Holy Spirit: Relationships, Roles, and Relevance* (Wheaton: Crossway, 2005); Andreas J. Köstenberger and Scott R. Swain, *Father, Son, and Spirit: The Trinity in John's Gospel* (Downers Grove, IL: IVP Academic, 2008).

[46] See Timothy George, ed., *God the Holy Trinity: Reflections on Christian Faith and Practice* (Grand Rapids: Baker Academic, 2006); and id, "Is Jesus a Baptist?" In *Southern Baptist Identity: The Future of an Evangelical Denomination*, ed. David S. Dockery (Wheaton: Crossway, 2009), 92–97.

by commending the Apostles', Nicene, and Athanasian creeds to our churches the next time we revise the Baptist Faith and Message.[47]

Southern Baptists and other Evangelicals share many beliefs that we need to bequeath to the next generation. But Southern Baptists must also pass on those distinctives that are uniquely emphasized by our tradition. This will be tougher than it sounds. Doug Weaver, my Baptist history professor in college, used to say that we live in a "post-denominational" era, and I think his claim is generally true.[48] I have studied Baptist history and identity at three Southern Baptist-related institutions, and now teach Baptist studies at a Southern Baptist seminary. While I have met some folks in the last decade who are excited about the SBC as a denomination, that attitude does not characterize the majority of my generational peers. Even the ones who *appreciate* the convention are not necessarily *excited* about it. Part of passing on the Southern Baptist faith will be convincing the next generation that the Southern Baptist faith is one worth having. I am afraid that the times are friendlier to our Evangelical friends on this point. But the task is not impossible and I remain hopeful for a vibrant future for the SBC, mostly because I am convinced that a basically baptistic identity is biblical and I continue to believe that the primary arena of God's redemptive activity is the local church.

---

[47] For a recent critical edition of this statement of faith, see Thomas Monck et al., "An Orthodox Creed or a Protestant Confession of Faith," *Southwestern Journal of Theology* 48, no. 2 (Spring 2006): 133–82. Another possibility is suggested by Beeson Divinity School theologian Steven Harmon, who argues that any future Baptist confession should be conceived as a Baptist exposition of the Nicene Creed. See Steven R. Harmon, "Baptist Confessions of Faith and the Patristic Tradition," in *Towards Baptist Catholicity: Essays on Tradition and the Baptist Vision*, ed. Steven R. Harmon, Studies in Baptist History and Thought, vol. 27 (Milton Keynes, UK, and Waynesboro, GA: Paternoster, 2006), 81–82.

[48] Weaver continues to emphasize the challenge that post-denominationalism poses for Baptist identity. See C. Douglas Weaver, "What Are the Top Challenges Facing Baptists Today," *Associated Baptist Press* (September 30, 2009), http://www.abpnews.com/index.php?option=com_content&task=view&id=4442&Itemid=9 (accessed October 7, 2009); Harry L. Poe, "Beyond the Denomination: Dean Addressed SBC Life in 'Postdenominational' Era," *The Alabama Baptist* (February 26, 1998): 6.

I argue in my classes that Baptist principles are simply the consistent application of the gospel to ecclesiological matters. We must pass on our belief that local churches, as communities of the gospel, ought to include only those individuals who give evidence of regeneration. We must pass on our conviction that believer's baptism by immersion publicly identifies a believer with Christ and marks him out for the community created by the gospel. We must pass on our conviction that we live out the gospel personally by embracing the principle of individual liberty of conscience, under the lordship of Christ, and in submission to Christian Scripture. We must pass on a healthy understanding of congregational polity that enables us to practice the gospel in community with one another. We must preserve the freedom of each gospel community to pursue its own gospel agenda by passing on our belief in local church autonomy. We must defend the preservation of gospel freedom by passing on the firm conviction that a free church best flourishes in a free state where religious liberty for all is a basic civil right.

There are several other priorities that Southern Baptists must instill in the next generation. We must teach them that redemptive church discipline and the adoption of local church covenants are two key means the Lord uses to preserve a regenerate church membership. We must pass on a commitment to a graciously confessional cooperation that builds a Southern Baptist consensus around primary issues while allowing for diversity in many secondary issues and all tertiary issues. (I say "many" secondary issues because some ecclesiological convictions that seem secondary to the Christian faith are in fact foundational to Baptist identity.) Although some of my generational peers might disagree, I think we must pass on a commitment to cooperative funding of missions and theological education through the Cooperative Program, which may not be perfect, but seems far better than any alternatives of which I am aware. We must instill in the next generation a zeal for Great Commission priorities that will result in an unwavering commitment to evangelism and church planting in every corner of North America and to the ends of the earth. I believe that with the right priorities, the Southern Baptist Convention can enjoy a bright future.[49]

But I also think there are some tendencies that both Evangelicals and Southern Baptists must not pass on to the next generation. To be as concise as possible, I will simply say of movement Evangelicalism that it must not pass on its *sometimes* unhealthy attraction to theological diversity and its *often* unhealthy overemphasis on parachurch ministries.[50] Evangelicalism must remain rooted in the gospel and strive to serve as a complement to local churches and denominations rather than their competition.

My greater concern, however, is with my own denomination. Southern Baptists must not pass on a cultural captivity that too often has confused Southern culture with biblical Christianity—America is too cosmopolitan for so myopic an approach. We must not hand down an ethnocentrism that is still present, albeit often subconsciously, in many quarters of our convention—America is too diverse for so prejudiced an approach. We must not pass on a denominational arrogance that has often assumed we are the greatest group of Christians in history just because we are the largest Protestant denomination in America (at least when we count all the dead people and Methodists on our church rolls). The nineteenth-century Georgia Baptist pastor C. D. Mallary warned against the "denominational pride and self-glorying" that he so aptly dubbed "denominational idolatry."[51] We would do well to heed Elder Mallary's advice in our own day. We must not pass on our sometimes sectarian and/or overconfident tendency to withdraw from other believers and go it alone, though we should

---

[49] I have elaborated on this theme elsewhere. See Nathan A. Finn, "Priorities for a Post-Resurgence Convention," in *Southern Baptist Identity*, 257–80.

[50] One recent book that overemphasizes the virtue of theological diversity is Kenneth J. Collin, *The Evangelical Moment: The Promise of an American Religion* (Grand Rapids: Baker Academic, 2005).

[51] C. D. Mallary, *Denominational Idolatry Reproved: The Introductory Sermon Preached before the Georgia Baptist Convention at Columbus, GA, April 22, 1859* (Charleston: Southern Baptist Publication Society, 1859), http://elbourne.org/baptist/mallary/idolatry/ (accessed October 2, 2009).

be prepared to face some considerable resistance on this point. Over the years, many Southern Baptists have considered themselves as "the last hope, the fairest hope, the only hope for evangelizing this world on New Testament principles," an attitude that does not lend itself to much in the way of interdenominational cooperation.[52] We must not impart a theological pragmatism that continues to influence not a few of our churches and denominational ministries. And we must not pass on our penchant for confusing bricks, budgets, baptisms, and bottoms with the blessing of the Almighty. Have you ever heard the old camping adage that you should leave the campsite in better shape than you found it? Southern Baptists should pass on a faith to the next generation that is even stronger than the one we have now.

Narrative: Passing On Our Stories

In addition to catechesis, Southern Baptists and Evangelicals must impart our faith to the next generation by means of *narrative*: passing on our stories. Movement Evangelicals must labor to pass on their stories to their younger counterparts. A generation of collegians was called to foreign mission work through the Student Volunteer Movement at the turn of the twentieth century. Theological conservatives in the North bravely battled modernism in the 1920s and 1930s, which helped give birth to a number of parachurch ministries and interdenominational networks. Countless thousands of Americans have come to faith in Christ through ministries such as Youth for Christ, InterVarsity Christian Fellowship, Campus Crusade for Christ, Young Life, and the Billy Graham Evangelistic Association. Missions-minded Evangelicals who wanted to take the gospel to the nations birthed dynamic ministries such as Wycliff Bible Translators, New Tribes Mission, and World Vision, while industrious Evangelicals who wanted to both win the lost and shape the culture launched periodicals such

---

[52] *Alabama Christian Advocate* (June 29, 1948): 2, cited in Bill J. Leonard, *God's Last and Only Hope: The Fragmentation of the Southern Baptist Convention* (Grand Rapids: Eerdmans, 1990), 2n1.

as *Christianity Today* and seminaries such as Fuller and Gordon-Conwell. Historically fundamentalist schools such as Wheaton College, Moody Bible Institute, and Dallas Theological Seminary embraced a more Evangelical outlook and prospered during the mid-twentieth century, expanding their influence worldwide. Conferences such as Urbana and Lausanne instilled in thousands of Evangelicals a Great Commission passion that continues. Evangelicals must also pass on the exploits of such figures as Billy Graham, Carl F. H. Henry, Harold John Ockenga, Jim Elliott, Bill Bright, Henrietta Mears, Bernard Ramm, Ralph Winter, James Montgomery Boice, Samuel Escobar, Joni Erickson Tada, and of course our British friends J. I. Packer and John Stott.[53]

We Southern Baptists have our own stories we need to pass on to the next generation. We are part of a tradition that advocated for full freedom of religion long before Jefferson's and Madison's grandparents were born. A number of traditions identified with locations such as Charleston, Sandy Creek, Georgia, Tennessee, and Texas give our denomination a unique ethos.[54] Our missionaries have been leaders in taking the gospel to the uttermost parts of the earth and nearly every corner of North America. Southern Baptist seminaries and denominational colleges and universities have played a unique role in shaping the tenor of our churches, sometimes for better and sometimes for worse. The Cooperative Program became an ingenious

---

[53] A number of books recount the growth and development of the postwar "new" evangelical movement. See Joel Carpenter, *Revive Us Again: The Reawakening of American Fundamentalism* (Oxford University Press, 1997); George M. Marsden, *Reforming Fundamentalism: Fuller Seminary and the New Evangelicalism* (Grand Rapids: Eerdmans, 1995); Jon R. Stone, *On the Boundaries of American Evangelicalism: The Postwar Evangelical Coalition* (New York: St. Martin's Press, 1997); John G. Turner, *Bill Bright and Campus Crusade for Christ: The Renewal of Evangelicalism in Postwar America* (Chapel Hill: The University of North Carolina Press, 2008); A. Donald McLeod, *C. Stacey Woods and the Evangelical Rediscovery of the University* (Downers Grove: IVP Academic, 2007); Rosell, *The Surprising Work of God.*

[54] See Walter B. Shurden, "The Southern Baptist Synthesis: Is It Cracking?" *Baptist History and Heritage* 16, no. 2 (April 1981): 2–11; H. Leon McBeth, "The Texas Tradition: A Study in Baptist Regionalism," *Baptist History and Heritage* 26, no. 1 (January 1991): 37–57.

way to fund our convention ministries and unite Southern Baptists all over the country in common cause.[55] We have transitioned from a regional denomination to a national denomination, from an ethnically homogeneous network of churches to an increasingly diverse network of churches, from a rural movement to an increasingly urban and suburban movement. We have undergone a Conservative Resurgence that has returned our convention to its theological roots and likely prevented a theological downgrade similar to those that have infected so many of the mainline denominations. We must tell these stories.

Like our Evangelical friends, we have our own heroes. We must tell the next generation about Jesse Mercer, W. B. Johnson, James P. Boyce, John Broadus, Lottie Moon, Annie Armstrong, Isaac Tichenor, E. Y. Mullins, Fannie Heck, J. B. Gambrell, George W. Truett, Herschel Hobbs, W. A. Criswell, Bill Wallace, Oscar Romo, Adrian Rogers, Emmanuel McCall, and Paul Pressler. We must also pass on the stories of Baptist heroes Thomas Helwys, John Bunyan, Thomas Grantham, William Carey, Andrew Fuller, Daniel Taylor, Isaac Backus, John Leland, Gerhard Oncken, Adoniram Judson and his *three* remarkable wives, Charles Spurgeon, Nannie Burroughs, W. B. Riley, and Martin Luther King Jr.[56]

Southern Baptists and movement Evangelicals have some common stories and heroes. Both movements were forged in the revival

---

[55] For more information about the Cooperative Program, see Chad Owen Brand and David E. Hankins, *One Sacred Effort: The Cooperative Program of Southern Baptists* (Nashville: B&H, 2005).

[56] Although it is a bit dated, the standard history of the Baptists remains H. Leon McBeth, *The Baptist Heritage: Four Centuries of Baptist Witness* (Nashville: Broadman, 1987). Other notable histories include Bill J. Leonard, *Baptist Ways: A History* (Valley Forge, PA: Judson, 2003); Tom Nettles, *The Baptists: Key People Involved in Forming a Baptist Identity*, 3 vols. (Fearn, Ross-Shire, Scotland: Christian Focus, 2005–7). The best reference work is William H. Brackney, *Historical Dictionary of the Baptists*, 2d ed. (Lanham, MD: Scarecrow, 2009). The best introduction to Baptist thought is James Leo Garrett, *Baptist Theology: A Four-Century Study* (Macon, GA: Mercer University Press, 2009).

fires of the First and Second Great Awakenings and similar stirrings.[57] Both movements experienced significant expansion during the nine-teenth century and were part of what Martin Marty has called a "righteous empire" of conservative Protestants.[58] Both movements endured the fundamentalist-modernist controversies of the early twentieth century, albeit in different ways and toward a different result.[59] Both movements have survived wars on American soil and dispatched soldiers and chaplains to wars on foreign soil. Both move-ments have discovered a penchant for political engagement in the last generation or two and both movements have sent presidents to the White House.[60] Of course both movements have shared some nota-ble figures such as Carl F. H. Henry, Jimmy Carter, Harold Lindsell, and that quintessential Southern Baptist Evangelical, Billy Graham. We must pass on their stories too.

Conclusion

When I first delivered this material in lecture form in the fall of 2009, we were celebrating the 400th anniversary of the beginning of the Baptist movement. Coincidentally, 2009 also marked the 60th anniversary of the 1949 Los Angeles Crusade that catapulted a young Southern Baptist evangelist named Billy Graham into Evan-gelical superstardom and made him the most well-known Protestant on earth. Interestingly, 2009 was also the 30th anniversary of the year a young Southern Baptist church planter named Rick Warren arrived in Saddleback Valley, California. When Warren's 2002 book

---

[57] See Jerry Tidwell's chapter in this book.

[58] Martin E. Marty, *Righteous Empire: The Protestant Experience in America* (New York: The Dial Press, 1970).

[59] See George M. Marsden, *Fundamentalism and American Culture*, new ed. (New York: Oxford University Press, 2006).

[60] See William Martin, *With God on our Side: The Rise of the Religious Right in America* (New York: Broadway, 1996); Hankins, *Uneasy in Babylon*. For a recent his-tory of Southern Baptist political engagement, albeit one written as an apologia for the denomination's current positions, see Jerry Sutton, *A Matter of Conviction: A His-tory of Southern Baptist Engagement with the Culture* (Nashville: B&H, 2008).

The Purpose-Driven Life became an international best seller, it was his "Los Angeles" moment, the event that made his a household name.[61] Fast-forward to August 2008. You no doubt remember that Saddleback Church hosted a live televised debate between presidential candidates Barack Obama and John McCain, with Warren as moderator. In an article published the day of the debate, editors of *The Economist* magazine dubbed Warren "the next Billy Graham," that is to say, the best candidate to replace Graham as "America's pastor."[62]

The comparison makes sense. Both Graham and Warren are popular authors with dynamic ministries, entrepreneurial spirits, and a desire to cooperate with all Evangelicals and at times even some outside the Evangelical fold. Both count presidents, business leaders, and Hollywood moguls among their friends. Critics accuse both men of being too shallow, too conservative, too ecumenical, too political, etc. Especially relevant to this chapter, both Graham and Warren are simultaneously Southern Baptists and card-carrying Evangelicals. Apparently, Billy Graham has passed his torch to the next generation. I sincerely hope that Southern Baptists, Evangelicals, and Southern Baptist Evangelicals will be able to pass on our faith to the next generation. After all, as Graham has reminded us on many occasions, God has no grandchildren.

---

[61] See Rick Warren, *The Purpose-Driven Life: What on Earth Am I Here For?* (Grand Rapids: Zondervan, 2002).

[62] "The Next Billy Graham," *The Economist* (August 16, 2008): 35.

Chapter 12

The Future of the Southern Baptist Convention

DANIEL AKIN, PRESIDENT, SOUTHEASTERN BAPTIST THEOLOGICAL SEMINARY

As we move into the second decade of the twenty-first century, Southern Baptists are at a crossroads. We find ourselves in the midst of seismic changes all across our convention of churches. Consider the following events that unfolded in just a five-month period in 2009:

1. In June, the Southern Baptist Convention meeting in Louisville, by a 95-percent vote, empowered its president, Dr. Johnny Hunt, to appoint a Great Commission Resurgence Task Force to study our convention and bring back recommendations as to how we can more efficiently fulfill the Great Commission. This occurred in spite of serious opposition by some groups, especially those who work for the denomination.
2. In August, Dr. Geoff Hammond resigned under pressure as president of the North American Mission Board.

3. In September, Dr. Jerry Rankin announced his retirement as president of the International Mission Board (effective June 2010).
4. In September, Dr. Morris Chapman announced his retirement as president of the Executive Committee (effective September 2010).

These four events are enough to make the point that we are experiencing a time of change. Add to this the decline in baptisms and membership of the Southern Baptist Convention in recent years, bizarre attempts to justify and paper over these declines, false rumors about and sustained opposition to the idea of a Great Commission Resurgence, distrust and a passion for the status quo on the part of some leaders, and it would not be difficult for one to be less than optimistic about the future of the SBC. The fact is that I am not optimistic. Nevertheless, I am hopeful—not because of my confidence in Southern Baptists, sinners saved by grace as we are, but because of my confidence in our God, His Word, and His promises. He has promised in Rev 7:9–10 (HCSB) that a day is coming in heaven when there will be "a vast multitude from every nation, tribe, people, and language, which no one could number, standing before the throne and before the Lamb." Now, the question that stares Southern Baptists in the face is this: will we join hands with our great God in seeing this awesome day come to pass, or will we find ourselves sitting on the sidelines watching? Or will we, as Pastor Al Jackson of Lakeview Baptist Church in Auburn, Alabama, has warned us, make the wrong investment (treasures on earth rather than treasures in heaven), have the wrong perspective (temporal rather than eternal), and love the wrong master (money rather than God)? The spiritual stakes are high. Of that no one should be in doubt.

This is the fourth time in five years that I have addressed some aspect of the future of the Southern Baptist Convention. I have some embarrassment at this point because I am not a prophet nor am I all that smart. There is no false humility here, just an honest self-evaluation and admission. Still, I will do my best to share my perspective on where we are and what we must do to have a "viable future" that will allow us to be a part of God's great and glorious plan of redemption. I will intentionally draw on my previous addresses, particularly "Axioms for a Great Commission Resurgence."[1] I do so because (1) I believe they chart a hopeful and positive agenda for the future and (2) nothing has transpired since I delivered these addresses that would cause me to change my perspective. I will also draw on conversations and experiences over these past several months that have only highlighted and made even more clear where the dangers to our future lie. I have eight points of observation for our consideration.

1. Southern Baptists have a hopeful future if we return to our first love and surrender fully to the lordship of Jesus Christ (Col 1:15–20; Rev 2:1–7).

I have experienced significant grief at how little attention has been paid to this first axiom of my spring address at Southeastern Baptist Theological Seminary. It was placed first for a reason. It must be first. It must set and establish the foundation for any future agenda for Southern Baptists. Yet, it has been passed over and quickly dismissed with the wave of a hand and words like, "We all believe that." Nevertheless, the question is not, Do we *believe* it? The question is, Do we *live* it?

Is Jesus Christ really our passion and priority? Do we truly aspire to both know Him and love Him fully? Do we long to see Him "come to have first place in everything" (Col 1:18 HCSB)? I fear we do not, and as a result we too often devolve into petty quarrels, territorialism, turfism, defensiveness, and personal agendas that find the Savior nowhere in sight. Jesus said, "The Son of Man has come to seek and to save the lost" (Luke 19:10 HCSB). Is that our passion? Our priority? Our agenda? His final words on earth are found in Matthew

---

[1] Daniel L. Akin, "Axioms for a Great Commission Resurgence," Convocation at Southeastern Baptist Theological Seminary, Wake Forest, NC, April 2009.

28:18–20 and Acts 1:4–8. Have we heard Him? Have we obeyed Him? Let me quickly add that a right reading of Scripture will not set these statements at odds with one another. Any appeal to Acts 1:8 to justify not getting more personnel and resources to the unreached nations is wrongheaded. Actually, it is shameful. Most of our Jerusalems have a gospel witness. Large portions of the uttermost parts of the earth do not. Who will tell them about Jesus?

George Barna is on target: "Most Christians don't act like Jesus because they don't think like Jesus."[2] Again, Jesus said, "The Son of Man has come to seek and to save the lost" (Luke 19:10 HCSB). Southern Baptists need to think like Jesus. Southern Baptists need to act like Jesus. His lordship requires it. It demands it. Any other agenda will get the first and most important thing wrong. If we fail here, we will fail everywhere.

2. Southern Baptists have a hopeful future if they continually make clear their commitment to the inerrant and infallible Word of God, affirming its sufficiency in all matters. (Matt 5:17–18; John 10:35; 17:17; 2 Tim 3:16–17; 2 Pet 1:20–21).

Southern Baptists won the "battle for the Bible" that began in 1979. Men of God such as Jimmy Draper, Paige Patterson, Paul Pressler, Adrian Rogers, and Jerry Vines put it all on the line because they saw what the poison of liberalism was doing to our convention and its institutions. These men are heroes of the faith, and what they did must be honored and never forgotten. We must keep reminding a new generation of what happened when they were small or not yet born. It is easy for young Southern Baptists "to forget Joseph," to forget the sacrifices of their fathers.

Nevertheless, the "battle for the Bible" will not end until Jesus returns. The war over the truthfulness of God's word began in the Garden of Eden when Satan asked, "Has God said?" The Word of

---

[2] "Barna: Biblical Worldview Held by Only 4 Percent of Adults," *Baptist Press* (December 2, 2003).

God will continue to be under assault, and we must ever be on guard and ready to answer those who question its veracity and accuracy (1 Pet 3:15). A younger generation of Southern Baptists will face this challenge, and they must be warned not to squander precious theological ground that is essential to a healthy and hopeful future for this convention.

Dr. Russ Bush, who is now with our Lord, was correct. I heard him say in a seminary classroom in the early 1980s, "The question of biblical inspiration is ultimately a question of christological identity." Why? Because Jesus believed the Holy Scriptures to be the true and trustworthy Word of God! Even Rudolf Bultmann said that about our Lord—he just believed Jesus got it wrong! To deny inerrancy is to say that Jesus was wrong or that He willfully deceived. That is both heresy and blasphemy. It is spiritually suicidal!

Do you doubt or deny the full truthfulness of the Bible? My counsel is to join another denomination. We will love you and pray for you, but we do not want you infecting our people with a spiritual disease that can be fatal to the church of the Lord Jesus. Inerrancy and the sufficiency of the Bible in all matters of faith and practice must never be up for debate in the Southern Baptist Convention.

3. Southern Baptists have a hopeful future if we will pursue a genuinely Word-based ministry that is theological in content and on fire in delivery (2 Tim 4:1–5).

We live in a culture that is increasingly biblically illiterate year by year. Sadly, Southern Baptists have not been immune to this spiritual malady. Even with the gains of the Conservative Resurgence, we have not seen a widespread revival of biblical preaching in our churches. This is both surprising and disappointing to many of us. While I am encouraged by what I see as a ravenous hunger for biblical/theological exposition in the younger generation, at the same time I am discouraged that so many of their models are non-Southern Baptists. Think of Alistair Begg, Mark Driscoll, John MacArthur, James McDonald, and John Piper. Thankfully, I can now add to these wonderful expositors Matt Chandler, Andy Davis, Mark Dever, J. D. Greear, Johnny Hunt, James Merritt, Al Mohler, and David Platt. This tribe must increase across our convention of churches if we are to have a healthy and fruitful future. So, what needs to happen?

- We need seminaries that teach an expositional model.
- We need pastor/theologians who model exposition.
- We need ministers who preach the whole counsel of God's Word (book, chapter, verse, phrase, word).
- We need preachers who value the calling of being theologians.
- We need men who are gospel saturated in their ministry of the Word, and faithfully proclaim Christ every time they stand to teach the Word of God.
- We need in our pulpits engaging expositors who are on fire as heralds of the unsearchable riches of Christ. Nothing is more exciting than theology. Nothing is more relevant than doctrine. No one is more beautiful than Christ. To proclaim these glorious truths in a dispassionate or boring manner is inexcusable. It is, I believe, sinful. If Southern Baptists have a future it will be rooted in the Word. If Southern Baptists experience a Great Commission Resurgence it will find its lifeblood in the Word.

4. Southern Baptists have a hopeful future if we can unite around and affirm the Baptist Faith and Message 2000 as a healthy and sufficient guide for building theological consensus that avoids the equally deadly extremes of liberalism and sectarianism (1 Tim 6:3–4).

What do Southern Baptists agree on doctrinally and theologically? I believe the answer is "quite a lot," and I would like to pinpoint a number of these:

- We affirm the inerrancy, infallibility, authority, and sufficiency of the Bible.
- We affirm the Triune God who is omnipotent, omniscient, and omnipresent.
- We affirm God as Creator and reject naturalistic evolution.

- We affirm both the dignity and depravity of humanity.
- We affirm the full deity, perfect humanity, and sinlessness of Jesus the Son of God.
- We affirm the penal substitutionary nature of the atonement as foundational for understanding the crucifixion of our Savior.
- We affirm the good news of the gospel as the exclusive and only means whereby any person is reconciled to God.
- We affirm the biblical nature of a regenerate church witnessed in believer's baptism by immersion.
- We affirm salvation by grace alone through faith alone in Christ alone for the glory of God alone.
- We affirm the reception of the Holy Spirit at the moment of regeneration/conversion and the blessing of spiritual gifts for the building up of the body of Christ.
- We affirm the literal, visible, and historical return of Jesus Christ to this earth when He will fully manifest His kingdom.
- We affirm the reality of an eternal heaven and an eternal hell, with Jesus as the only difference.
- We affirm a "sanctity of life" ethic from conception to natural death.
- We affirm the sanctity of heterosexual marriage, the goodness of sex in marriage, and the gift of children, lots of them!
- We affirm the complementary nature of male/female relationships, rejoicing in the divine ordering of them for the home and the church.

Now, there are some things on which we do not agree doctrinally and theologically. For example:

- The exact nature of human depravity and transmission of the sin nature.
- The precise constitution of the human person.
- The issue of whether Christ could have sinned. (We agree He didn't!)

- The *ordo salutis* ("order of salvation").
- The number of elders and the precise nature of congregational governance.
- The continuance of certain spiritual gifts and their nature.
- Does baptism require only right *member* (born again), right *meaning* (believer's), and right *mode* (immersion), or does it also require a right *administrator* (however that is defined)?
- Time of the rapture (pre, mid, post, partial rapture or prewrath rapture).
- The nature of the millennium (pre, amill, or post).
- And, of course, we are not in full agreement about Calvinism and how many points one should affirm or redefine and then affirm!

Now, what are we to make of all this? Can we move forward, work together, and pursue the Great Commission as one united army of believers under the command of King Jesus, and if so, how? No one has been more helpful in getting us to think rightly and wisely in this area than Dr. Al Mohler of Southern Baptist Theological Seminary. I believe his paradigm of "theological triage" gets to the heart of how we can think well theologically.[3] Furthermore, the apostle Paul affirms in 1 Cor 15:3 that there are theological matters of first importance, and in 1 Tim 6:4–5 that there are lesser issues that ought not drive us to engage in "word wars" which lead to "envy, strife, reviling, evil suspicions and useless wrangling. . . ."

First-order doctrines are those that are essential to the Christian faith. These include the full deity and humanity of Christ, the Trinity, the atonement, and justification by faith alone. Where such doctrines are compromised, the Christian faith falls. *Second-order doctrines* are essential to church life and the ordering of the local church but, in themselves, do not define the gospel. Here theological differences make it difficult to function together in the local congregation.

---

[3] R. Albert Mohler Jr., "The Pastor as Theologian," in *A Theology for the Church*, ed. Daniel L. Akin, (Nashville: B&H Publishers, 2007), 930–31.

Third-order doctrines may be the ground for fruitful theological discussion and debate but do not threaten the fellowship of the local congregation or the denomination.

Now, let me make my position and convictions crystal clear. Some things are worth fighting over and dying over. Some things are not. Some things are worth dividing over. Some things are not. At the Building Bridges Conference in November 2007, I put it like this, and I have not changed my mind:

> Our agreement on the BFM 2000 is an asset, not a weakness. It is a plus and not a minus. If I were to pen my own confession it would not look exactly like the BFM 2000. But then I do not want nor do I need people exactly like me in order to work together for the proclamation of the gospel of Jesus Christ and the building of His church. Our confession is a solid foundation for a sound theology that avoids the pitfalls and quicksand of a straightjacket theology. Do we want or need a theology that rules out of bounds open theism, universalism and inclusivism, faulty perspectives on the atonement, gender-role confusion, works salvation, apostasy of true believers, infant baptism and non-congregational ecclesiologies just to name a few? Yes, we do. These theological errors have never characterized who we are as Southern Baptists and they have no place in our denomination today. Inerrancy is not up for debate. The deity of Jesus and His sinless life are not up for debate. The triune nature of God as Father, Son and Holy Spirit is not up for debate. The perfect atoning work of Christ as a penal substitute for sinners is not up for debate. Salvation by grace alone through faith alone in Christ alone is not up for debate. A regenerate church is not up for debate.[4]

I am convinced we have an adequate and healthy theological consensus for coming together for the purpose of fulfilling the Great Commission.

---

[4] Daniel L. Akin, "Answering the Call to a Great Commission Resurgence," in *Calvinism: A Southern Baptist Dialogue*, ed. E. Ray Clendenen and Brad J. Waggoner (Nashville: B&H Academic, 2008), 252–53.

5. Southern Baptists have a hopeful future if our denomination at all levels begins to reflect the demographic and racial makeup of our nation and the nations.

Southern Baptists were born, in part, out of a racist context and have a racist heritage. That will forever be to our shame. To deny or ignore this is foolish and dishonest. By God's grace and the Spirit's conviction, we publically repented of this sin in 1995 on our 150th anniversary, but there is still much work to be done. To my dismay, some still refuse to own up to our transgression, perhaps because the seeds of this sin are scattered across too much of our denomination, especially in the South where most of our people live. We must confront the sobering reality that the Southern Baptist Convention remains a mostly middle-class, mostly white network of mostly declining churches in the South. If you doubt what I am saying, visit most state conventions, attend an annual Southern Baptist Convention meeting, or drop in on 99 percent of our churches on any given Sunday. We can integrate the military, athletics, and the workplace, but we can't integrate the body of Christ! The lack of urgency and concern in this area is mind-boggling. It is spiritually inexcusable.

Until we get right about race, I am convinced, God will not visit us with revival. The plea for a Great Commission Resurgence will not move heaven, and it will be scoffed at by the world as a sham. Starting at home, we must pursue a vision for our churches that looks like heaven. Yes, we must go around the world to reach Asians and Europeans, Africans and South Americans. But we must also go across the street, down the road, and into every corner of our local mission field where God in His grace has brought the nations to us.

Now please hear carefully what I am about to say. I plead with you to consider its merit. This call to reach the *ethne* here in America and around the globe will demand a greater commitment and a greater devotion, especially on the part of men. Reaching, for example, Muslim men, will require Christian men! More men must have a Christ-centered passion and gospel-centered priorities. More men must leave our country and go to the nations as our sisters in Christ have been doing for generations! This will demand a radical reorienting of lifestyles, choices, commitments, and perspectives. Business as usual as a denomination and as individuals will not be an option if a real Great Commission Resurgence is to take place. Fathers and grandfathers must have lives that will inspire their children, especially their sons and grandsons, to do something great for God.

6. Southern Baptists have a hopeful future if we have the courage to rethink our convention structure at every level, clarify our mission so that we maximize our energy and resources for the fulfilling of the Great Commission, and provide a compelling vision that inspires our people to do something great for God.

Are Southern Baptists a Great Commission people? If you listen to our rhetoric, then the answer is yes. Yet, although Southern Baptists gave $12 billion last year through the local church, only between two and three cents on the dollar ever left the United States. Further, North America church planting in the unreached and underserved areas of our nation is little more than a trickle! Why we plant more churches in Georgia, Alabama, South Carolina, North Carolina, and Tennessee than we do in New York, Illinois, Michigan, Pennsylvania, Washington, and California is incomprehensible.

Recent days have convinced me of an undeniable truth. The future of Southern Baptists will depend on the type of leaders we choose to follow. The need of the hour is for aggressive, visionary leaders who are daring and courageous, men who understand the times and are willing, as William Carey said, to attempt great things for God and believe great things from God. Why do I say this? Because many Southern Baptists are trapped in a time warp. They are aiming at a culture that went out of existence years ago. They use mid-twentieth-century methods and pine for a nostalgic golden age. They are convinced that if we would just go back "to the way things were" we would experience a spiritual renaissance that would restore the good ole days. Such a perspective is a prime example of denial and a refusal to live in the real world. We cannot go back. We are not going back. We will move forward into the future whether we like it or not. How we move ahead is the question yet to be answered. Those who lead us will play a significant role in that answer.

We have built bureaucracies and little kingdoms that are the primary objects of our affections, concerns, and reasons for existence. We are slowly dying but refuse to admit that we are even sick. The time, energy, personnel, and resources that we keep at home, especially in the deep South, is hard to explain or accept for a rapidly growing number, and I fear how we will justify ourselves when we stand before our Lord. Some may say this is "dramatic rhetoric" merely designed to "fan the emotions." Call it what you will, my concern is what will the God of heaven say about so much staying in church-saturated regions in America? Jesus said, "To whom much has been given, much will be required" (Luke 12:48 NRSV). God will, no doubt, require much of Southern Baptists when He asks what we did with what He gave us to reach the nations and penetrate the lostness of this world.

Thom Rainer has challenged us to do *simple church*.[5] This is good counsel. Once more I want to challenge us to do *simple convention*. We must streamline our structure, clarify our identity, and maximize our resources. A younger generation wants a leaner, quicker, and more missional convention that pursues the unreached and underserved in our nation and around the world. That is where younger people are going, and our leadership at every level will either get on board or be left behind. We will change the way we operate whether we like it or not. The SBC of 2010 will not look like the SBC of 2020, and certainly not 2030. Again, I would raise some hard questions we must consider in the immediate future.

1. Is the name "Southern Baptist Convention" best for identifying who we are and what we want to be in the future? I believe the answer is no.

---

[5] Thom S. Rainer and Eric Geiger, *Simple Church: Returning to God's Process for Making Disciples* (Nashville: Broadman Press, 2006).

2. Do we have unnecessary overlap and duplication in our denomination that can be corrected for greater efficiency and better stewardship? Yes.

3. Do we have a healthy and strategic structure and mechanism for planting churches in unreached and underserved areas that will thrive and survive past a few years? I am doubtful, but hopeful that will change quickly in the near future.

4. Should we dismantle the Cooperative Program because it does not work? No, because such a perspective is simply untrue. I cannot find anyone who thinks like this. Now, this does not mean we shouldn't be open to studying the Cooperative Program and making improvements if possible. Such a mind-set is essential if we are to be responsible stewards of the gifts of God's people.

5. Are we technologically up to date, living on the cutting edge of advances being made at a rapidly increasing pace? Doubtful.

6. Are we distracted by doing many good things but not giving full attention to the best things? No doubt. Church planting in the unreached and underserved population centers in North America, pioneer missions around the world, and theological education that permeates every sphere of our convention and serves our churches is a three-legged stool that will excite and inspire our people to serve more and to give more. Of that I have no doubt.

Our mission in the future will require aggressive and intentional *church planting*. Rick Warren is right, "Starting new congregations is the fastest way to fulfill the Great Commission."[6] The churches we plant must be sound in their doctrine, contextual in their forms, and aggressive in their evangelistic and mission orientation. In order to make this work, we need a new and compelling

---

[6] Rick Warren, *The Purpose-Driven Church* (Grand Rapids: Zondervan, 1995), 180.

vision for our churches, local associations, state conventions, and national entities.

Timothy George is correct, "The exchanging of one bureaucracy for another bureaucracy does not make a revolution."[7] For a revolution or a revival to occur, we need to kill and bury all sacred cows; we need to be willing to put on the altar for sacrifice our dreams, goals, ministries, and entities if doing so will further the Great Commission. For me personally, that would include the dismantling and closing of Southeastern Baptist Theological Seminary if that would further the goals of world evangelization. For me to think any other way would be shortsighted. It would also be hypocritical.

7. Southern Baptists have a hopeful future if we raise up a generation of pastors who lead their churches to see themselves as gospel missions agencies who equip and train all their people as missionaries for Jesus regardless of location or vocation (Eph 4:11–16).

The headquarters of the Southern Baptist Convention is the local church. All associations, conventions, and national entities exist to serve them, not the reverse. Further, these agencies and entities exist to assist the churches in fulfilling the Great Commission.

Missions is not a ministry of the church. It is at the heart of the church's identity and essence. No Great Commission passion means no genuine NT church. The strategic and biblical importance of the local church in this regard must be recaptured. The local church is to be ground zero for the *missio dei*. Here is the "spiritual outpost" for the invasion of enemy territory as we reclaim lost ground for its rightful owner—King Jesus. A new vision that I pray will grip the churches of the Southern Baptist Convention is, "Every church a church-planting church and every church a Great Commission church." This must be more than a slogan. It must be a reality.

---

[7] Personal conversation with Dr. George.

Pastors must be seized by a vision for the strategic importance of their calling as the head of a gospel missions agency called the local church. This will involve:

1. Rightly defining the Great Commission and missions. The shibboleth that "everything we do is missions" is without biblical warrant and is theologically flawed.

2. Being used by God to call out the called who have an overseas calling given by our commander in chief, the Lord Jesus.

3. Partnering in strategic and vibrant church planting that assaults the major population centers of North America, following closely the pattern of the apostle Paul revealed in the book of Acts. Again, this will inspire and energize a younger generation because of the excitement entailed in new works. For too long we have neglected the great urban centers such as New York, Washington, DC, Boston, Los Angeles, and Seattle, cities that are almost completely bereft of Evangelical influence. This cannot continue or we will face a future of irrelevance and insignificance.

4. Working to help revitalize existing congregations so we do not lose a meaningful past and squander massive assets built by our parents and grandparents.

5. Training all our people to see themselves as God-called missionaries no matter what their vocations or locations. God has gifted them, and we must equip them for their service of ministry and missions in their communities, schools, workplaces, and places of recreation. Religious practices and traditions are not the same as missionary and gospel living. We must recognize the difference. We must help our people recognize the difference.

6. Motivating our people to give the funds to match the missions strategy plan that is in place to reach the nations. That will require funding 8,000 missionaries, not the 5,700 we had in 2009 and the 5,000 projected for the immediate future.

Money follows vision. Jim Henry is correct, "Many of our faithful people are more than ready to move into reproducing their church; but let's face it, they can only go as far as the pastor's passion and support for the project will allow."[8]

8. Southern Baptists have a hopeful future if we can devote ourselves to a cooperation that is gospel-centered and built around a biblical and theological core—not methodological consensus or agreement (Phil 2:1–5; 4:2–9; Eph 4:1–6).

When I delivered the axioms message at Southeastern Baptist Theological Seminary in the spring, this axiom caused hesitation and concern for some. Therefore, let me take another run at it.

There are essential and nonnegotiable components of biblical worship and work. The Word proclaimed, the ordinances administered, singing, praying, and mutual service are necessary components of authentic church life. Nevertheless—and we must be clear on this—there is no specific biblical style or method ordained by our God. Within biblically defined parameters there is room for variety and difference. Is this not self-evident?

What will unite Southern Baptists will not be style, methodology, and liturgy. Any past hegemony of methods and programs is gone, and it is not coming back. How we do things will be expansive and diverse, and that is OK. The key, and please hear this, will be that what we do is filtered through the purifying waters of Scripture so that we honor Jesus and glorify the Father in all that we do. Nothing should distract or detract from the gospel of a crucified and risen Savior. Nothing!

Different contexts will demand different strategies and methods. Cultivating the mind of a missionary, we will ask, "What is the best way to reach with the gospel the people I live among?" Waycross, Georgia, will look different from Las Vegas, Nevada. Montgomery,

---

[8] Jim Henry, "Casting a Vision for Reproduction of Your Church," in *Reaching a Nation through Church Planting*, comp. Richard H. Harris (Alpharetta: North American Mission Board, 2005), 86.

Alabama, will look different from Portland, Oregon. Boston will be different from Dallas. Memphis will have a different strategy from Miami. Reaching Liberty, Missouri, is not the same as reaching Seattle, Washington. Various ethnic believers and social/cultural tribes will worship the same God, adore the same Jesus, believe the same Bible, preach the same gospel, and seek to glorify the one true and living God. Nevertheless, they may meet in different kinds of structure, wear different kinds of clothes, sing different kinds of songs, and engage in different kinds of gospel-centered ministries. The point is this: we must treat the United States missiologically, and do so with the same seriousness that our international missionaries treat their people groups missiologically. As long as it is done for the glory of God and has biblical warrant and theological integrity, I say, Praise the Lord! It is foolish to gripe about organs, choirs and choir robes, guitars, drums, coats and ties. It is also a waste of time. It is time to move on with the real issue of the Great Commission!

If we build a consensus around style or methods we will continue to Balkanize, fracture, and lose important ground. If we build a consensus around Jesus and the gospel, we can and we will cooperate for the advancement of God's kingdom and He will bless us. Theology should drive our cooperation, not tradition. The message of the gospel will unite us, not methods!

Conclusion

Recently I was studying the life of the wonderful C.I.M. (China Inland Mission) missionary James Fraser. A brilliant engineer and gifted pianist, he left the comforts of England to spend his adult life in western China among the Lisu people. What moved him to make such a radical, life-changing decision? It was a small tract placed in his hands in 1906 when he was only 20 years old. Hear the words that have brought in hundreds of thousands of believers among a rural mountain people group that had no hope until James Fraser came to help them.

A command has been given: "Go ye into all the world and preach the Gospel to every creature." It has not been obeyed. More than half the people in the world have never yet heard the Gospel. What are we to say to this? Surely it concerns us Christians very seriously. For we are the people who are responsible. . . . If our Master returned today to find millions of people un-evangelised, and looked as of course He would look, to us for an explanation, I cannot imagine what explanation we should have to give. . . . Of one thing I am certain—that most of the excuses we are accustomed to make with such good conscience now, we should be wholly ashamed of then.[9]

These words haunt me. I hope they haunt you. They moved James Fraser to live out the Great Commission. I pray they move me. I pray they move you. I pray they move Southern Baptists. If they do, our future is bright. If they don't, we do not deserve a future.

---

[9] Eileen Crossman, *Mountain Rain* (Sevenoaks, UK: OMF Books, 1982), 4.

Chapter 13

Southern Baptists, Evangelicals, and the Future of Denominationalism

R. ALBERT MOHLER JR., PRESIDENT, THE SOUTHERN BAPTIST THEOLOGICAL SEMINARY

The Lord Jesus Christ asked His disciples, "When the Son of Man comes, will He find faith on the earth?" (Luke 18:8 NASB). This haunting question brings a disturbance and shock to followers of Christ. In the context, Jesus was pointing to a powerful demonstration of faithfulness and asking the disciples, "Will I see faith when I come?"

Southern Baptists and Evangelicalism

From 1989 to 1990, Southern Baptists were involved in some very specific discussions which were forged in the midst of a longer and larger controversy that had consumed large portions of denominational energy. This controversy required answering questions about our theological identity as we determined who we were and who our friends were. At that time, it was necessary to answer some questions that now seem rather odd.

One question was, "Are Southern Baptists Evangelicals?" Some Southern Baptists argued that "Evangelical" was a Yankee term and foreign from the identity of the SBC. They knew there were liberals within Evangelicalism, and so believed the SBC was somehow outside the Evangelical dynamic. Others argued that the SBC was most certainly part of Evangelicalism, and it was better to seize Evangelical identity lest the SBC be found with no identity at all.

It was on the campus of The Southern Baptist Theological Seminary that this conversation was formalized through a series of discussions resulting in a book, *Southern Baptists and American Evangelicals: The Conversation Continues*. In that work, edited by David Dockery, I contributed a chapter titled, "A Call for Baptist Evangelicals and Evangelical Baptists: Communities of Faith and a Common Quest for Identity."[1] Even now as we revisit some of those questions, it is fascinating to look back after two decades and see where we are today.

The SBC was then embroiled in a controversy over the inerrancy of Scripture that would cause us to look beyond ourselves, in many ways for the first time. Going back to the midpoint of the twentieth century, Southern Baptists were an insulated people, talking to each other and publishing all our own material. There existed within the SBC a cradle-to-grave Baptist experience. In fact, SBC Sunday schools in the 1950s enrolled unborn babies, literally providing a womb-to-tomb approach to SBC identity. In my office, I have a framed certificate that enrolled me in pre-cradle roll.

The SBC was a solitary, unitary franchise. It seemed there was no reason to look outside the denomination for either resources or relationships. Nevertheless, as the SBC debated some of the most essential issues of the Christian faith and the Christian gospel in the 1980s, it became necessary to look outside the SBC for others who

---

[1] R. Albert Mohler Jr., "A Call for Baptist Evangelicals and Evangelical Baptists: Communities of Faith and a Common Quest for Identity," in *Southern Baptists and American Evangelicals: The Conversation Continues*, ed. David S. Dockery (Nashville: Broadman and Holman, 1993), 224–39.

could help. Although the battle for the Bible emerged in the SBC in the late 1970s and throughout the 1980s, this conversation had been progressing for a long time among American Evangelicals.

Concurrent with the debate over Scripture in the 1980s, some argued that the term "Evangelical" was too much of a contested concept, rendering it useless. They said that because the term was used in so many ways and lacked any objective meaning or substantial content, it would be better to jettison the term and come up with something new. As a result, for the last three or four decades, different groups have attempted to come up with a new word.

The problem with this is that the media reduce American Protestantism into three types: liberals, Evangelicals, and everybody else. The SBC does not want to be among "everybody else," or to be classified with the mainline liberal denominations. Therefore, like it or not, as far as the media are concerned, the only place that the SBC fits is within the Evangelical camp.

The term "Evangelical" continues to have a great deal of meaning and value, as many people desire to use it as a self descriptor. For this reason, the term must have specific content. It cannot simply be used to describe anyone who wants to use it. This same issue and debate is going on now, even as it was in 1989, and the question of Evangelical identity will continue into the future.

Twenty years ago, I argued that the SBC was in a dynamic of controversy between two parties: a truth party and a liberty party. Although some tried to join both, ultimately the controversy forced a choice because the issues became so narrowly focused and so intense in application. The broader Evangelical world saw similar division between the "experience" party and the "doctrine" party. Again, the basic issue was whether it was enough to claim to be related to Christ, or whether some very specific truths must also be embraced.

First, the truth party understood doctrine to be the most basic issue confronting the denomination. They were suspicious that heterodoxy had entered the ranks of Southern Baptists, and they had documentation to back up their claims—reports from students at colleges, universities, and seminaries. Soon, what had begun as a grassroots concern became an organized movement, convinced that truth must not be compromised, or all would eventually be lost.

Second, the liberty party might best be described with what became a bumper sticker slogan: "Baptist Means Freedom!" The problem is that being free can mean almost anything, for you do not even have to be a Christian to use "freedom" as your overarching theme. Nevertheless, Baptist identity *must* mean more than simply being free, for in a vacuum of doctrinal content there will be no spiritual grandchildren in the faith.

Twenty years ago, one of the ways we looked at these questions was by thinking through what logicians and phenomenologists call "set theory."[2] Is the set, or group, established by a center? If so, is the lordship of Christ the center? Is the gospel itself that which draws us together? If so, then do all the iron filings drawn toward that role constitute the group?

We answered those questions in the affirmative, believing that we are united around truths that both transform our lives and change our eternal destination. These truths are an essential part of what it means to be an Evangelical and what it means to be a Southern Baptist.

In time, Southern Baptists came to understand that being a centered set was not enough. Without clear and adequate boundaries, the center does not hold. A healthy structure requires both the robust embrace of the center and a healthy respect for the boundaries.

The background to the SBC conversation was, and is, the trajectory of the mainline Protestant denominations. Even back in the 1980s, the liberal denominations sowed the seed of their own destruction. Continuing down this path, they have abandoned the great truths on which they were established, forfeiting their claim to

---

[2] R. Albert Mohler Jr., "Has Theology a Future in the Southern Baptist Convention? Toward a Renewed Theological Framework," in *Beyond the Impasse? Scripture, Interpretation, and Theology in Baptist Life*, eds. Robison B. James and David S. Dockery (Nashville: Broadman and Holman, 1992), 107–8.

any definite doctrines and declining into nothingness and irrelevance. There is no new thing they will not try, and they are best characterized as being "tossed to and fro by the waves and carried about by every wind of doctrine" (Eph 4:14, ESV).

In 1990, *The Wall Street Journal* published an editorial by Wade Clark Roof titled, "The Episcopalian Goes the Way of the Dodo," explaining the decline of mainline denominations.[3] Yet, just two decades later, these same mainline Protestant denominations are engaged in conversations that would have been unthinkable even in 1990. Although the trajectory was clear at that time, the disaster is now even more apparent.

In summation, Southern Baptists in 1989 determined that the future of the SBC must be a future in conversation with American Evangelicals. Theologians, biblical scholars, and other figures worked hard on this, and theological resources were developed. It was good to discover that the SBC had theological friends and allies. At that very crucial turning point in the history of the denomination, it was profitable to know that as Southern Baptists, we too were Evangelical, and we were not alone.

In *Southern Baptists and American Evangelicals*, I argued that it was important to seize Evangelical identity, for otherwise we would have *no* identity. Although I still agree with every word that I wrote then, I would not write the same chapter today. If twenty years ago I believed that the imperative was to say to Southern Baptists that we really are Evangelicals, then the imperative that now falls on us is to say to Southern Baptists that we really are Baptists.

The younger generation already knows that the Southern Baptist Convention is located somewhere within the great Evangelical tradition. The issue today, however, is that the Evangelical movement is now in more trouble than the SBC. What the Evangelical movement needs is for Southern Baptists to be authentically Baptist, and to give

---

[3] Wade Clark Roof, "The Episcopalian Goes the Way of the Dodo," *Wall Street Journal*, July 20, 1990.

our witness in a clear way. As we look to the future of the SBC, the real issue is whether we will be Baptists, and what that would mean as we look to the generation ahead.

Southern Baptist Confessionalism in a Secularized, Neo-Pagan World

Consider how the world has shifted over the past two decades, especially in terms of its intellectual patterns and predictions. Twenty years ago, those who talked about the future of American society and advanced industrial societies were convinced that religion would pass away. They predicted that Christianity would become part of the cultural memory. The argument, known as the theory of secularization, said that as nations became more advanced, as people became more educated, and as humanity became more in control of the universe—building dams, splitting the atom, sending people into space, and such—there would be less need for God and faith.

Peter Berger, a sociologist and one of the formative figures in the theory of secularization, recently came back and said that the world is not becoming more secular, except in two places: in Europe and among the cultural elites in the United States. Berger and his associates conducted a study of relative religiosity across cultures. They discovered that the most religious people in the world were those in India, and that the least religious people were the citizens of Sweden. Berger then made his oft-quoted statement of explanation about the United States, "The American situation can be described as a large population of 'Indians' sat upon by a cultural elite of 'Swedes.'"[4]

Although secularization did not go as predicted, the world has witnessed massive changes in technology, communications, the rise of social media, and the collapse of distant social networking. Disenchantment and confusion abounded as the culture has shifted from

---

[4] Peter Berger, Grace Davie, and Effie Fokas, *Religious America, Secular Europe? A Theme and Variations* (London: Ashgate Press, 2008), 12.

modernity to postmodernity. People are asking the most basic questions about the meaning of life and the habits of the heart, looking to discover and to understand the good, the beautiful, and the true.

Among American Evangelicals, there is further confusion. We take note of the contest over the brand, aging institutions, generational tensions, emergence of new challenges. We understand things such as the Emergent Church and Emergent Christianity. These were not discussed twenty years ago because they were not yet on our screen as they are today. Examining the weaknesses of Evangelicalism, with its essentially parachurch structure, one wonders whether it has enough cohesion to survive. The debate over Evangelical identity remains even today, and this conversation has ongoing ramifications within the SBC.

Our discussion of the SBC is not a dispassionate discourse about one denomination among others. Rather, Southern Baptists are searching their hearts and looking at their denomination because they love it and care for it and are deeply concerned about it. We recognize that the SBC too often has been characterized by denominational bravado and pride. It has been too easy to look at statistical graphs from mainline denominations that show their decline in membership, while pointing to graphs that show growth for the SBC. The problem is that although the SBC has continued to produce graphs that indicate greater numbers and growth, the statistics do not hold up under scrutiny. So many people on the rolls of SBC churches can't even be located. All of a sudden, the numbers are not going up.

The Southern Baptist Convention is asking important questions at a strategic moment in its history. Although we can be thankful that these are not the questions of a denomination in disaster, they *are* the questions of a denomination headed toward, or already in, a crisis. This is not the inerrancy crisis of the 1970s and 1980s. The younger generation is the beneficiary of that controversy, having inherited a denomination that knows where it stands on the doctrine of Scripture. Nevertheless, the challenge for the forthcoming generation is to join in the work of forging a new identity. Although statistics and numbers are not without significance, the primary concerns should center on the heart of the denomination, the clarity of our vision, and the essential importance of our mission.

The SBC is now experiencing the death of cultural Christianity. For a long time, the SBC saw its growth in conjunction with the growth of the Bible Belt. People became involved in SBC churches and SBC programs because that was simply what was done. Nevertheless, this is no longer the normative practice. Although there are pockets of cultural Christianity in the world today, they are disappearing fast. Any denomination that bases its future on a foundation of cultural Christianity deserves to die with that culture when it dies.

Financial and institutional challenges confront the SBC even as it experiences a clear generational crisis. The present challenges will not find remedy with a new slogan. Indeed, there *is* a need for a resurgence of Great Commission passion, vision, commitment, and energy in our denomination.

In 1845, when Baptists gathered in Augusta, Georgia, they determined to establish a convention to unite the energy, conviction, and passion of the churches from which they came. They established what we would now call a mission statement, by explaining that the formation of the Southern Baptist Convention was "for the eliciting, combining, and directing of the energies of the denomination for the propagation of the gospel."[5] Only the cause of the gospel is sufficient as a reason for us to be together in mission.

Although the world has changed, the gospel has not. Today's challenges are more complicated than those from past eras, but the gospel remains the only message that saves. The gospel resurgence needed in the SBC will not begin with a slogan, nor will it result in a program. New publicity and fresh approaches to public relations will not bring this awakening. Rather, a gospel resurgence must come from the hearts of Southern Baptists, as individuals and churches

---

[5] Southern Baptist Convention, "Constitution," available at http://www.sbc.net/aboutus/legal/constitution.asp.

renew their passion to take the glory of Christ to their neighbors and to the nations.

This resurgence will be costly because Southern Baptists will have to ask questions that we have not asked for many generations. We must look at issues we have not conceived of and have not considered for far too long, but this is what the church of the Lord Jesus Christ is called to do.

When evaluating strategies, we cannot merely receive what has been handed to us, confirming past ideas because of brand loyalty. The SBC has been called to be a body of churches on mission. The grand vision before us is not the perpetuation of the SBC, but the call to the nations to exalt in the name of the Lord Jesus Christ. The great passion of the SBC cannot be to make sure our statistics are healthy and that our charts point ever upward. Rather, our passion must be for the glory of God to be evident in persons hearing and responding to the gospel of the Lord Jesus Christ. In that way, the gospel work would be manifested in the establishment of godly churches that are ruled by Christ through His Word, bearing the fruits of righteousness and the power of the gospel.

Understanding the Mind-set and Empowering the Mission of the Coming Generation

It is of vital importance that the SBC understands the historical significance and consequence of the coming generation. This generation will determine the future of the local church, and hence the SBC. The future witness to the Lord Jesus Christ will be largely determined by what this generation does in service to the gospel of Christ.

First, in the providence of God, the coming generation is a strategic, hinge generation of history. They arrived after the Cold War, Vietnam, and Watergate. They came of age in a postmodern world. They are digital natives with a global mind-set.

Second, they are a generation of social transformation. They have experienced it and are the fruit of it. They will become participants in the establishment of a "new normal" of social values and mores. All this will take place under the close observation of politicians, marketers, and merchandisers who are eager to discover and capitalize on prevailing trends. Over the next 20 years, the church will discover what this coming generation thinks about the church. How will they understand the basic definition and mission of the church? Within the SBC, the dynamic energy of the convention will flow from the current generation of leadership to the generation that is coming.

Third, they are a generation of global responsibility. They have unprecedented connectivity and access to transportation. They understand that they can be anywhere in the world by tomorrow afternoon. As such, our prayer is that they will be a generation willing to go anywhere for the cause of the gospel. Even as they inherit the leadership of churches and the denomination, our hope is that they will be doing even more for the cause of Christ, and that the glory of God will be more evident in their lives of faithfulness.

Fourth, they are a generation of spiritual confusion. Certainly, many have been seized by the substance of the Christian faith and are committed to Christ. They know the transforming power of Christ and have a passion to see others experience new life in Christ. Yet, as their witness goes forth in this nation and beyond, they will speak to people whose basic response may not be rejection of the gospel, but merely a shrug. These people think religion is little more than a person's private hobby or personal project.

Christian Smith, a sociologist who has observed and written much about this generation, says that the religion of young people in America today can be reduced to moralistic, therapeutic deism. They think God wants people to be happy and good—however those terms happen to be defined. They say they believe there is a god, but not a god who would be actively engaged in their everyday affairs, or who would be a creator, or a judge.[6]

---

[6] Christian Smith and Melina Duncan, *Soul Searching: The Religious and Spiritual Lives of American Teenagers* (New York: Oxford University Press, 2005), 118–71.

This is not a generation of radical secularists and atheists. The "new atheists" have made very few inroads here, in terms of convincing young people that there is no God. These questions appear unimportant to the younger generation. In his latest book, *Souls in Transition*, Smith says young adults still hold to moralistic, therapeutic deism, but they are even less sure about the deism part.[7]

Fifth, they are a generation of institutional lack of interest. Although it is natural that commitment to institutional forms tends to come later in life, the younger generation says with consistency that they are not interested in institutions. Nevertheless, these institutions will one day be theirs, and they will decide what to do with them.

A Challenge to the Coming Generation

If the Southern Baptist Convention is not where you can most effectively demonstrate the glory of God, reach the world with the gospel of Christ, or see the nurturing of faithful Christians, then the solution is to find the denomination and context that is. You should not give your life to the SBC simply because your grandmother was a Southern Baptist. You should not invest your energies in the SBC because you think the denomination is worth saving as an important artifact of American religion in Southern culture. Instead, first give yourself to faithfulness in your local church, and second, give yourself to cooperative efforts with churches who also desire to reach the world for the glory of God.

By God's grace, the SBC can be a denomination transformed by a resurgence of Great Commission passion. The Conservative Resurgence in the SBC salvaged the convention, but it did not redeem it. We must redeem what has been lost, and strengthen what remains. We must bring our passion and insights into service for the cause of

---

[7] Christian Smith, *Souls in Transition: The Religious and Spiritual Lives of Emerging Adults* (Oxford: Oxford University Press, 2009), 154–65.

Christ. The SBC must be the kind of denomination that is known not for its name and its brand, but rather for the glory of God. People should be able to taste and savor the Lord Jesus Christ present in SBC life and practice.

Members and ministers of the SBC must give themselves over to a lifetime of service to Christ, not the SBC. This is a Christianity lived out in the midst of the local church, in fellowship with other believers and mutual accountability to the lordship of Christ. As the members discover what it means to be faithful in the local church, they will discover what they can do in cooperation with other gospel churches. They will discover that there are things one church cannot do alone.

Each generation faces the reality that they are a generation of perishable promise. There are only a few years in which each generation will determine the future for their local church, for the denomination, and for so much beyond. The decisions each generation makes in a relatively short time will determine the shape of the future. Each generation is both the beneficiary of what has come before and the steward of the future. The SBC of the present and future must challenge each other to go deep in ecclesiology, conviction, passion, devotion, discipleship, missions, and fellowship. We must recapture the Baptist vision of regenerate church membership, the centrality of Scripture, believer's baptism, and congregationalism, but not merely for the sake of Baptist history and heritage. Rather, such convictions are how we must understand what faithfulness to Christ would require, and that is where we can find deep identity together.

On both individual and denominational levels, participants in the SBC can bless the larger Evangelical family by knowing who we are and by knowing that we will work in unison with all Great Commission people to do Great Commission work. There can be no minimalism, dropping back to some lowest common denominator of Christianity. There can be no easy believism. There can be no cultural captivity. In a world headed for hell and breaking apart at the seams, there is no time for us to worry about recapturing a denominational culture and brand that is lost. Cultural Christianity built many institutions and nurtured much bureaucracy, but it has now evaporated. Rebuilding lost culture is not the cause of the gospel.

The Hope of the Future

The cause of the gospel compels us to see that the glory of God is manifested in the call to the nations and the establishment of godly churches here and abroad. We pray for a revitalization of Christianity that demonstrates and manifests the glory of God wherever believers are found. Nothing will do but faithfulness.

The Lord Jesus Christ asked, "When the Son of Man returns will he find faith on the earth?" I am haunted by that question. That question drives and impassions me, even as I serve as president of a theological seminary and as I think about the future of the SBC. Indeed, my hope and prayer are that when the Lord returns He will find us faithful. The Lord answers that question in Matt 16:18 (HCSB) when He declares, "And I also say to you that you are Peter, and on this rock I will build My church, and the forces of Hades will not overpower it." The ministry of the church is not conducted in desperation or panic. We are confident that Christ will accomplish His purposes and will glorify Himself in His gospel. We are absolutely, positively, and unshakably confident that the gospel saves—indeed, that Jesus saves.

Name Index

Scripture Index

Psalms
110:1 *163*
119:105 *85*

Isaiah
61:1–2 *163*

Jeremiah
31:31–34 *165*

Daniel
7:13–14 *164*

Matthew
4:23–25 *163*
5:17–18 *264*
5:21–22 *140*
6:33 *xvi*
11:4–6 *163*
16:18 *xvi, 291*
17:1–9 *161*
18:15 *127*
26:64 *163–64*
28:18 *164*
28:18–19 *165*
28:18–20 *264*

Luke
4:18–19 *163*
12:48 *272*
18:8 *279*
19:10 *263–64*
20:44 *163*
24:25–27 *161*
24:44–49 *162*

John
1:1 *153*
1:12 *151*
1:14 *153*
3:1–8 *151*
3:2 *163*
3:16 *150*
10:3–4 *130*
10:10 *150, 153*
10:11–15 *118*
10:35 *264*
14:2 *163*
14:3 *153*
14:6 *85, 151*
14:7 *163*
14:20 *163*
14:23 *164*
16:5–7 *163*
16:13–15 *163*
16:28 *163*
17:1–5 *163*
17:17 *264*
20:17 *164*

Acts
1:4–8 *264*
1:8 *264*
3:19 *153*
4 *144*
6 *123*
14:15–17 *167*
17:22–31 *168*
20:18–21 *122*
20:28 *122, 127, 130*
20:31 *130*